Routledge Revivals

Behind The Wall

Originally published in English in 1964, this volume describes the ghettos which formed medieval enclaves in the cities of Renaissance and post-Renaissance Europe. In their overcrowded quarter where the only protection against disease and epidemics was their own religious rules, the Jews were constantly exposed to violent attack, looting, and arson. Yet despite these conditions, the period of the ghetto was one of the richest eras of Jewish exile. The Bible was read and closely studied, culture and learning flourished and philosophical ideas were discussed and debated. The ghetto gave birth to Spinoza.

Behind The Wall
The Story of the Ghetto

Poul Borchsenius

First published in English in 1964 by George Allen & Unwin Ltd.

This edition first published in 2024 by Routledge
4 Park Square, Milton Park, Abingdon, Oxon, OX14 4RN
and by Routledge
605 Third Avenue, New York, NY 10158.

Routledge is an imprint of the Taylor & Francis Group, an informa business

© 1960 English Translation George Allen & Unwin Ltd.

The right of Poul Borchsenius to be identified as the author of this work has been asserted by him in accordance with sections 77 and 78 of the Copyright, Designs and Patents Act 1988.

All rights reserved. No part of this book may be reprinted or reproduced or utilised in any form or by any electronic, mechanical, or other means, now known or hereafter invented, including photocopying and recording, or in any information storage or retrieval system, without permission in writing from the publishers.

ISBN 13: 978-1-032-91070-3 (hbk)
ISBN 13: 978-1-003-56118-7 (ebk)
ISBN 13: 978-1-032-91074-1 (pbk)
Book DOI 10.4324/9781003561187

BEHIND THE WALL

THE STORY OF THE GHETTO

POUL BORCHSENIUS

TRANSLATED BY REGINALD SPINK

London
GEORGE ALLEN & UNWIN LTD
RUSKIN HOUSE MUSEUM STREET

FIRST PUBLISHED IN 1964

This book is copyright under the Berne Convention. Apart from any fair dealing for the purposes of private study, research, criticism or review, as permitted under the Copyright Act 1956, no portion may be reproduced by any process without written permission. Enquiry should be made to the publishers.

This Translation © George Allen & Unwin Ltd, 1960

Translated from the Danish
BAG MUREN
© H. Hirschsprungs Forlag, Copenhagen 1957

PRINTED IN GREAT BRITAIN
in 11 on 12 point Juliana type
by EAST MIDLAND PRINTING CO. LTD.
BURY ST. EDMUNDS

CONTENTS

I	The Ghetto	9
II	Open Doors	29
III	Excommunicated	47
IV	Safad	67
V	Italy	83
VI	Germany	107
VII	Poland	131
VIII	The Third Temple	144
IX	Destruction	169
X	A Vision that Faded	180
XI	Narrow Paths	193
XII	Hasidism	204
XIII	Living Ruins	213

I

THE GHETTO

THREE long tables had been placed together in a row running through the door, and reaching almost from the wall of one room to the wall of the next. A snow-white cloth covered the long festive board and many flickering candles illuminated it, casting reflections from the cut glasses which held red wine. Bowls of bitter herbs and dishes of *mazot*, the white unleavened bread of the Passover, stood on the tables.

It was the first evening of the Passover in the year 5273 after the Creation, by the Christian reckoning 1513, and the house was one of the largest in the Judengasse of the old Rhineland town of Worms. It was in fact the ghetto, the quarter to which Jews were confined by a wall, the gates of which were locked and guarded at night to ensure that no Jew went out and no Christian went in. The wall was a dividing line between Jews and Christians.

Seated at the head of the top table was the host: a long-bearded, dignified, and pious rabbi named Bezalel ben Chaim, a man respected by the entire ghetto. A true aristocrat, he believed himself to be of royal blood, able to trace his ancestry in a direct line back to King David. At his right sat the mistress of the house, and on his left, according to custom at the Passover, his youngest son. Looking along the table, he could see, first his other children, then relatives and friends, and, down at the bottom end, the local poor; for at the Passover it is the rule that the poor shall come and eat. The face of everybody present was flushed with good food and wine and the guests were leaning comfortably back in their chairs On the eve of the Passover when they celebrate their memorable deliverance out of Egypt, the Jews are truly lords.

All had gone as it should on a *Seder*. The *Haggadah* containing the account of the deliverance had been read; the bread had been broken and the wine drunk; and the exultant tones of the thanksgiving psalms had sounded through the open windows. They had come now to the most solemn moment of every *Seder* evening. At the elbow of the head of the family stands a cup of wine which is left undrunk; and, rising from his seat, the youngest son opens the doors on to the street. At this time on the evening of a Passover the prophet Elijah will come and announce to some Jewish home that at long last the Messiah is at hand; and should he come on this *Seder* to this house they must show that they are expecting him and that he is welcome.

At the point of rising, however, the boy suddenly stopped; for something alarming had occurred. All turned quickly to the mistress of the house, as she collapsed with a groan. She had sat at her husband's side through the long meal heavy with pregnancy, and now her time had come and she was giving birth. Some of the women helped her to the bedroom and got her into bed, while two of the men ran out for a midwife.

It was a calm, spring-like evening. The moon hung large and round in the sky, and lights were shining from the small square windows of every house in the narrow streets of the ghetto. As they ran along the street the two men saw a stranger carrying a large oblong parcel. When he observed them he hurried off down a side street and they, thinking that he was a thief, followed him. At that moment a night watchman appeared on the scene and they called him. The man was arrested and taken off to court.

The bundle contained a child's body with the throat cut. Conscious of his awkward situation, the man confessed that some Christians had bribed him to smuggle the body into Bezalel's cellar. They would then arrange for a search to be made by the watch, and when the body was found there would be an excellent pretext for attacking the Jews and looting their homes. Incredible though such methods may seem now, in those days it was not uncommon to arrange so-called Jewish ritual murders, and the week of the Passover, the classical period of Jewish persecution, was the favourite time. On this particular Passover evening, however, the trick failed.

That same night Bezalel's wife gave birth to a son and the father named him Jehudah Löw, after the words of Jacob: 'Judah is a lion's whelp'. To the whole ghetto it seemed a lucky omen that the boy had saved Israel from deadly peril even before his birth, and the omen proved true: Jehudah Löw was to become one of the great and celebrated Jews of the ghetto period, for many years a rabbi in Prague, where he died at the age of ninety-seven. As a teacher, he received by Jewish custom a special name, which was Maharal, and which was formed from the initials of Moreinu Harav Rabbi Löw; that is to say, 'Our Teacher, the Lord Rabbi Löw'. Alternatively, he was known as *'der hohe'*, or 'the great one'. Few men have been so greatly loved by ordinary people, and his memory is associated with many legends. Let us look at a few of these; for they provide an excellent introduction into the psychology of the ghetto.

First there is the story of his love affair, which is full of romance. His parents betrothed him, according to the contemporary custom—for in matters of this kind the persons concerned were not consulted—to a charming girl from Posnan, whose name was Perl. Both parties had agreed to the marriage contract, all seemed to be in order, and Löw, far away at a *yeshiva*, a Talmudic school, was concentrating on his studies, in order to complete them before the wedding. It so happened, however, that Perl's father lost his fortune and so was unable to pay the arranged dowry. Writing to Löw, he released him from all his obligations. Löw, however, was in love with the girl and trusted that God would put everything right; and so for over ten years he waited patiently for something to happen.

In the meantime, Perl helped her improverished parents by looking after a stall at which she sold bread and cakes. One day a body of soldiers came riding through the ghetto and the officer thrust his lance into Perl's loaves; one of them stuck on the tip, and he rode off waving it and laughing. Running after him the girl cried that she was poor and could not spare the cost of the bread, but the officer curtly replied that he had no money with him. She persisted, however, and to escape from the crowd which had by now gathered round them, he flung her his saddle bag, saying that she could keep it as security and he would return and pay her the next day, failing which, the bag would be hers. He did not return; and sewn into the bag Perl found a purse full of gold ducats. Here was the marriage portion. The girl concluded that the officer was the prophet Elijah who had come to her aid.

The strangest of all the legends connected with the renowned Rabbi Löw are the stories about the *Golem*. The background to these will already be apparent. In those days a danger threatened every Jew: the charge, at the Passover, of stealing a Christian child, cutting its throat, and using the blood for the unleavened bread. Accusations of ritual murder, clinging evilly to the Jews right from the Dispersal, have carried over into modern times. They were whispered in the corners of every town and city in the Middle Ages, and little more was needed to spark off an explosion. In order to remain alive and free, Jews had constantly to be on the alert. None was more so than Rabbi Löw; as we shall see in the legend of his *golem*.

'Golem' is a Hebrew word which means 'a thing incomplete'. It can be a needle without an eye; and it can be a child unborn. A woman before she has borne a child is a *golem*. What is it that completes the embryo? What is it that breathes life into a thing that is formless? These problems have been speculated on by writers of every age; and in the Middle Ages there was a legend that credited Virgil with the power to give a dead statue life, so that it both moved and obeyed his instructions. The legend of the *golem* is a manifestation of the same idea in Jewish folklore, where it has provided the material for both poetry and drama. The Hebrew play *The Golem*, by Leiwik, belongs to the permanent repertoire of the Habimah Theatre in Tel Aviv, and has been played by the company all over the world.

To return to Rabbi Löw and his *golem*. Löw had now spent many years as a rabbi in Prague, where the Jews were bitterly persecuted by the priest Thaddaeus. He hatched endless plots against them and there was no limit to their baseness so long

THE GHETTO

as they attained their desired objective. In despair, Rabbi Löw appealed to Heaven, and his prayers were answered. The response took the form of ten words in Hebrew, arranged alphabetically according to their initials, and meaning:
'Make a *golem* of earth to destroy the enemies of Israel!'

To appreciate the deep impression made upon the devout rabbi by this reply it is necessary to know something about the paramount role of letters in Jewish mysticism. According to the Cabbala, letters were the cryptic tools which God brought with Him when He created the world; and so Rabbi Löw knew immediately that the letters and the words which he had heard contained hidden secrets that would enable him to create life out of death, and provide protection for the ghetto.

First, however, he had to find assistants, and not everyone would do. He made a long search before choosing the two right ones. The fact is that it takes the four elements of *esh, majim, ruah,* and *aphar* (fire, water, air, and earth) to create a *golem*. At last, he found an assistant who was like fire and another who resembled water; he himself was air, and the *golem* would be earth.

For seven days and nights Löw and his assistants cleansed their bodies and souls by bathing, fasting, and praying; and then, on the second day of the month of *adar* in the year 5340 after the Creation (or 1580), they left the city and went down to the river Vltava. There, from the clay of the earth, they shaped the figure of a man, six foot tall, lying, a dead and motionless form, on his back. Seven times they walked round it, from the right and from the left, murmuring mystic formulas; then, behold! the *golem* began to glow and breathe, while hair and nails grew on it.

Finally, Rabbi Löw thrust into its mouth a piece of parchment, bearing the four most potent letters, JHVH, which stand for the *hashem*, or name of God. With one voice the men then recited the words from Genesis: 'And the Lord God formed man of the dust of the ground, and breathed into his nostrils the breath of life; and man became a living soul'. Whereupon the figure blinked its eyes, opened them, and looked wonderingly round.

'Stand up on your legs!' Rabbi Löw commanded.

And the figure obediently rose and put on the clothes the men had brought with them. Then all made their way back to the city. Three had left Prague, but four returned.

On the way Rabbi Löw said to his *golem*:

'Know that you are made of earth; your name is Joseph and your mission is to protect the Jews. You shall obey me in all things that I command, go through fire and water, even leap down from the roof, and be my *shamash*—my servant.'

The *golem* was unable to speak; the letter which imparts the gift of speech was missing from among those that Rabbi Löw had received from God. But it is understood what Rabbi Löw said to it and possessed a rare ability to perceive sounds, being able to detect even the faintest and most distant. This rendered it doubly useful as a sentinal in the ghetto, which was its purpose. Countless stories are told of its alertness and many a time it thwarted the wicked designs of the scheming Thaddaeus. Every sabbath eve Rabbi Löw would remove the paper containing the *hashem* from the *golem's* mouth and it would then lie inanimate until the *hashem* was replaced on the Saturday evening.

All in the ghetto rejoiced in the *golem* for many years, but then things went wrong. One Friday afternoon Rabbi Löw forgot to take the *hashem* out of the *golem's* mouth and went off to the synagogue; and suddenly the *golem* ran riot, upset everything in the house, and then rushed into the street, breaking windows, throwing stones, and threatening the whole city with destruction. Terrified people ran in search of Löw, and found him in the synagogue, preparing for the sabbath. If the *golem* was to be stopped, it would have to be done in seconds; for it could not be done on the Sabbath, when no man may take life. Rushing into the street, Rabbi Löw managed at the last moment to snatch the paper from the *golem's* mouth, and at once the creature fell down and lay as though dead.

Rabbi Löw could take no more risks with his *golem*, and so the lifeless creature was carried into the loft of the synagogue. Nobody has ventured up there since, but doubtless it is still there.

It is a pity that the personality of Rabbi Löw has been so tangled in legend, because he seems to have been a truly great

THE GHETTO

man, both a brilliant scholar and unusually broad-minded for a resident of the ghetto. His friends, many of them outside the ghetto, included the celebrated astronomers Johannes Kepler and Tycho Brahe, the latter having settled in Prague after his exile from Denmark. Löw actually met the Emperor, Rudolph the Second; and for a Jew of the despised ghetto to be received by such a ruler was an extraordinary event. It naturally added something to the mythology. According to the new legend which arose, the Emperor visited Rabbi Löw, together with Tycho Brahe, at his house in the ghetto, where, in order that he might feel more at home, his host conjured up Hradcany Castle.

Prague was in those days one of the principal centres of European Jewry and the capital of the kingdom of Bohemia, which was an important member State of the Holy Roman Empire, as well as a personal apanage of the Habsburg rulers. In 1571, when Vienna was seriously threatened by the advance of the Turks, Prague also became the Imperial residence.

It has been estimated that as many as 10,000 Jews lived in Prague in the sixteenth century, and it is one of the few European cities which have had Jewish populations almost continuously from the Middle Ages down to the present century. The Judenstadt, or ghetto, was a city within the city, where Jews lived isolated from the rest of the inhabitants and had their own judicial system and their own prison. The *Meistergericht* was their supreme court. Prague was also the only city where Jews had their own Town Hall: a handsome building with a tower, and a clock on it which had Hebraic figures and hands that moved 'anti-clockwise', Hebrew being read from right to left.

First and last, there was in Prague the splendid old synagogue of *Altneuschule*, a name which suggests that a new synagogue had been erected on the site of an old one. But it is unwise to rely on the most obvious explanations where Jews are concerned. Very often there is a hidden meaning besides the obvious one; and such is the case here.

Some hold the belief that *Altneuschule* signifies something altogether greater than 'Old New School'. They say that its foundation was laid by fugitives from Jerusalem after its destruction by Titus's legions in the year 70; and that the dispersed people had brought stones from the ruins of the old Temple and used them for building the foundations of their new synagogue in Prague. What is more, they made the stipulation (in Hebrew *tenai*) that this new house of prayer should be pulled down at the coming of the Messiah and the stones taken back to Zion, for building the new Temple at the latter day. The Hebrew words *al tenai* mean 'on condition'; and as a reminder they called the synagogue *Al tenai*, a name which in course of time became Germanized to *Altneu*.

These stories help us to envisage life as it was lived in the ghetto 300 and 400 years ago. There is much that is strange and unbelievable, but the ghetto was truly a world unto itself. It is like entering a home for the first time. We open the door and look inside, and perhaps our eye falls first on the things that are peculiar: a picture in bad taste, an 'off' colour, an odd knick-knack, an ugly vase. But once inside, seated in the best chair, we begin to take a proper look. Perhaps then we find that after all the room is of a piece, that features which before looked out of place now fit into their surroundings. The visitor who in time becomes a friend, calling at the house often, finally comes to like all of it, but especially the atmosphere, the general tone of the place and its occupants. The truth is that a home is not merely a thing of the present; it is a record of changing periods, of pleasures and of tribulations, in the lives of those who shaped it. Learning about all these, the outsider gradually understands how it came to be what it is, with all its peculiarities.

The ghetto was a home; a refuge, over the centuries, from an alien and hostile world outside. Behind its walls, in the tiny houses and narrow streets, its people passed their lives from their first faltering steps of childhood until their bones were laid to moulder in a poorly provided burial ground beneath crooked grey stones with their Hebrew inscriptions. The ghetto was the scene of hope and of despair; its weathered walls bore witness to tears and supplication, but also, and far oftener than we are inclined to think, to both wit and mordant satire.

So far we have just opened the door of this house and got

THE GHETTO

a first impression of the home inside, a home such as the world has never known. We must go in and appreciate its good sides and bad. But first we must pause on the threshold and begin by studying the door-plate. It bears the word 'ghetto', a word we have already heard. What does it mean?

Its origin is obscure and the scholars have disagreed about it. Some believe that 'ghetto' is the ending of the Italian word *borghetto*, which is the diminutive of *borgo*, meaning 'town'. Thus if this theory is correct a ghetto is a small town. According to another theory, the name derives from the Hebrew word *get*, which means 'separation'. If this is correct, the ghetto, instead of being the quarter behind the wall, is the wall itself. A German origin has also been suggested. According to this theory, the derivation is the word *Gitter*, or 'bars'; meaning the bars of a cage. In addition to the theories I have mentioned many others have been suggested, some of them highly fanciful. They all have one thing in common: they cannot stand critical examination. To find the right derivation we must go to Venice.

For centuries the city of Venice was known as the 'Queen of the Adriatic'. Up to the discovery of the New World by Columbus she controlled the commerce of Europe, and as 'the city of the lagoons' she grew rich and beautiful. To the Jews the gates of Venice were locked and barred; not so much for religious reasons in this case, as for reasons of commercial policy. The Jews were dangerous commercial rivals, and so were forbidden either to travel by Venetian ships or to forward merchandise by them.

Because of the position which Jewish merchants gained at the close of the Middle Ages, however, both in the Italian peninsula and especially in Turkey, this negative policy could not in the long run be maintained. Jewish merchants from Germany and the Levant could not be prevented from occasionally visiting Venice. In such cases the Senate would relax the regulations, though it insisted that they should neither live nor keep their merchandise in the city centre. Their business had to be restricted to the island of Spinalunga, and in time this came to be known as *Giudecca*, a derivative of *giudeo*, the Italian word for 'Jew'. They had to live in the neighbouring town of Mestre, on the mainland,

and were allowed to visit Venice across the lagoon only fourteen days in a year, paying heavily for the privilege. It took dramatic events in international affairs to make Venice alter its Jewish policy, which it did suddenly and radically.

In 1508 the city faced great danger. Instigated by the Emperor Maximilian, the League of Cambrai despatched its army of papal, German, and Spanish troops to conquer and divide the republic. The army advanced swiftly, laying waste the cities of Verona, Padua, and Treviso, and leaving a trail of smoking ruins. The German and Spanish troops were fanatical Catholics, and their first victims at each stage of their advance were the unbelieving Jews; and Jews, fleeing panic-stricken before them, poured into the capital. Their only hope was to put the sea between them and the enemy: and Venice allowed them to cross the water and find a refuge there.

After the war they stayed in Venice, though the priests, fulminating against them from every pulpit, demanded their ejection. But Mestre across the lagoon lay in ruins. Where were they to go? Finally, Venice issued a safe-conduct, a *condotta*, which entitled them to stay. It was costly and was valid for only three years; when it fell due for renewal the charge was raised. But that is how the Jewish settlement in Venice began.

It was thought dangerous, however, to have Jews in a Christian city and there were strict canonical laws which forbade Christians to associate with them. The only way was to segregate them; and to this problem the Venetian Senate found a solution.

There was a small island near the city, separated from the other districts by canals and approached by only a drawbridge. Here a foundry had been built; it was called *geto nuova*, the 'new foundry', and was surrounded by a protecting wall. This was the ideal place to put Jews, and they were directed to settle there. The site being very cramped, the city afterwards gave them a neighbouring island, where there had also been a foundry, one older than the first, and therefore called *geto vecchio*, the 'old foundry'.

This Jewish quarter in Venice is the oldest of its kind in the world. There the Jews were required to live behind the

THE GHETTO

wall; no Christian was allowed to dwell there, and the gates were locked at night. This took place in the year 1516, and the *geto* at Venice not only provided the pattern for the ghetto system in general, it also gave it its name. *Geto* became ghetto.

We shall return later to the Venetian ghetto. It was destined to be one of the most celebrated, and a rich and distinctive life developed there. Suffice it at this point to establish the fact that it was at Venice that the ghetto got its name.

The establishment of the ghetto at Venice in 1516 was only the final stage in an evolution that had been going on ever since the Jews had settled abroad. It had begun probably in 63 B.C. when Jerusalem was captured by Pompey, long before its destruction. He took captives to Rome, and they were followed by merchants and artisans. The Jewish colony in Rome, dating from the time of Pompey, had been the first embryonic ghetto.

It was a voluntary one, however. There was no order which segregated the Jews; they congregated spontaneously, and there is nothing very remarkable in that fact. Similar developments have taken place in all periods, and are familiar even today, when American cities have their 'black belts' and even London its coloured districts. Many cities in the world have Polish and Italian quarters, to say nothing of Chinatowns. It is a natural tendency for compatriots to form colonies in a foreign environment.

Jews did the same. Where there were many the cities soon developed streets with a Jewish character. There would be *kosher* butchers selling ritually slaughtered meat; shop signs would carry Hebrew names such as Abraham, Jacob, Levi, and Samuel; Jewish types would be noticeable among the children at play or the women shopping. In one of the side streets there would be a synagogue. Whole districts would be named after them: the *vicus judaerum*, or 'Street of the Jews', in ancient Rome; the Judengasse in Germany; the Juiverie in France; the Jewry in England. The Jew was an alien wherever he went, and particularly so in the Middle Ages, when everybody had his native and restricted locality, the serf bound to his lord, the lord to his overlord, the overlord to his king, and the merchant and artisan to their company or guild. How the Jews were fitted into this rigid system is another story, irrelevant to our present theme. I would only emphasize how natural it was that Jewish quarters should evolve in the cities where Jews lived.

This was especially so because the Jews form a separate group of people having their own traditions and their own taboos, unintelligible to other people. Why should one abstain from eating pork? Why should animals have to be slaughtered in such a seemingly barbaric way? What is wrong with using the same dishes for both meat and milk? They were strange people who celebrated the sabbath on a Saturday and worked on the Sunday, and to whom the Christian holidays were ordinary working days, their mysterious festivals being celebrated at other times. They never married except among themselves, and every house in the small Jewish quarter was related to the next. Though they learnt to speak the language of the country in which they lived, they introduced so many Hebrew words into it that it soon degenerated into a special Jewish dialect or idiom.

Fear also promoted Jewish isolation. They had every reason to be afraid; for in the brief life of the individual as well as in the long history of his people there were evil memories of a hostility which would break out into violence, with looting and murder as the consequence. There was wisdom in drawing closer together; for then in times of trouble they could better defend themselves.

While the Jews drew together, however, of their own free will, living voluntarily in the same street, and regarding it as their right to do so, the Jewish quarter was not a ghetto as we understand it. That came when it was forced upon them and they were driven behind the wall.

It is one of history's paradoxes that at the time when Christendom was emerging from what we call the Dark Ages the Middle Ages were beginning to descend in earnest on Judaism. When the inhabitants of Europe were groping their way in the twilight the Jews had been perhaps the most enlightened people in the world. The Spanish Jews, proud inheritors of Classical and Arab culture, had assimilated and transmitted it to the developing centres of European culture,

THE GHETTO

and so in a very real sense had helped to promote both the Renaissance and the Reformation. Yet when these two great movements were gathering momentum, soon to revolutionize the life of Europe, the windows of Jewry were blacked out and a period of gloom began. The Jewish Middle Ages did not ebb out until the French Revolution was in sight. It is the tragic centuries in between, the age of the ghetto, that are the theme of this book.

During the millennium and a half in which they were exiles and aliens, the Jews, wherever they appeared, caused first surprise and wonder, then vigilance and fear of rivalry, and finally, with the rising power of the Church, the horror and detestation of its priests. The first manifestations of hatred were the appalling massacres of German Jews by the pious Crusaders before they turned on their outside enemies in the Orient. In those tragic years the Jews learnt by bitter experience that a spear is a weapon with two ends: a handle held by the Christian and a point aimed at the Jew.

The next stage in the evolutionary process was the Lateran Council of 1215, which introduced the emblem of Jewry. The hostility of the Church had become obvious; and from then on every Jew was compelled to wear a red or yellow badge proclaiming his race and warning others against associating with him. This was the mark of Cain; wherever the aggressive Church could enforce the regulation in full the Jew was branded as an outsider. It robbed him of his former pride and made him a second-class citizen. This was apparent in his gait, as he slouched with bent back and cringing looks through the streets, and urchins bombarded him and the mob jeered at him. Even to himself he soon began to appear as the contemptible and miserable wretch the priests did all they could to make him.

It was not everywhere, however, that the Church had the power, and it was only briefly and occasionally that it succeeded in making the badge universal. On the whole, the Jews came through the Middle Ages relatively unscathed; it was about 1500 that the storm broke calamitously about their heads. In 1492 the Jews of Spain, Israel's pride, were expelled from the land where their forefathers had lived for more than a thousand years, as the Counter-Reformation mobilized the resources of the Catholic Church in a great effort to stamp out heresy. The Jews went down with it; and, what is more, they fared no better on the opposite front. After a brief period of good will, the countries which adopted the Reformation proved as hostile as Catholic countries.

The standard-bearer of the Counter-Reformation, about the middle of the sixteenth century, was Paul the Fourth. In Jewish history his record is nearly as black as that of Innocent the Third, who introduced the emblem of Jewry.

On July 12, 1555, a date which will ever remain a black one in the annals of the Christian Church, Pope Paul the Third issued the bull *Cum nimis absurdum*. Cruelly noting in its opening sentence the absurdity of past lenience towards the Jews, he revived, down to the smallest detail, the rigorous and cunningly devised regulations aimed against them. They were forbidden to keep Christian servants, to serve as doctors to Christians, to hold a respectable occupation, to own fixed property; they were to bear the emblem of Jewry, and the ghetto was to be made compulsory. As in the ghetto of Venice, they were to be segregated and surrounded by a wall, which was to be kept locked from sunset until the following morning.

The age of the ghetto had begun.

Entering by the gate, we find the ghetto inside, with its narrow streets, dark and gloomy even in the middle of the day. On either side the houses tower to a great height, shutting out the sun from the streets and courtyards. Medieval streets had always been like this; but Jewish quarters were forced to maintain their medieval character long after the surrounding cities had opened up their streets and rendered them more habitable.

The street or area set aside for the ghetto was cramped and in the fullest sense closed, because in the evening the entrance was locked and barred. The inhabitants were herded together; and while the population grew, the ghetto became increasingly congested, the houses being raised in height to accommodate them, the streets getting steadily narrower. The Jewish street in Cologne was actually called *Enge Gasse*—

THE GHETTO

'Narrow Alley'. If such a street was not a slum to start with, it soon became one.

The obvious consequence was fearful overcrowding, of which we shall hear more when we come to consider the ghettos individually. A further consequence was bad sanitation and frequent epidemics. His unhealthy life left its marks on the Jew's physique; he aged early, looked lean and emaciated; and was noticeable for his flabbiness, sickly complexion, narrow chest, and bent back. Prevalent inbreeding also affected his general health.

The ghetto produced, too, a particular state of mind: a chronic sense of insecurity, and a dread of the envy and hatred which lurked on the other side of the wall. To begin with, no doubt, the ghetto wall had implied some protection against the mob; but in actual fact it had the opposite effect. Now the mob always knew where to find the Jews; and so the ghetto became a trap, enclosing its defenceless inmates like sheep in a fold.

Moreover, it shut the Jew off from the world, forming a cultural backwater impervious to outside influences. A whole people thus turned in on itself, to exist on its inherited resources. The spiritual segregation proved to be as serious as the physical confinement of narrow streets and back alleys. In this environment religion became the all-in-all basis of everything, and permeated the whole atmosphere. Inside the walls, the voice of doubt and the warnings of criticism went unheard. What profound human tragedies were engendered in this stifling climate we shall shortly see.

A river when it is dammed forces an outlet at the weakest point. When the Jewish people, who in ancient times had lived by farming, following the changing rhythms of nature, were shut in behind their wall, their bodies fettered, they had only the spiritual life to sustain them. Consequently, there was a vigorous development of the intellect and extreme intellectualism. Not for nothing was it said:

'God save us from the hand of the heathen and the head of the Jew!'

Moreover, his religion was shot through with logic. The inmates of the ghetto read and studied, and they also sharpened their wits in interminable debates on the Talmud.

They engrossed themselves in the Talmud, reading it with such deep concentration that they would thoughtlessly pluck the hairs from their beards, leaving them between the pages as future proof of the zeal with which they had read it. Of course there was also a reverse tendency. Dreams and visions are not contained by wretchedness and poverty, nor are they nurtured by logic and debate. They flourished like weeds, and with the same vigour as the old Oriental myths which bred them, when they did not degenerate into grotesque superstitions and medieval magic. False messiahs achieved great and easy successes. Sorcery and black magic abounded. At the same time, there was the true mysticism which provided the religious revivals that in evil times help to make life worth living.

So far we have chiefly considered the darker aspects of the ghetto. But it also had its brighter side, for life is unquenchable, and the eternally questing Jewish mind cannot be confined entirely by prison walls. There were certain encouraging signs, which though faint were nevertheless unmistakable. Just as when, standing by a pool, one sees the sudden leap of a fish, catching a glimpse of a clean and supple body and the momentary white streak which it leaves on the grey surface, so flashes of life can be discerned rising from the grey surface of the ghetto.

It was so with the mystics. To comfort themselves in their wretchedness they had wonderful legends which, passing from father to son, told of ancient greatness. There was, for example, the story of the mystic who had saved a ghetto against attack by attaching cabbalistic charms to the gate and so preventing the enemy from getting in. Many tales were told of steadfastness under pressure of baptism; and there was also one about a baptized Jew who, on the day preceding his ordination as a priest, heard the bells ring for the Messiah, and at once became aware of his shameful defection. Above all, there was the story of the Jew who was elected Pope. This one was sure to provoke bursts of laughter.

There was wit, humour, and keen satire in the ghetto. This was the smile which helped to hold back the tears. It has its roots in the Bible, and for a thousand years it could be

THE GHETTO

a sharp sword in Jewish hands. A dry humour and a mordant philosophy of life are revealed, for example, in this Hassidic adage:

'A man is young for as long as a woman can make him happy or unhappy. He is middle-aged when a woman can make him happy but not unhappy. And he is old when a woman can make him neither happy nor unhappy.'

There is also a hint of a smile in the accounts, springing from the ghetto itself, of the strange types that were frequently found in the alleys and the back streets. Amid the general poverty, beggars of all kinds were common, as they are in every city where there are slums; and among them there was the clear-sighted man who sat in the street with a sign marked 'Blind', and was handed a coin by a passer-by.

'God bless you,' he cried after the man. 'I saw straight away that you were a good man.'

There is one kind of beggar who is in a class apart; namely, the *schnorrer*. This man does not stand on the pavement holding out his hand, nor does he cringe and whine. He knows that alms are his due. A *schnorrer* feels no shame at all in begging; it is the duty of the rich to give him *mazot* at the Passover, fuel in winter, and a coin occasionally; and in his own eyes he is one of the steps of Jacob's ladder by which the wealthy ascend to Heaven. Like a real philosopher, too, he does not expect to be thanked for his help, for he knows that virtue is its own reward.

If, however, the gift is not voluntarily forthcoming he feels that he must use every means to enforce it, and then he is not squeamish; gentleness, indeed, is not his strong point. On the contrary, the *schnorrer* has developed a remarkable ability in furthering his profession, and he is both impudent and persistent—though always smilingly. This is what is known in the vernacular of the ghetto as *chutzpa*; that is to say, a mixture of resourcefulness and sheer cheek. To anybody who has a sense of humour there is something irresistible in hearing a beggar switch over like lightning from impudence to wit.

To take one example among thousands, there was a *schnorrer* who had dined at an inn, and of course had no money with which to pay for his meal.

'Give me half-an-hour's credit,' he said to the innkeeper, 'and I'll go and beg the money.'

'How am I to know you'll come back?' the inkeeper asked.

'If you don't believe me, you can come with me,' the *schnorrer* replied in a tone of injured innocence.

At which the innkeeper cried in alarm:

'Do you think I can be seen in company with a beggar?'

Quick as lightning came the answer:

'All right, then go out and beg the money yourself, while I wait here.'

There were other types. A *schlemihl* is always unlucky; a fumbler, he continually gets in the way of others, and is a failure in everything. A *schlemihl* becomes really ridiculous when he has to contend with a shrewish wife; one of those of whom it says in Proverbs: 'It is better to dwell in the corner of the housetop than with a brawling woman and in a wide house.' Here, indeed, is a source of entertainment. Take the story of the *schlemihl* who had visitors, and the wife who wanted to show who was in charge.

'Sit down under the table!' she ordered him.

And obediently he crawled under it.

'Come out again!' she commanded.

But from below came the reply:

'Oh no; I'll show you who's master in this house.'

The *schlemihl* had a sort of first cousin, who was called a *schlimazl*. It is a typically Yiddish word, made up of the German *schlimm* (bad) and Hebrew *mazl* (luck); in short, he was the man of bad luck. Not that he was devoid of cleverness and ability; he was just unlucky. The difference between the two was generally expressed as follows:

'A *schlemihl* spills the tureen of hot soup on to the *schlimazl*.'

How these two coped with their difficult life was a riddle. They seemed to live on air. Accordingly, from them developed a further ghetto type: the *luftmensch*, or 'man of air'. We shall encounter him later on.

Ein Jude und ein Schwein
dürfen hier nicht herein.

THE GHETTO

This sign ('Jews and pigs not admitted') stood at the entrance to a public park in Hanover, not many years ago. It indicates the general attitude in Christendom to Jewry through the whole period of the ghetto. He slunk through the world a despised man, the mark of Cain on his forehead.

But there was one place on earth where he felt free to breathe: in his own home. There he was king; and however condemned outside the ghetto, at home he could cherish his wife and children.

Then, when the sabbath came round, he would throw off his rags, bathe, and put on his finest clothes. On that day the home was a temple; the table its altar. It was decked with a shining white cloth and the candles burnt over the two twisted loaves. A small glass of wine was drained to the glory of God and His holy day; prayers were sung, and afterwards gay songs. On that day of the week the Jew felt that he was one of God's chosen people.

Here we have the miracle of the ghetto. However grim the degradation on the other days of the week, here was the relief that none could take away. The solemn words of the old prophets of Judah were like beacons. On the long weekdays of the world outside the wall they would flicker and seem about to be extinguished by winds of contempt, but on the sabbath, in his own home, they flared up radiantly triumphant. He knew that one day he would be delivered. He served his God through a long and dark night; but the night would have an end, and one morning God would vouchsafe him the dawn. On that day the Messiah would come; and all his sufferings would be forgotten.

Expectation of the One to come was the deep breathing of the ghetto.

We have taken a quick look at the chequered world of the ghetto and have formed some tentative impressions. It can now be left to relate its own long and scattered history. First, however, we must lay down some sort of plan that will assist us on our way.

I concluded my book *The Three Rings* by describing how the Jews of Spain, the *Sephardim*, were expelled from that country and sought refuge elsewhere. They were followed, later on, by other streams of exiles from Spain, the *Maranos*, those forcibly baptized Jews who wanted to escape to a country where they could freely profess the faith of their forefathers. Some of these 'Portuguese' Jews, as in time they were called, went first to Amsterdam and afterwards to London and many other cities. Wherever they went they took with them the best features of the Spanish culture of that period, and there were times when they were to play a vital role in the countries which had admitted them. It seems natural to begin with them, therefore.

The great majority of the *Sephardim* took the route along the Mediterranean coast, and some reached Palestine. We will go with these to Safad, the city in the mountains of Galilee, where, devoting their lives to mysticism, they created a strange culture which was later to send its sparks far and wide, lighting beacons in distant lands.

From there we will proceed on a round tour of the old Jewish communities; first in Italy, then the settlements of the Ashkenazi Jews in Germany, and finally in Poland, where the ghetto was to develop the proudest period of Jewish culture, but which was also to end in disaster.

We shall find fortunes so incredible that no writer would dare to imagine them, but which nevertheless were carved out of the hard rock of reality. In doing so we shall find that, despite all the ghetto's degradation and wretchedness, this extraordinary people were to confer gifts on their neighbours which were drawn from the riches of their poverty, and from the poverty of their riches.

II

OPEN DOORS

THE fierce weather had gone on for weeks and there had been nothing like it within living memory; for many years to come, the people of Holland were to talk of the equinoctial gales in that autumn of 1596. In seemingly never-ending columns the grey waves of the North Sea surged and battered against the low-lying dikes, as ragged black clouds raced across the sky and howling winds whipped up the sea, scattering the flecks of grey-white foam in all directions before the hungry waves finally swallowed them again.

To guard the dikes in such a storm was hazardous work. Small black figures in long sea-boots and with sou'westers pulled well over their heads were posted at threatened points, where they could be seen leaning against the wind or seeking the little shelter that was to be found behind the sea-wall. Alert eyes kept close watch on the buffetings of the sea; and if at any point they made inroads into the fragile wall, men would come hurrying with their spades and sandbags to repair it. During those tempestuous nights disaster was averted; the dikes held out.

Suddenly, the winds dropped; as the end of September approached calm followed storm, and the sun shone once more from a cloudless blue sky. The days grew light and warm, and the end of September brought with it one of those gracious Indian summers that are appreciated far more than summer itself.

In the streets of Amsterdam people awoke to new life. During the storm they had kept inside their solidly built houses and watched it rage from behind the small bow windows, but now the sun recalled them into the open air. Wrenched-off tiles lay scattered about the streets and chimney-pots had been blown down. Large trees had been snapped in two and the yellowed autumn foliage stripped off those which had survived. The flaked leaves had danced across the cobbled streets and found a final resting place in the grey water of the canals. The cleanly Amsterdammers got busy tidying up the streets and gardens which they kept so neat. There was plenty to discuss with the neighbours, both gale damage and shipwreck and the latest local news.

Suddenly, however, the bustle and the talking stopped. Something was going on down the street. The men placed their shovels and rakes against the walls and the women came into the street to have a look. Windows were thrown open and well-nourished matrons in caps leant out of them to see what was afoot. And there they came: a company of the civic guard marching quickly through the streets. They were not in step; for they were free men who could do as they pleased and the officers were of their own kind. But there was strength in the ample figures; and though their large, heavy features and impassive blue eyes suggested slow thinking and deliberate action, they could hurry if need be. These were not review troops, and indeed they had seen war and victory against the armies of the King of Spain, the most celebrated in Europe. Tried and tested, they grasped their halberds and firearms.

On the outskirts of the city, hidden behind the languishing fruit-trees of an old garden, stood a small house, and this was their destination. As soon as it came within sight the captain in charge called a halt. He had orders to go carefully and show caution. None of those he had come for was to get away.

Two detachments were sent round to the other side of the house along side streets, and soon it was surrounded. Then at a blast from the captain's whistle the men advanced from all sides. In a matter of seconds a close cordon encircled the house. The Spanish papists were caught.

With pistol in one hand and drawn sword in the other the captain strode to the door, kicked it open, and crossed the threshold, his men supporting him. They gazed into a small room, lit by a few candles. Twenty or thirty men were scattered about the room, all wearing hats, and with white shawls over their shoulders. On approaching the door the captain had heard the murmured chanting of prayers in an unintelligible language. Now he saw they were reading them from old-looking rolls of parchment.

As the heavily armed soldiers burst into the prayer house panic broke out among the congregation. Staring, terror-stricken eyes were turned on the troops and a single shrill cry went up:

'The Inquisition!'

Their terror gave them wings, and with incredible agility they sprang on to the forms, wrenched open the windows, and leapt out. But then they fell back on to the floor again, the blood drained from their despairing faces. Halbardiers also blocked the windows, barring their flight that way as well. They were helplessly trapped.

The officer ordered them into a corner of the room, and then the house search began. There would surely be Catholic ritual books, holy-water pitchers, and altar vessels. But the Dutch soldiers found nothing but rolls of parchment and well-thumbed prayer books, printed in a script they could not read; in Hebrew, as the officer afterwards learnt. He looked round bewildered.

Early that morning he had been summoned to the Town Hall and told that the police had tracked down a secret haunt of Catholics, probably a Spanish spy centre; it was a clear case of treason. During the past few months neighbours had observed strange goings-on in the old house. Every Friday evening, and several times on Saturday, a number of people would gather there. They were not Dutchmen; that was obvious, for their long black hair hung in elaborately arranged locks over their shoulders, they had fine features, and there was something aristocratic about the elegant van Dyke beards which some of them wore. Their dress, too, differed from the plain, uncoloured clothes usually worn by citizens of Amsterdam; they wore colourful silk doublets, immaculate ruffs, and broad hats. Moreover, they had been heard to use strange-sounding Spanish names when they met before arriving at the house. They would swing their hats in a broad sweep, bowing and gracefully greeting one another by name: Juan Martinez de Cabbaleria, Rodrigo Ramirez de Ribera, Lope de Vera y Alarcon. The good citizens of Amsterdam nearly twisted their tongues trying to repeat the names, so as to remember them. In short, it all looked highly suspicious, recalling the hated Spanish noblemen who had lorded it over the Netherlands not very long ago.

If they were Spaniards they must also be Catholics; but oddly enough, there was nothing in the house that resembled popery. The captain beckoned to a distinguished-looking old man who appeared to be in charge. The old man bowed ceremoniously and gave his name: Jacob Tirado. But he could not speak Dutch; and the captain did not understand when he tried Latin. There was nothing else for it but to take the whole assembly to the Town Hall for examination through an interpreter.

Once more the clearing-up operations stopped in the storm-ravaged streets as the company marched back, this time escorting prisoners. Hundreds of inquisitive eyes followed the soldiers and the despairing captives. There was lively talk, and all manner of conjectures were exchanged across the garden hedges as the plump men and women discussed the occurrence they had been lucky to witness. But when, towards evening, they saw all the prisoners return, talking happily together, their curiosity increased. Strange things must have happened.

As indeed they had; for when Jacob Tirado had established contact with the police through an interpreter, up at the Town Hall, he had had a singular tale to tell. It was true that they had come from Spain; or rather Portugal, for it was three generations since their ancestors had been forced to leave Spain. It was also true that they were Catholics; but only by compulsion and in appearance. Their popery had been assumed in order to save their lives, and in fact they were Jews. And that day, to the Dutch an ordinary weekday, was the most sacred of the year: namely *Yom Kippur*, the great Day of Atonement. It was their principal service that the police had disturbed.

When Jacob Tirado spoke of the ceremonies on the Day of Atonement an understanding smile had spread across the police officer's face. The devout reformed Christian was well versed in the Old Testament and remembered the story of the sacrificial animal on whose back the chief priest loaded the sins of the people before driving it into the wilderness.

Contact between the two men was thus established and the old Jew waxed so eloquent that the interpreter could hardly keep pace. With great volubility and eloquent gestures he explained that they hated the Inquisition even more than did the Dutch. They had good reason. For more than a century the Inquisition had kept a vigilant eye on the *Maranos*, as the forcibly baptized Jews of Spain and Portugal were called by an abusive name which meant 'swine'. Thousands of them had suffered on Dominican racks, or had been burnt at the stake in the *autos-da-fé*. Those who had so far escaped lived in perpetual fear of the day when the Inquisition would swoop on them.

This group, however, had escaped, having been allowed to leave the country on the pretext that they were going on pilgrimage to Rome. When well out of sight of land they had turned, not south to Gibraltar and Italy, but north; for it had long been whispered among them that far to the north was a country called Holland where there was that rare thing, religious freedom. The refugees had sailed through the English Channel and cruised about the North Sea, looking for a chance to land. For weeks they had sailed to and fro along the coast between Amsterdam and Hamburg, the captain being unable to decide where to venture ashore. Then a sudden storm had forced them into the harbour at Emden.

They had inquired their way to the house of a rabbi, called Moses Uri Levi, and had asked him to circumcize them and teach them the religion of their fathers.

But Moses had been full of misgivings. In that Protestant town they might arouse dangerous attention. So many Jews from an arch-Catholic country: that would never do. He advised them to sail to Amsterdam; and he went with them and there admitted them to the Covenant. When the rich and distinguished old Manuel Rodrigues Vega was circumsized, he changed his name to the Jewish one of Jacob Tirado. The community of which he was now the leader had been holding their secret meetings in the old house, which they used as a synagogue.

As a result of the inquiry the prisoners were at once released, and they hurried off home, overwhelmed with joy. During the following days, however, Jacob Tirado paid frequent visits to the Town Hall, where, assisted by the envoy of the Sultan of Morocco, himself of Spanish-Jewish extraction, he explained to the city fathers the advantages to Holland in opening its doors to the Spanish and Portuguese *Maranos*. Many of these were wealthy; and they would smuggle their riches out of Portugal, and so transfer considerable capital to the Netherlands. They were also men of ability, both intellectuals and merchants with international trade connections.

Tirado was shrewd enough not to appeal in the first instance to humanitarian feelings, knowing that the down-to-earth Dutch would think primarily of their own practical interests. But fortunately commercial advantages and idealism coincided, and he skilfully exploited the situation. In the course of a few days, the Amsterdam Corporation granted the Jewish fugitives right of residence and free religious instruction. When a year or two later they built their first synagogue in the city they named it Beth Jacob (or 'House of Jacob') in honour of Jacob Tirado.

Holland had been a storm centre for many years; and for a long period the united Netherlands, comprising present-day Holland and Belgium, had formed a part of the mighty Spanish Empire. The idea of the Reformation, however, had at an early date won the support of the nobility, the burghers, and the farmers; and the great majority of the population in the northern provinces, the Netherlands of today, had embraced the new faith. They responded to the ideas, not of Luther but of Calvin, and the Dutch congregations consequently belonged to the branch of Protestantism known as the Reformed Church.

The Netherlands were unfortunate in having as their absolute ruler the bigoted Philip the Second, great-grandson of Isabella the Catholic; the king who said that, come what may, he would never rule over heretics. Accordingly, the Inquisition soon lit its fires in Dutch towns and cities and launched a campaign of extermination against the Evangelicals.

The citizens of Holland refused to submit and rebelled. The year 1568 saw the start of the war of independence; the most romantic and heroic that the world has ever seen; 'the weak against the strong, the few against the many'. The revolt can only be compared to the war of the Maccabees in ancient times against the mad Antiochus Epiphanes, or to David's struggle against Goliath. And the miracle occurred; the dikes of Holland held out against the raging seas. Little by little the citizens drove the swarthy fanatical armies from their land, along with the Inquisition and all its horrors.

By the time that Jacob Tirado and his companions were allowed to settle in Amsterdam the war had been virtually won. In 1588 swift English warships had destroyed King Philip's invincible Armada; it was a crushing blow which also settled the fate of Holland, for the power of Spain had been broken. Blue skies and bright sunshine returned to the storm-ravaged but now liberated country, though the war was not quite over, and new storms were to descend on Holland before final victory was won. It was in 1648—after eighty years of war—that the peace at length came which formally recognized Holland's independence.

But Holland's Golden Age began in 1600. And the Jewish refugees from Spain and Portugal were an important contributing element.

Their start was, as we have seen, dramatic; but the Dutch had every reason to remember the sacrifices and sufferings their victory had cost them, and anything connected with Spain was bound to be suspect. Once they had realized that the *Maranos* hated their Spanish rulers and the Inquisition as much as they did themselves, they threw their doors wide open. Tens of thousands of *Maranos* passed through.

The fires of the *autos-da-fé* had blazed for centuries in the public squares of Spain and Portugal, and Thomas Torquemada, Isabella's cruel Grand Inquisitor, could retire satisfied after fifteen years of work, leaving others to continue what he had so well begun. He could look back on a record of 10,000 Jews burnt at the stake, as well as 10,000 *reconciliados* whom his men had forced by means of torture to accept baptism and surrender their possessions. Fear of these activities spread like wildfire, and many who were weak in the faith hurriedly sought safety under the Catholic wing.

These luckless neo-Christians, however, who did not call themselves *Maranos* but *anussim* ('unfree'), remained wards of the Inquisition for the rest of their lives. Its spies kept vigilant watch on all their movements, and woe betide the relapsed heretics. The tribunals were ready waiting in every town and city to remove them 'mercifully and without bloodshed'—a euphemism which meant death at the stake.

The Inquisition's powers were boundless, its subterfuges as cynical and as sadistic as those resorted to later on by the Gestapo, its disciple. Nevertheless, it failed to achieve its final aim; for Spanish Jewry survived in secret. Generation after generation its watchword was: Pay lip service to Christianity but honour God in your heart; pretend to be a Christian but remain secretly a Jew! Young children were brought up as Catholics, but when they reached maturity they were initiated into the Jewish faith. Outwardly, the *Maranos*, parents as well as children, had to be professing Christians. They attended church, and went to confession and Communion; when strangers were present they even ate pork. But in their homes, at least when the servants were not watching, they observed Jewish customs and celebrated the festivals as well as they could.

The *Maranos* were a chronic problem to the Church. Secret Jews were everywhere: among the nobility, the highest officials, and the clergy. They even included bishops, as well as inquisitors who are known to have clung, in their heart of hearts, to their ancestral faith.

But they went in perpetual fear of their lives, and were everywhere under the surveillance of the Inquisition's secret police. If at Easter-time they bought radishes in the market place they could endanger their lives, since the ritual of the Passover included the use of 'bitter herbs'. The minions of the Church had a list of thirty-four signs that were regarded as 'Judaizing propensities'. Thus it was incriminating to buy unleavened bread at Easter, to wash hands before a meal, to put on clean linen on a Friday evening, and to avoid eating meat and butter at the same meal. No one could feel safe.

The Jews had been attached to the Iberian peninsula by the ties of a thousand years. Nowhere, during their exile, had they felt so much at home as in Spain, where Jewish culture had borne some of its fairest flowers. Now, however, bright day had given way to the blackest of nights, and, grievous though the decision was, the *Maranos* had no option but to sever their ties with Spain; their only hope of a decent existence was to get out. So for centuries there was a steady stream of Jewish emigrants from Spain and Portugal. Most of those who could went to the new Turkish Empire in the Levant. We, however, have planned to go with those large numbers who, attracted by the reports of freedom in Holland, sailed north.

Many, of course, came to a tragic end on their flight and vanished into the great unknown; and those who managed to reach a haven of safety never forgot the adventures and the suspense they had been through. The stories were recounted by generation after generation. First, there was the ingenuity they had had to display in making all their preparations, among them the conversion of their property into liquid assets, which would usually take the form of diamonds—and here we have the beginnings of the diamond industry of Amsterdam. Then there was the risky procedure of chartering a ship and getting exit permits, which perhaps had to be false. Even when they had succeeded in putting to sea they might encounter hostile ships of war, a privateer, or a hurricane. The following escape story suggests both the adventures and the horrors of such a flight.

A young man named Manuel Lopez Pereira was travelling north in a Spanish ship, along with his sister, the beautiful Maria Nunez, and many other *Maranos*, when they were intercepted by an English frigate. England and Spain were at war, and so naturally the Spanish ship was seized and taken in prize to London. There, however, Cupid took a hand in the game. The English captain was none other than the Earl of Essex, and, captivated by the exotic beauty of the black-eyed Portuguese girl, he courted her.

When Queen Elizabeth heard the story she desired to see Maria Nunez who had won the heart of her loyal servant, and sent for her. She, too, was struck by Maria's charms. But the Jewish girl refused the earl, saying that she could not marry a Christian. The old book which tells the story says that 'she forsook England's pomp for the sake of Jewry'. Seeing her steadfastness, the queen ordered the release of the ship and its passengers, and they sailed on to Amsterdam.

The story has a happy ending. In Amsterdam Maria consented to marry one of her fellow-fugitives who had long loved her, and thus was celebrated the first Jewish wedding in Amsterdam. No fewer than twenty-four cousins of the bride and bridegroom attended the ball.

The Jews settled in the southern part of Amsterdam, where the River Amstel, which gives the city its name, enters it. The quarter was of course named after them; Joodenburt, it was called, and it was a kind of voluntary, self-chosen ghetto.

Joodenburt was a world unto itself. Entering it one passed from the regularly built and tidily kept Amsterdam into a veritable Oriental quarter, exotic and noisy. In neighbouring streets, quiet, fair-haired, muscular men and women walked slowly and rather solemnly. In the Joodenburt there was constant excitement, as everyone talked, laughed, shouted and bustled, except for the white-bearded old men who sat outside the houses, dozing or chatting with their neighbours. The streets were narrow and not nearly so well kept as the Dutch streets. Splendid houses with magnificent Oriental features stood alongside tumbledown tenements; tall and narrow buildings which already resembled slums and were overpopulated with thin, pale people and swarms of black-headed children. It was to be many years before the rich Jewish merchants would move out of the Joodenburt and build themselves stately houses in Christian quarters.

Even the language was strange. The immigrant Jews remained loyal to the melodious tongue of Castile; and in the evening, in gardens where young people gathered, Andalusian folk-songs would be heard. Slow to understand the rougher language of their northern neighbours, they took even longer to speak it. Centuries were to pass before their poets would get the feel of it, learn to write it, and borrow its words with which to express their dreams and ideas. The vernacular of the Joodenburt remained for long the Spanish dialect known as *Ladino*.

Every year more shiploads of refugees would arrive in the port of Amsterdam, and as time went on the Dutch Jews became very numerous. One synagogue was insufficient to meet their needs, and more were built. But they remained in the Joodenburt, forming a separate enclave in the midst of their Dutch surroundings. The responsibility for this was not all theirs. Holland was the first state in modern times to proclaim freedom of religious worship. It was in 1579, at the Union of Utrecht, that the insurgent provinces issued their declaration that 'every citizen is at liberty to choose his own religion, and no man shall be penalized because of his faith'. The declaration of the principle of religious liberty was unique for those times; and Jews flocked to take advantage of it.

A principle so advanced could not, of course, be fully realized all at once. Strict Calvinism was in power, and it was for that that the people of Holland had fought and died. It was no more than human that many should think that the religious freedom they had struggled for so bitterly should be reserved for the Calvinist Reformed Church. The belief that diversity of religious faith demoralized a nation belonged to the spirit of the times. So in the treatment of religious minorities Holland fluctuated between tolerance and severity. Those who were oppressed would bitterly equate 'Orange' with 'Spanish'.

How great, nevertheless, was the difference between Holland and the rest of Europe! When there was official interference it was never against the freedom of belief, which was inviolable, but against public statement and action. All were free to worship God in their own way at home; and the Jews throughout enjoyed the freedom that was promised them, subject to a few clear limitations: they had to refrain from religious propaganda; they were excluded from public offices; they were not allowed to marry Christians; and there were certain occupational restrictions. They did not obtain civic rights until 1667; and it was to take another two hundred years for them to achieve full equality. Yet even during the period of the ghetto they had ample opportunity to display their skill and energy; and they played their part in making the small country of Holland a great nation.

A period of prosperity followed on the victorious war; and the power of Holland reached out to the furthest parts of the earth. Commercial and naval strength rendered her the equal of the Great Powers, and kings and statesmen sought her favours. Numerous ships brought home the wealth of the Orient from the East Indies, and the riches of the Levant streamed into her ports. Thrift and civic virtues preserved what courage and industry had achieved, though of course affluence had its vices, among them greed, uncontrolled speculation, and finally the pursuit of doubtful enterprises. 'When Mijnheer Satan pays, he must be punctually served,' as the saying went.

The great economic expansion was accompanied by a cultural one, and Dutch painting, above all, rose to heights that have never since been equalled. Rembrandt, the greatest of the painters, lived for many years in Breedstraat in Amsterdam, near to the Joodenburt, and he has left some vivid pictures of Jewish life in the Amsterdam of three hundred years go. He found many of his models in the Jewish quarter, depicting its old men as the patriarchs of the Bible, and Jewish leaders and young women with such psychological insight that we almost seem to hear them speak.

But, with a few exceptions, it was not in cultural spheres that the Jews repaid the Dutch for their hospitality. Most of them entered trade and industry, for which they were well suited. It was no empty boast when Jacob Tirado told the Amsterdam city fathers of their far-flung trade connections. Over many generations they had developed contacts with their fellow-Jews in the Orient. Those contacts they took with them to Holland. These Spanish Jews were no small-town tradesmen but did business on a world scale and thought in terms of commercial policies. Having both capital and initiative, they were soon active in the two principal instruments of Dutch overseas trade, the West Indies and East Indies companies.

Many Dutch Jews became very wealthy; and Jews in distant countries began to call Amsterdam the New Jerusalem. Far-sighted men in other European countries became alive to the great benefits conferred on Holland by the Jews, and the open-door policy was adopted there as well. We come now to those pioneers who succeeded in opening the doors of England.

Manasseh ben Israel's origins were typical of those Jews who found an asylum in Amsterdam. His parents came of old *Marano* families in Lisbon and his father was imprisoned by the Inquisition, and though he made a miraculous escape, he bore the marks of the rack for the rest of his life. Maltreated and fever-ridden, he succeeded in escaping from Portugal and, with his pregnant wife, reached La Rochelle in France. After Manasseh's birth there, they went on to Amsterdam, where Manasseh ben Israel was to spend the greater part of his life.

An infant prodigy, he astonished his teachers by acquiring a store of knowledge well above his years. Having obtained an extensive Hebrew education while still a boy, he advanced to the 'higher sciences', as Christian and Latin literature were called by Jews. He preached his first sermon in the synagogue when he was eighteen.

It was as a preacher that he first became known, his eloquence making him the most popular rabbi in Amsterdam, where he rivalled the former favourite, Isak Aboab. In spite of their piety, rabbis, like Christian ministers, tend to compete with one another, the rivalry between them being followed with keen interest by their congregations. One such spectator has left a letter in which he awarded points to the two rivals in these words: 'Manasseh said what he knew; Aboab knew what he said.'

Manasseh married early, as Jews are required to do; and the marriage was a fruitful one, with a new baby every year. The family income, however, failed to keep pace with its increasing size; so many mouths could not be fed by preaching and private teaching. But luckily Manasseh was a practical man, and he established the first Hebrew book-printing press in Amsterdam, which tided him over his financial difficulties. Whether it was the urge to write which inspired him to become a printer, or it was the printing works which cried out for manuscripts, no one now knows. But certain it is that he developed into both a fertile writer and a fine printer. Such is the quality of his best products as a printer that, according to experts, they have never been excelled, in spite of technical progress.

Book-printing, of course, forms an important chapter in Jewish history. This old book-reading people eagerly took to the new craft which made it possible to take books to the widest circles far more cheaply and more effectively than before. The Jews called it 'the art of writing with many pens'. The first printers regarded their craft as 'sacred work'. Old Hebrew books give not only the author's name, but also the printer's and the proof-reader's. And they went to a good deal of trouble to find allusions to book-printing in the Talmud! It is a fact that this refers to various methods of easing and expediting transcriptions by means of copies; but of course it had nothing to say about printing. When this was at length discovered, the Jews were among the first to use and develop it. That was even before they were driven out of Portugal; but a real advance came when the Jews arrived in Italy. Manasseh was the man who introduced it into the rapidly developing Jewish centre of Amsterdam.

Admired though he was as preacher and printer, Manasseh was happiest of all when seated in his study between his tightly packed shelves. His appetite for reading was insatiable. Like so many scholars of the seventeenth century, he was the typical polyhistor, reading omnivorously and spreading himself over too many fields; nothing human was foreign to him. Of course, such all-round and almost encyclopedic reading did not go deep. But in Manasseh ben Israel great knowledge became the servant of rare rhetorical gifts, and the combination naturally made him an easy writer, easy to read, and extremely productive. Book after book came from his desk. None of them is distinguished by originality; his gifts were those of the reporter rather than the creator. Yet two of his books acquired European importance.

While still a young man he wrote the *Conciliador*—the word means 'reconciler'. In this book he examines all the passages in the Pentateuch which seem mutually contradictory; and as the title implies, he seeks to reconcile the contradictions, endeavouring by means of ingenious dialectic to harmonize them. The book is written in fine Spanish and in it Manasseh displays all his persuasive eloquence.

The *Conciliador* was an epoch-making book. The first Jewish book to deal in a modern language with subjects of interest to churchmen, it was written to be read, not by Jews, but by Christians. As indeed it was read; it aroused wide interest, and was translated into Latin and English. The *Conciliador* secured for its author a unique position as the friend of almost every Protestant scholar. All through life he conducted a lively correspondence with virtually every important man in northern Europe.

We know exactly what Manasseh ben Israel looked like in those fertile years of his youth. He was a close friend of Rembrandt; Rembrandt's portrait of him hangs in the Rijksmuseum in Amsterdam, and he was also the model for the celebrated picture of an Amsterdam rabbi.

These portraits tell us more about Manasseh ben Israel than many words. We stand before a great man who knew he was great and bore himself like a great man. He meditated daily on the Torah and the Talmud and interpreted their mysteries; but not only had he a mind, he also had a heart. From his Spanish ancestors he learnt to dip into that deep and wonderful art that we call mysticism, and that over the centuries had become interwoven with Jewish thought. Moreover, Manasseh ben Israel was deeply versed in the Cabbala, though, for all his eloquence, he was remarkably reserved about this when writing to non-Christians. The truth is, the Cabbala is concerned with esoteric knowledge intended only for the initiated, and is so intensely Jewish that it is improper to reveal it to the Gentile.

At no time, however, did he conceal his belief in the early advent of the Messiah; and it was through this that he was to make history. In an extraordinary book entitled *The Hope of Israel*, written in 1650, he sets out to prove that the Indians inhabiting the newly discovered continent of America were descended from the ten tribes of Israel that were lost when the Northern Kingdom was destroyed by the Assyrians in the year 722 B.C. and their people were led into exile. His theory was based on the loosest of foundations. He had heard that there was an Indian word which resembled the Hebrew

Shma, the opening word in the Jewish creed concerning the one-ness of God. The whole book is full of such absurdities; yet it was to inspire great things.

According to Manasseh, the Messiah cannot arrive until there are Jews in every country in the world. It was now obvious that Jews had lived in America since early times. Therefore it behoved all those countries which had hitherto excluded them to open their gates and let them in, so that the coming of the Latter Day could be hastened. Looking out across Europe he turned his gaze on Sweden; and he began to correspond with Queen Christina, trying to persuade her to call in Jews to her kingdom. Christina was not interested, and so he turned his attentions to England. That choice proved to be a lucky one.

England had witnessed dramatic events. The king had lost his head and a Commonwealth had been set up; and Oliver Cromwell, who ruled it, was a simple and devout man as well as a great soldier and a brilliant statesman. The Puritans found inspiration in the warrior heroes of the Bible: Moses and Joshua, Gideon and Saul. They sang the psalms of David when they went into battle, and politicians at Whitehall talked like prophets of Israel. The English had become a Bible-reading people. What could be more natural than to expect of Cromwell that he would raise the ban on the descendants of the biblical heroes and prophets?

The Jews had been banished from England for more than 350 years, expelled by royal decree in 1290. Old street names, like Old Jewry in the City of London and Jewry in York and Canterbury, still survive as reminders of medieval Jewish settlements, but for centuries no Jews had lived there. Shakespeare, when he wrote *The Merchant of Venice*, had never seen a Jew, the character of Shylock having been based on the popular ideas about them.

It was in Shakespeare's time that something had occurred in England to prove that frontiers cannot shut out the things of the spirit, and that 'the wind bloweth where it listeth'. A French rabbi, David Kimhi, of Narbonne, wrote in the Middle Ages some celebrated Bible Commentaries, which found their way to the studies of British theologians, and were an invaluable help to the men who made the translation of the Bible, King James's version of 1611. It is a remarkable fact that, at a time when Jews were not tolerated in England, one of the great Jewish theologians was present in spirit at Westminster, helping to translate for the British people the Bible which had first been his.

Now, under Cromwell, the old ban was about to be lifted, and in fact it had already lapsed, as a small group of *Maranos* had actually settled in London and had been tacitly allowed to stay. Of course they professed to be Christians, but they were only awaiting an opportunity to disclose themselves. Incidentally, they had rendered the Government an important service, when one of their number, a leading merchant named Antonio Fernandez Carjaval (a Spanish name once more) had transmitted information relating to Spanish designs on England.

Manasseh ben Israel was not only a scholar, he was also a visionary, and he was very much a statesman. With a sure eye for strategy, he concentrated on securing a new home for his people in England. He caused *The Hope of Israel* to be translated into English, and he dedicated it to the English Parliament.

It fell on fertile ground among the Puritans, and especially among the Fifth-Monarchy Men, those Puritan mystics who looked forward to the early coming of the Jewish and Christian Messiah, in the fifth and final kingdom on earth, successor to the first four—the Assyrian, the Persian, the Greek, and the Roman.

There can be little doubt that Cromwell sympathized with Manasseh's plans; and when the war between England and Holland ended in 1655 he invited Manasseh to visit London, where the latter handed to the Lord Protector his famous 'Humble Address', in which he argued eloquently in favour of a Jewish asylum in England. The fruit seemed to be ripe for the picking; and Cromwell convened a conference of politicians and theologians at Whitehall to consider the matter. The conference, however, was a failure. Theological doubts and the fear of Jewish competition encouraged so many intrigues that Cromwell in irritation dissolved the assembly. Manasseh's path had not been strewn with roses;

and tired and disheartened, he returned home to Amsterdam, to die soon after, in 1657.

In actual fact, however, the issue had been settled and his ideas were about to be crowned with success. The only pity was that he did not live to see it. England now opened her doors, and she did so in true British fashion. No laws were passed and no formal decrees promulgated; but casually and as if by chance a few permits were granted for residence in London; then permission was given to build a synagogue and later to lay out a burial ground. It may not sound much; but a bridgehead had been established that could later be opened out. When in 1956 the Jews of Britain celebrated the tricentenary of these events it could truly be said that the seed planted on the banks of the Thames by Manasseh ben Israel had grown into a fine tree.

That is how the exiled Spanish Jews found open doors in Northern Europe; first in Holland, and then in England. And because those very countries succeeded to the declining dominion of Spain, history can safely say that the Inquisition had expelled some of its best citizens and driven them into the arms of its rivals, which had taken them in and allowed them free scope for their skill and industry.

A beginning once made, other countries followed suit. One of these was Denmark, whose king, Christian the Fourth, allowed some of the exiles to settle at Altona and Glückstadt in Holstein; not for idealistic reasons, but because he wanted to build up Danish competition to the growing trade of Hamburg. More and more Jews, however, found their way across the ocean to the New World, where they helped to create New Amsterdam (now New York) and other cities of the United States, which is today not only the strongest power in the world but also has the largest Jewish population.

Doors were indeed opened to the exiled people; yet most countries were at that time building ghettos and shutting the Jews in behind their walls. And while the Jews of Amsterdam never had walls built round their Joodenburt, they erected invisible barriers between themselves and the world outside. We come now to the tragic chapter of how they thrust two of their finest spirits outside those barriers.

III

EXCOMMUNICATED

URIEL DA COSTA was originally called Gabriel da Costa. This was the name he was baptized under in the Jesuit church at Oporto in Portugal, the city where he was born in 1585 into a rich and distinguished family of *Maranos*. To this family the Catholic faith was more than a mere semblance; they had taken it to their hearts and could truly be called former Jews.

Young da Costa, though slight of build, was strong and handsome; with his long black hair reaching down to his yellow doublet, he seemed when mounted on the thoroughbred horse on which—like other Portuguese youths of good family—he loved to ride in the country, to form a part of it. What first attracted those who saw him, however, was his eyes; gay, but with melancholy underlying their gaiety, they proclaimed a young man of charm and spirit. It is true that no picture of him has survived; but if one were to deduce his appearance from his life and his ideas, that is what he must have looked like.

He was sent by his father to study ecclesiastical law and scholastic philosophy at the Jesuit college of Coimbra, which was the path to greater wealth and equality with the aristocracy. But with his father's early death the carefree days of youth came to a sudden end; for, as the eldest son, Gabriel was responsible for supporting his mother and his brothers. Reluctantly, he took the post of canon and treasurer (which meant administrator) of a church in Oporto, and there he came into intimate daily contact with the ways and doctrines of the Catholic Church.

It was there, too, that he received his first shock. His keen and sensitive spirit could not reconcile itself to the dogma of the Catholic Church, with its assertion of original sin and the everlasting torments of Hell and flames of Purgatory; and his restless mind revolted against the formalistic routine of its ritual. For long and bitter years he wrestled with profound and intense doubt.

Possibly it was his Jewish blood and heritage which asserted themselves and led him to read the Old Testament books that were so remote from the Catholic Church of those days. It is a fact frequently experienced that in spite of their desperate efforts to become assimilated to their Christian environment Jews have great difficulty in shedding the religious tradition and experience of many generations.

However that may be, he found in the Old Testament a spirit that was more sympathetic, and in the message and the visions of the prophets ideas that were more attractive than the direful warnings and unhealthy mysticism, as he saw it, of the Catholic Church. The earthy, healthy, life which emerged from every page of the Old Testament induced him to continue with his studies.

He was well aware that he was embarking upon a dangerous course. The spies of the Inquisition were constantly on the look-out for hidden Jews, and it could mean his death. With doors locked and blinds drawn, he sat, night after night, studying the biblical scrolls that had been passed on from generation to generation in his family. Finally, he realized that without knowing it he had been a Jew before he had been a Catholic. The Judaism of the Old Testament seemed to him now a Paradise regained; and he resolved to accept all the consequences which sprang from that realization.

Da Costa began slowly and cautiously to plan his escape to Holland, the country that had thrown off the papal yoke and where it was safe to live because—as it was whispered in Portugal—it was 'more of a ship than a land'. Carefully sounding his mother and his brothers, he found to his great joy that they were willing to sever their ties with Portugal and accompany him into an uncertain future. Nothing is known about their escape, except that it was successful and

EXCOMMUNICATED

that one day, in 1517, their ship entered the port of Amsterdam.

Scarcely had the vessel docked when da Costa sprang ashore and, running into the streets, breathlessly inquired the way to the Joodenburt. A few minutes later he stood in front of the Portuguese synagogue, and felt like a pilgrim when, after great risks and hardships, he catches his first glimpse of the Holy Land. He trembled with excitement and his eyes dimmed with tears; for there, standing openly and in broad daylight, was a synagogue.

As quickly as they could the da Costa brothers went through the formalities required to forswear Catholicism and be admitted to Judaism; and on the day of his circumcision Gabriel changed his name to Uriel. Uriel da Costa is the name by which he is known to history. It also heads the chapter of one of the bitterest tragedies in the history of religion.

Never has a convert practised his new faith with such enthusiasm as da Costa; and never has a man suffered such a sudden and complete disappointment. The one-time Jesuit student knew Judaism only through the Bible, and had never experienced Jewish daily life. His zeal had been nourished by the dreams and fantasies of a remote age, not by present reality; and the visions of Moses and Isaiah were things of the past. In place of their lofty spirit, sublime visions, and inspiration, he found among the Jews of Amsterdam a rigid and narrow set of precepts and rituals, interpreting the Law literally 'line for line, and commandment for commandment'. He realized that he had only exchanged one dogma for another; and he found himself bound by elaborate rules and observances more irksome than the Catholic ones. Eating, drinking, undressing, sleeping, rising, washing, working, loving, and the most ordinary of everyday activities were subject to innumerable restrictions. The Law of Moses with its involved code of 613 commandments and prohibitions he knew; but here in Amsterdam tens of thousands of new ones had arisen, forming, with their countless ramifications, a parasitic growth entangling all the closest and most intimate things of life. Was it for this that he had abandoned the ceremony of Catholicism, which at least had been stately?

Da Costa was one of those men who have no eye for the finer shades, but who see everything as either black or white, and who fail to perceive, too, that there can be right and wrong on both sides. Nor could he see the Jewish life, among which he suddenly found himself, in its historical perspective. Had he done so, he would have found that all this ritual was of historical and national importance rather than religious. He had had no experience of the crucible of suffering which had moulded the faith of Israel over the centuries into the rigid forms his fellow-Jews would have him conform to.

He did not intend to yield; nor did he nurse his disappointment in silence. Refusing categorically to comply with some of the conventional observances, he had the courage to declare his belief that they were without biblical foundation and were the inventions of Pharisees. The application of this Christian term to the Amsterdam rabbis provoked a sensational reaction and isolated da Costa almost from the start. The abyss to which his path was to lead him will by now be apparent. In fact, his whole career has some of the inevitability of a Greek tragedy.

An ardent and tempestuous spirit is irked by solitude even when it has been brought on by his own actions. Turn as he may in Amsterdam, da Costa found only resentment and animosity. Who did he think he was, this Jesuit upstart? Did he—a late convert—imagine he could bend the accepted doctrines to suit himself? Quickly realizing that he would find no response for his ideas in Amsterdam, da Costa began to cast around for some other place to live, where he would not be so isolated.

His younger brothers, who had remained orthodox Jews and never took to the heretical ideas of Uriel, had established a trading company, with a branch at Hamburg, where there was a small Sephardi settlement. When one of his brothers went to run the branch there, Uriel accompanied him, and he spent several years in the free city of Hamburg. But his turbulence went with him; and the bitterness and the cold-shouldering that he also experienced there aggravated it. Pondering on the difference between the faith of the Bible and contemporary Jewish doctrine, he resolved to launch an attack on Judaism in its modern form.

EXCOMMUNICATED

His first book, *Theses contra Traditio*n, was an impassioned protest against the oral tradition. In it this representative of the old Sadducees challenged the new Pharisees; and with his usual courage he sent the book to the Sephardi community in Venice, which was the leading citadel of Rabbinism. He would strike where the enemy was strongest.

The challenge was accepted and the battle between old and new joined. By a strange quirk of fate the man charged with the task of replying was Leon de Modena, a remarkable and highly gifted man of whom we shall hear more later on. It is a tragic fact that de Modena was as much a modern doubter as da Costa was, but he held his tongue. Openly an orthodox Jew, he sharply opposed da Costa. As a result, Venice had recourse to the ultimate weapon: it excommunicated the uncompromising doubter. He was expelled from the ranks of Israel, and the same fate threatened all who dared to have dealings with him.

Although the Venetian ban was so far without effect in northern Europe, it could become effective at any time, and da Costa hurried home to Amsterdam to seek protection. His brothers were by now wealthy merchants and occupied high positions in the religious community. Perhaps they could help him.

Of course in Amsterdam he should have gone softly and shown caution. But—as Jeremiah said—can a leopard change his spots? He was still unrepentant, believing that it was the others who were wrong. He went further. Delving ever deeper into the problems, his tireless mind finally led him to extreme radicalism; no longer opposed merely to traditions and rituals, he now doubted the dogmas themselves. Soon he had written a new book, in which he argued that the Old Testament said nothing about retribution after death.

The reply was given even before the book was printed. With his usual carelessness, he had read some of the manuscript to supposed friends, and one of them at once published a book attacking his latest heresies.

No longer a matter which concerned only Venice, it had become a public issue at home in Amsterdam. With all due deference to da Costa's family, the heads of the community—the *Parnassim*—felt compelled to put down this dangerous heretic. Uriel da Costa was entering the bitterest phase of his life, which he might have described, in biblical terms, as the valley of the shadow of death.

One May day in the year 1623 the streets of the Joodenburt lay silent and deserted; everyone who could walk or crawl had gone off early that morning to the synagogue. The building was packed. On the floor where the men had their places they stood shoulder to shoulder: thousands of pale and staring faces. It was a study in human destinies. Many of them were themselves fugitives from Spain or Portugal, when they were not the sons of *Maranos* who had fled the Inquisition. There were former priests and monks, even a bishop of Portugal; and there were rich, distinguished merchants, doctors, and professors from well-nigh every town in the old country. They had found their one refuge here in Amsterdam; and now this rabid da Costa was about to destroy everything by his fantastic and blasphemous agitation. Praise God he would now be expelled from the fellowship of Israel. From the women's balcony the same thoughts were reflected in hundreds of other staring faces: bitter, rancorous, implacable.

The whispering ceased as the five heads of the community strode slowly into the synagogue and walked solemnly to their places facing the congregation. Their names are known; and they are the same mixture of Hebrew and Spanish names always found in the Sephardi communities: Samuel Avravanel, Binjamin Israel, Abraham Curiel, Joseph Abeniacar, and Raphael Jeshurun. Though self-controlled, they could not conceal the consternation which filled them all at the terrible act they were about to perform. The many candles that were burning in various parts of the synagogue had all been draped in black crape, so that it looked as though a funeral was about to take place. Such, in a way, was the case; but first there would be the 'execution'. One of Israel's finest and most sensitive spirits was about to be crushed.

The service opened with the congregation singing the ancient penitential psalms that were appropriate to the occasion. The sad and plaintive tones were heart-rending. At last came the moment for which they had all been waiting, as

EXCOMMUNICATED

the singing ceased and the principal elder rose from his seat. The last excited whisper died away as he slowly ascended the steps of the dais from which the sacred words of the Torah were always read. In his hand was a large roll of parchment, from which hung the five seals of the elders.

Solemnly unrolling the parchment, he began to read, and at the sound of the first words the attendants began to extinguish the candles. One by one as he read on they were put out, and gloom descended on the synagogue. The text opened with these words:

'The representatives of the Jewish people herewith declare that Uriel da Costa, already proclaimed a heretic and excommunicated for false and heretical views in Venice, shall be cast out.'

Slowly he read on, the awful words falling heavily on the minds of his audience:

'Let him be excommunicated by the judgment of the Lord of Lords in the two courts, the higher and the lower. Let troubles rain upon him. Let dragons dwell in his house. Let the heavens eclipse his star and be cruel and terrible to him. Let his body be consigned to the flames. Let all his silver and gold be taken from him. Let his wife be given to another and let other men live with her. Let him be cursed by the lips of Addirion and Ahtariel, Gabriel and Sepharim. Let him fall and rise no more. Let him remain under this ban, and let it be his heritage. And let the peace and blessing of the Lord descend over all Israel!'

At the sound of the last words all the lights in the room were extinguished, symbolizing that the accursed Uriel da Costa had been deprived of the light of Heaven. From now on he was known colloquially as Uriel Abadat—Uriel the Lost.

But that was not all. A few weeks later the elders accused da Costa before the city Corporation of spreading dangerous disbelief. He was gaoled and his writings publicly burnt. Though released after a week, he was fined the sum of 300 guilders.

BEHIND THE WALL

From now on he found himself in a vacuum. No man or woman, no child, dared to speak to him or come nearer than eight feet. Beggars in the street refused his alms; street traders spat at him when he passed. His house was shunned; no one ever knocked at his door; it was as though it had borne the mark of the plague. Boys flung stones through the windows.

To a sensitive mind such as his this was intolerable. Moreover, his wife being dead, he wished to remarry; and that would be impossible in Amsterdam. So he fled back to Hamburg. There, however, it was no different, and he could not speak German. For fifteen years he lived in this appalling isolation.

Then he could stand it no longer, and he decided to submit. Writing humbly to the Parnassim in Amsterdam, he offered to retract his false ideas and in future accept the precepts of the faith. And the elders gave him absolution and revoked the ban.

But Uriel da Costa had not changed. He said bitterly as he submitted his retraction that he was becoming an ape among apes. And he got more and more radical in his ideas. At first he had at least believed in the divine inspiration of the Law of Moses. But as time went on he came to doubt even that, and in the end he arrived at a kind of natural religion devoid of outward forms and stripped of ceremony and ritual. God ruled the world and nature taught peace and harmony; while the official religions resorted to the stake and excommunication.

Unfortunately for himself, Uriel da Costa never learnt to dissemble, but broke the rabbinical precepts openly and even violated the sabbath and the laws of eating. Though people talked, he never concealed his indifference to such outward forms. The family were perturbed and his brothers did what they could to persuade him into observing what everyone else observed, but it was all of no use.

What finally made the cup flow over was a chance and thoughtless remark made to two young Christians who appealed to him for advice with a view to going over to Judaism. His reply that by becoming Jews they would be taking up an intolerable yoke became common knowledge and there was general indignation. The elders summoned him

EXCOMMUNICATED

to appear before them and do public penance in the synagogue; but he stood by his opinion, convinced that he was right. Things took their inevitable course, and once more he was excommunicated.

Once more he had to endure an isolation that was complete and overwhelming. For seven years he went through purgatory, but then he broke down and begged for mercy. This time, however, the return of the prodigal son was not to be so easy. He was forced to do public penance, and submit to the painful and undignified ceremony which went with it.

Once again the synagogue was packed with curious men and women, as the penitent ascended the dais and, in a loud voice, read out the document in which he pleaded guilty to a thousand deadly sins against the faith and promised to do all that was required of him to obtain forgiveness.

In a corner of the synagogue he stripped to the waist and his hands were tied to a pillar. Then taking his belt, which a Jew wears over his caftan and which divides the higher and nobler parts of the body from the baser, an attendant flogged him on his bared back, administering the thirty-nine strokes, the ancient punishment known as the forty strokes less one. As he did so, the congregation sang one of the psalms.

Finally, one of the elders stepped forward and declared the excommunication to be revoked. The bitterest part of the punishment, however, was yet to come. Putting on his clothes, he was led to the entrance, where he lay down on the threshold as the congregation left the synagogue, the hundreds of men, women, and children trampling on him as they passed out. He lay there perfectly still, his face pressing against the floor, an occasional quiver passing through his body, but otherwise concealing his stinging humiliation, especially that of being 'under the heel of women'. When the last of them had gone, the attendant helped him to his feet and brushed the dust off his clothes.

Outside, small groups of the congregation stood by the canal side, casting inquisitive glances at him as he passed. Seeing nobody, he staggered off like a man in a dream, yet like a Spanish noble with his shoulders back and his head high. His nostrils quivered and his face was as white as death.

No one ever saw him alive again. Shutting himself up in

his house, he feverishly put his last book on paper. Entitled *Attempt at a Human Life*, it is the story of his own life. It was his final, blistering attack on his fellow-Jews.

Then he loaded two pistols; and the next day he kept watch at the window. There was another account to settle: with his cousin, who had made the last accusation to the elders. He would avenge the humiliation he had inflicted on him. Da Costa had often seen his cousin pass through that street; and he sat at the window and waited for him.

At length the cousin arrived. Throwing the window wide open, Uriel da Costa took aim with trembling hands, and fired. The shot missed, and his cousin fled in terror.

A minute or two later a fresh shot sounded inside the house. Then all was still.

When they broke into the house a few days later, they found da Costa's body lying on the floor by his desk. His blood was spattered across the last manuscript.

A few days after da Costa's body had been taken from the house, a boy slipped through the city gate and walked a few miles south along the road to Ouwerkerk, a village not far from Amsterdam. Here was the Jewish burial ground, of which his father had charge. At home he had heard his father speak of the shattering events connected with da Costa's end, the pious man's voice trembling as he told the tragedy. The Joodenburt had seethed with excitement and there had never been so much agitation.

The boy could not tell what drove him to Ouwerkerk; he only knew that he had to stand by da Costa's grave. And no one had to know. So he did not ask the custodian where they had laid the suicide: he walked round the burial ground looking for a freshly-dug grave, which he would recognize as da Costa's. But there was no new grave there: and he remembered that a suicide may not be buried with other dead. So the boy went outside the burial ground; and there he found the object of his search. Close to the wall lay those who had died by their own hands, and da Costa's grave was there among the rest.

For a long time he stood looking down at the grave, where there was nothing visible but the black earth; for no flowers had been laid on it. What could have occupied the thoughts

EXCOMMUNICATED

of this precocious and highly intelligent boy? Did he have a feeling of kinship for the dead man? Did he suspect that, nine years later, he too would be excommunicated in the great synagogue of the Joodenburt? Perhaps he swore that he would never falter, as the unfortunate dead man before him had faltered?

Breaking a branch of white blossom from a nearby bush, he laid it carefully on the grave, and returned home.

The boy was Baruch Spinoza.

The Spinozas had originally been called d'Espinoza, after the Spanish town of Espinoza near Burgos. There are d'Espinozas still living in Spain. But both Baruch's father and his grandfather had fled to Amsterdam, where the boy had been born in 1632. Baruch means 'blessed', and he changed the name later to Benedictus, which has the same meaning.

Little is known about his parents, and there is no mention of his mother, who died when he was an infant. His father suffered many domestic afflictions, losing three wives and four children; only two of his children, his daughter Rebecca and Baruch, survived him. Michael d'Espinoza, the father, was a merchant, well-to-do without being actually rich, and highly respected in the Sephardi community for his integrity, piety, and wisdom. The house at No. 41 Waterlooplein in Amsterdam (formerly the Houtgragt of the Joodenburt) where Baruch grew up may still be seen.

The pride of the Sephardi community was the school, which had been founded in 1636 and at which the best teachers and the most learned rabbis used to teach, taking their pupils in the course of seven years from a grounding in the Torah up to the subtleties of Talmudic disquisition. The curriculum was restricted to Jewish subjects, there being no Latin in a Jewish school and no instruction in Dutch, or in profane history and geography. The language spoken, as everywhere in the Joodenburt, was Ladino; but the Bible and the Talmud were read in the original Hebrew, and all instruction in the top classes was in that language. The headmaster was Manasseh ben Israel and the principal teacher was Saul Morteira, the community's chief rabbi, who was later to play a ruthless part in Spinoza's life.

BEHIND THE WALL

For the first seven years Spinoza spent every morning from 8 to 11, and every afternoon from 2 to 5, at school, except in the winter months when it closed at dusk because it was unlighted. The foundations of a biblical education which this school laid influenced Spinoza for life. There he heard the word of the prophets, the Psalms, and the poetry of Job, and his mind was whetted and steeled in its most receptive years.

Christian theologians as well as Orientalists read the Bible in quite another way from the way a Jewish boy reads it. They, approaching it from without, acquire laboriously, little by little, knowledge which the Jew imbibes with his mother's milk. Spinoza breathed its air both at home and at school; his daily prayers were said in Hebrew and he picked up Jewish history without having to learn it. It was all a part of the everyday life, and was reinforced in conversation and in the feasts. The life of the Bible was thus the bone of his bone, and the flesh of his flesh. Hence the great knowledge of the language and grammar of the Bible, its history and its ideas, of which his writings bear evidence.

At a school such as this the boys' wits were sharpened. The teaching alternated between question and answer, problem and solution, and obscure textual points were studied and interpreted, all sorts of objections tried and tested. Teachers would sometimes find it hard to match their more intelligent boys. Before he was fifteen, Spinoza was asking questions that his teachers could not answer. There is no wonder that great things were expected of him, and that he was seen as the coming luminary of Judaism. The predictions were to be right, but not in the way that had been expected, or the rabbis desired.

After school, his father wanted him to become a merchant like himself; but young Spinoza felt drawn to other and higher things than the buying and selling of goods, the chartering of ships, and the exchanging of money. An insatiable thirst for knowledge impelled him towards a scientific career. In those days that meant theology. Official positions were closed to Jews; and unless he was to be a physician, the only course open was to become a rabbi and theologian.

The school was only a beginning, and was followed by further, voluntary studies, which Spinoza eagerly pursued.

EXCOMMUNICATED

First he read the great religious philosophers whom I have introduced in my book *The Three Rings*. But he arrived at different conclusions! In the celebrated work of Maimonides, *Guide of the Erring*, he found more error than guide; and it seemed to him that the great scholar asked more questions than he could answer. Abraham ibn Ezra, a writer who lived six hundred years before Spinoza, he found far more attractive; and it was that old thinker, the father of biblical criticism, who was to sow the first seeds of doubt in Spinoza's mind. In his work biblical contradictions were noted and the problems, they raised left open as insoluble. Reading on, Spinoza became increasingly sceptical of the faith of his ancestors. At the same time, in ibn Ezra he found ideas, contradictory to Judaism, which led him to the pantheism that was to be his final philosophy. 'God is the One that is in all,' he wrote, quoting from the critic; 'and He is in all, and all is in Him.'

Mysticism repelled him. He had seen it at close quarters, for his two principal teachers, Manasseh ben Israel and Morteira, had both been ardent Cabbalists. Despite this early influence, the complexities and innumerable self-contradictions of the Cabbala had made no appeal to a brain as clear as Spinoza's. Where his teachers fell prostrate before its wisdom, he found only fine-sounding but hollow words. His dislike of the Cabbala developed in time into contempt. He had already got far from the narrow confines of the Joodenburt.

He now found his way into the world of Christianity. The key which opened the door to this was Latin, the *lingua franca* of those days. His teacher was a Dutch polyhistor and adventurer, by name Franciscus van den Ende, a restless spirit who had travelled the world and had aroused interest and anger by the frankness of his opinions. What is more, he had caused his pupils to perform the frivolous plays of Terence, a conduct which in those days marked him out as a libertine. Van den Ende came to a tragic end, when during the war between France and Holland he hatched a plot in Paris to depose Louis the Fourteenth and lay France open to invasion by a Dutch army, while Admiral Tromp cruised off the Normandy coast. The conspiracy was exposed and van den Ende was hanged.

But he taught Spinoza Latin; and the young student fell in love with his pretty daughter, Klara Maria. For some months she was a serious rival to the Latin; but then another and richer suitor presented her with a precious necklace and won her hand. The bitter disappointment led Spinoza to devote his entire life to philosophy; he was destined never to marry.

Through Latin—and a little Greek—he familiarized himself with classical literature, and its infinite riches of poetry, philosophy, mathematics, and natural science became a part of his life. The massive works of the Scholastic philosophers also influenced him; but an even greater influence was that of the modern philosophers: Giordano Bruno, who was burnt at the stake by the Inquisition; and, above all, Descartes, the favourite philosopher of the time, who was known as 'the morning star of the new philosophy'.

Spinoza admired the lucidity which he found in Descartes, and was also impressed by his understanding of human nature. More than anything else, however, Descartes' bold break with tradition, together with the free and independent thought which resulted from it, was a revelation to him.

A deep gulf opened up between Spinoza and the orthodox Jewish community in which he had been brought up. He himself felt that it was as if he had gone aboard a ship and, casting off its moorings, was steering away from his childhood shores. Further and further he travelled into free and open seas, charting a course for future generations to follow. Yet however far he travelled, he never forgot the language of his fathers, and he remained in his heart of hearts a Jew.

Spinoza hesitated for a long time before allowing his breach with the synagogue to become an open one. A thousand invisible strands bound him to Jewry, and there was a powerful one that he dared not cut; his affection for his father. Spinoza knew that his defection would give mortal offence to his father. But in 1654 Michael d'Espinoza died and so was spared from seeing his only surviving son's apostasy and excommunication. The son's filial piety was so strong that he allowed the year of mourning to end before changing his ways. He continued to attend the synagogue as usual, and on

EXCOMMUNICATED

the anniversary of his father's death he read the *kaddish*—the prayer which the eldest son says annually on the day of his father's death.

But then rumours began to circulate about him. To some presumed friends he had heretically observed that the soul is not immortal, making the same mistake for which da Costa had been excommunicated. The 'friends' were not slow to leak the sensation. Worse, however, he openly broke the sabbath and the rules of eating, was rarely seen in the synagogue, and—worst of all—was seen among Christians and at their services. These Christians were members of a small sect rather like the Quakers, and they had their headquarters at Rijnsburg near Leiden. Among them Spinoza found what the prophets and psalms had proclaimed: that religion does not consist in unintelligible ceremonies but resides in the heart; that love of God is manifested in love of one's neighbour; and that God may be found by those who seek Him with a pure heart and a pious mind. All these positive ideas recur in Spinoza's writings.

The conflict with the synagogue was now an open one. Its first result was that Spinoza left the family home. After his father's death he had lived there with his sister and her husband; but realizing that the gap could not be bridged, he moved. Horrified by his behaviour, they struck hard at the apostate and denied him a share in their father's inheritance; he was no longer a son of the house. To obtain recognition as an heir Spinoza had to take legal proceedings; but having won his case, he contented himself with the choice of a bed out of the estate and renounced the rest. To him it had been not a matter of money, but of right or wrong.

He now moved into the house of his teacher van den Ende and taught in his school, at the same time turning to the craft which, by Jewish tradition, he had learnt. Since the time of the Talmud, learned Jews have earned their bread by the work of their hands, being forbidden to accept payment for teaching, as that would be 'to use the Law as a spade'. Spinoza was a grinder of optical lenses. With his precision and sense of mathematics he became skilled at his craft and the finished lenses left when he died fetched high prices. By this means he became independent and made a frugal living for the rest of his days. But it shortened his life. A long-standing tuberculosis, probably contracted from his mother who died of the disease, was aggravated by the glass dust inhaled while at work.

The synagogue's judicial machine came into play. Spinoza was summoned before the *beth din*: the court of which the judges were the chief rabbis and elders. The men to whom Spinoza had revealed his views were called as witnesses and duly testified; they affirmed their evidence and Spinoza acknowledged his words. His old teacher Saul Morteira intervened and endeavoured to mediate, offering Spinoza on behalf of the synagogue an annual pension of 1000 florins if he would undertake not to publish his heretical opinions. Spinoza immediately refused, declaring that he was not to be bought.

Thereupon the first blow fell. At a weekday service—so dire an act could not be carried out on a sabbath—Spinoza was solemnly condemned to *minor* excommunication. Excommunication had been since ancient times the severest punishment of Judaism; but a distinction was made between minor and major excommunication, or *herem* as it is called in Hebrew. Minor excommunication lasts for only thirty days; but major excommunication is indefinite and may last for the rest of the person's life unless he repents. The origins of the institution are in the Bible, and the Catholic Church adopted it.

To the Jews excommunication was a horrible thing, and we have seen how it was used to crush da Costa's resistance. No one may go nearer to an excommunicated person than eight feet, and no one may eat in his presence. He has to wear mourning; he may not bathe, cut his hair or his beard, or wear shoes. A stone is laid on his coffin when he dies and his family may not mourn in the customary manner; for example, by rending their clothes.

The minor excommunication was a reform measure, of course; having tasted its terrible fruits the sinner would usually relent. Not so Spinoza, however.

Once again, therefore, the Jewish community of Amsterdam witnessed the dramatic spectacle of a major excommunication in their synagogue. The date was the sixth day of

EXCOMMUNICATED

the month of *Ab* in the Jewish year 5416, or, according to the Christian reckoning, the 27th of June, 1656. As the candles were slowly extinguished and the plaintive notes of the horn were sounded, Saul Morteira read the proclamation of excommunication over his former pupil. The wording, though rather different from that used in the case of Uriel da Costa, was the same in substance:

'Accursed be he by day, and accursed by night; accursed when sleeping and accursed when waking. May the Lord never forgive him; may His wrath burn upon him and heap on him all the curses that are written in the Book of the Law. May the Lord destroy him under the heavens, and cut him off for his offence from all the twelve tribes of Israel with every curse in the firmament!'

Spinoza was absent from the synagogue during the act of excommunication, but the document was brought to him. After reading it, he quietly observed:

'You are not compelling me to do anything that I did not mean to do anyway.'

One dark evening a few days later, however, he was attacked in the street by a fanatic who tried to stab him, and it was only by turning quickly that he escaped with a cut in his neck. He preserved the slashed cloak for the rest of his life as a relic of his former fellows.

But a sharper knife than the assassin's had struck him. Under the excommunication, he had been cut off from Israel. From that day and until his death no Jew spoke to him again. He responded by changing his name from the Hebrew Baruch to the Latin Benedictus.

At the time of his excommunication he was barely twenty-four.

The first few years after the break Spinoza lived at Ouwerkerk, near to the Jewish burial ground where both da Costa and his parents lay, in the house of some members of the Mennonite sect, When they moved to Rijnsburg, the centre of this Christian sect, he went with them, living in a house which still stands, in a street that now bears his name. A few years later he moved again, first to a suburb of The Hague, and then into The Hague itself. There he spent the rest of his life.

After the rough storm he had weathered, they were quiet and peaceful years. His hosts felt great affection for the modest, mild-mannered man, and were always glad when he looked in, chatting and smoking his pipe, before going up to his room in the evening; for, in spite of the grandeur of his thought, he preserved the ability to talk with ordinary people.

He worked hard; and in his small room created an imposing collection of works. As he ground his lenses, he would be pondering on the problems of life. A wide reader, he left an extensive library, in spite of his modest means. For hours on end, day and night, he stood at his desk, writing his great books.

Among these, the two which count as his principal works are the *Theological-Political Treatise* and the *Ethics*. The former work, which acquired historical importance by its views on biblical criticism and its modern ideas on the freedom of thought and conscience, civil as well as religious, makes remarkable reading even today. For 300 years, however, these ideas were revolutionary, and their author risked his life in publishing them. Though the book was published anonymously, its authorship could not be concealed. There was an outcry both from the political reactionaries and from the orthodox Reformed Church, and the synods demanded its confiscation. Because of these violent reactions, Spinoza published his later books under a pseudonym.

The *Ethics* was not published until after his death. The manuscript was found in his desk, and under his will was sent to his publisher. It appeared, undated, the year after his death; and the publisher did not dare to inscribe it with the name of the author, the publisher, or the printer.

It is chiefly in the *Ethics*, the major work of the new philosophy, that we can study Spinoza's speculative pantheism, and note how far he had departed from his Jewish training. Nature and thought he sees as 'attributes' of the ultimate 'Substance', or God, whom Spinoza firmly relates to the law of necessity. In Judaism, however, there is a personal God,

EXCOMMUNICATED

and the world bears the marks of His creative hand. It follows that man has freedom of will.

Yet Judaism had been his starting-point, and he never departed from its inmost core. The Spanish author Unamuno has said of Spinoza that he suffered from 'the ache of God', which, like toothache or earache, would give him no rest. His thoughts centred continually on the supreme and ultimate problem of God. That is truly Jewish.

Spinoza experienced few dramatic events in those peaceful years of work. It was a great shock to him when his friend, the Dutch statesman Jan de Witt, was murdered by the mob in the disastrous war with France, and he nearly got involved in it himself. The Prince of Condé, the commander-in-chief of the invading French army, invited the famous philosopher to meet him, and, with a safe-conduct, Spinoza passed through the French lines. When he returned, the air was thick with rumours, and for some days he went in danger of his life, accused of being a spy. It was soon realized, however, that he was only a harmless philosopher, having nothing to do with practical politics.

Spinoza found many friends throughout Europe and carried on a voluminous correspondence. His fame reached great heights. The German philosopher Leibnitz paid him a widely discussed visit and Karl Ludwig, the liberal Elector Palatine, offered him an honourable post as professor of philosophy in the University of Heidelberg. The offer was declined because Spinoza refused to accept the condition that he should abstain from undermining accepted religious faith.

Spinoza's health steadily declined over the years; his hacking cough got worse, and soon it was clear that he could not last much longer. So reconciling himself to an early death, he made his arrangements accordingly.

The end came in 1677. It was a Sunday, January 20th, and the family had gone to church, Spinoza having assured them he felt well and that a friend, who was a physician, would be with him. They returned to find him dead in his friend's arms. A sudden haemorrhage had put an end to his life. He was only forty-four when he died.

When David Ben-Gurion at the end of 1952 relinquished

the post of Prime Minister of Israel and withdrew to the desert settlement of Sde Boker, the first sign of life to come from him in his retreat was an article on Spinoza. In this article he recommended the annulment of the excommunication passed on the philosopher and his rightful rehabilitation as one of the great Jewish thinkers.

A number of leading philosophers supported the recommendation; and one of them said that excommunication could only be for life, since God took charge after death.

And so, on the three hundredth anniversary of that sombre day in the synagogue of Amsterdam in 1656 a stone of black basalt, quarried in Galilee, and bearing the Hebrew inscription *Amka* (Thy people), was built into the monument over Spinoza's grave at The Hague.

Orthodox Jews, however, opposed both Ben-Gurion's idea and the ceremony at the graveside, and Jewry is still divided in its attitude to its greatest thinker.

The doors of the synagogue at Amsterdam closed with a bang. First they excluded Uriel da Costa, and then Baruch Spinoza. Erecting its defence works, Jewry confined the hearts and minds of its people behind invisible walls.

It took place in the freest city in Europe only three hundred years ago.

IV

SAFAD

'So this King Ferdinand, who depopulates his own lands in order to enrich mine, you call "the wise"?'

The first victims of the repressive anti-Jewish policy of Ferdinand and Isabella had just arrived in the Turkish capital of Constantinople, and the speaker was the Sultan Bajazet.

Eight hundred years earlier, the stream of fleeing Jews had flowed from east to west across the Mediterranean Sea, and hundreds of thousands of them coming from Babylon had been washed ashore in Spain. Now a new storm centre had arisen, and like driftwood on the waves the exiles were carried back the way they had come.

The Spanish Jews found many changes in their ancient homelands. The new Turkey manifested in the mighty Ottoman Empire was in the ascendant. In 1453 the Turks had captured Constantinople, an event celebrated by Jews everywhere as a judgment on Christendom. To them it seemed a supernatural occurrence which might presage the coming of the Messiah. Christendom itself trembled at the sight of its bitterest foe mounting invincible armies under the Crescent banner and directing them against the heart of Europe, while Turkish fleets held control of the Mediterranean. For a long time the fate of Europe hung in the balance, and it was only after a fierce struggle that the scales were eventually tipped against Islam.

Turkey needed the Jews. It had warriors and it had peasants, but what it lacked was merchants. It found these among the Armenians, the Greeks, and in particular the Spanish Jews whom it warmly welcomed. It was about this time that a Jewish author, Joseph Cohen, wrote *The Valley of Tears*, a terrible book describing the persecutions of his people, and he called Turkey an asylum. It offered shelter to the Jews, and soon there were hundreds of thousands of them in the new empire. Some attained to great power; and as Hasdai ibn Shabrut had done in tenth-century Cordova, Jewish statesmen exerted in sixteenth-century Constantinople an influence in international affairs. Their careers, romantic like the tales of *A Thousand and One Nights*, provide a clear picture of the Jewish world after the great disaster in Spain. Here are two of the best known.

Mendes is the name of an old Spanish-Jewish family which has survived in France, where one of those who bear it is M. Pierre Mendès-France, the political leader. Franciscus Mendes was one of those forcibly baptized Jews, the *Maranos*, who continued to observe Judaism in secret. The head of a large business house in Lisbon, he numbered among his customers such prominent people as Charles the Fifth and the King of France. He died young, but his widow, Beatrice Luna Mendesia, carried on the business, and it was she who made the family name famous.

Remaining at heart a Jew, and fearing the Inquisition, she transferred the business to Antwerp, and it is there that we first hear of Joâo Miquez, her nephew, the head of a world-wide banking firm, and himself a *Marano*. Both charming and good-looking, they enjoyed the favour of Queen Maria, the Regent of the Netherlands. But that came to a sudden end when the queen asked for the hand of Beatrice's young daughter, Reyna, for one of her courtiers and the mother curtly replied that she would rather see the girl dead than married to the man in question.

After this embarrassing incident the family found it advisable to change their abode. With a large retinue, Beatrice and Miguez passed through Europe and eventually arrived in Venice. There, however, the Council of the Republic threw Beatrice into prison and confiscated all her belongings in chests and coffers. The charge was that she was a secret Jew, which, as we already know, was a highly serious matter in the Venice of those days. The King of France was behind the plot. It was an easy way of ridding himself of his debt to her;

and as a large part of her vast fortune was invested in France he confiscated that, with the result that his exchequer suddenly swelled. But both France and Venice rejoiced too early.

The energetic Miguez at once got in touch with Constantinople. Through the sultan's physician, himself a Jew, he made contact with the Government, informing it that a rich and distinguished Jewish widow, on her way to Turkey with large treasures, was imprisoned in Venice, where the money had been confiscated. The Sublime Porte acted at once and dispatched an ambassador to Venice with threatening demands. The upshot was that the whole family got out to Constantinople. At long last they were able to throw off their disguise and declare themselves Jews. They also changed their baptismal names, she becoming known as Gracia Mendesia, her nephew as Joseph Nassi. He soon married the beautiful Reyna. But these events form only the first act of the drama.

The word 'drama', however, applies only to Joseph Nassi. Life for Gracia Mendesia slipped into smooth water. But it was a rich and vital life, and her goodness and solicitude for Jews who had fared ill, even in distant lands, are legendary. She was a noble and warm-hearted woman to whom the honourable name 'a mother of Israel' may be applied. 'To describe all her good deeds and virtues would take many books,' it was said.

Joseph Nassi, her nephew, acquired power. A born diplomat, he knew how to manoeuvre cleverly among the intrigues and cabals which throve at the sultan's court. The floors were slippery, sometimes with blood, but Joseph Nassi came through it all alive. He had much to offer the sultan: a razor-sharp intelligence, many years' intimate knowledge of the diplomatic labyrinths of Europe, and a gigantic fortune which he knew how to multiply. Quickly achieving exalted positions, he was made Duke of Naxos and nearly became King of Cyprus.

The kings of Europe felt the long arm of Joseph Nassi, who amply repaid them for humiliations inflicted on his family and people. In the Netherlands his agents fanned the flames of revolt which the King of Spain never managed to stamp out. And the French king had to repay the Mendes family many times over what he had robbed them of. Joseph

Nassi simply had French ships seized by the Turkish fleet in the Mediterranean and regarded them as his lawful prizes. Nor was Venice forgotten. Through his highly developed intelligence service he learnt that the great arsenal of the doges had been destroyed by fire, and he prompted the sultan to seize the opportunity while the proud republic was suddenly unarmed. In a lightning war the Turks captured Cyprus from Venice. It remained in Turkish possession for the next three hundred years.

In one respect Joseph Nassi was well ahead of his times. He was a Zionist in the modern sense of that word, four hundred years before true Zionism developed. His dearest wish was to establish an independent Jewish State in Palestine. And, no mere visionary, Nassi went far towards realizing his amazing plan.

Interested in his invaluable servant's ideas, the sultan presented him with the town of Tiberias on the Lake of Gennesaret, where Moses Maimonides was buried. Then, appealing to Jews everywhere to return to the land of their forefathers, Nassi offered to provide ships for the voyage.

Realpolitiker as he was, he knew that an emotional appeal was not enough, and that good living conditions would have to be provided for the prospective immigrants. He accordingly rebuilt Tiberias, restored its crumbling walls, founded textile factories, planted mulberries for silkworms, laid out plantations, and imported sheep from Spain in order to develop farming. A few impoverished Jews in the Papal States responded to his appeal, but failed to reach their destination, as their ships were wrecked on the way, or were captured by sea-rovers.

The project was a failure, and centuries were to elapse before the time would prove ripe for such an enterprise. Even so, it was a brave and forward-looking experiment.

Constantinople, with its cosmopolitan atmosphere, and its intriguing court and harems, was not the place to provide a setting for Jewish life in its real sense. Joseph Nassi had the right idea when he looked towards Palestine, which the Turks had conquered in 1517, and where many Spanish refugees had settled. His aim was to grant them political liberty, when all that they wanted was the freedom to live as Jews. Once

SAFAD

they obtained that, Jewry threw up fertile new growths.

The place where it took place was the small mountain city of Safad in Galilee.

The northward view from the Lake of Gennesaret and the hilly country which lies between Tiberias and Nazareth is blocked by a range of mountains, the highlands of Galilee, which rise to a height of 3,000 feet above sea-level. On the highest peak, perched like a bird's nest near the summit, a cluster of white houses can be seen. This is Safad, and may have been the town alluded to by Jesus when He said that a city on the side of a mountain could not be hidden. In biblical times a beacon shone from it every month when the Synedrium announced the new moon by lighting bonfires on the mountain sides.

There are places where time stands still and the present merges into the past to appear as it did to those who walked that way hundreds of years before. Whenever I have passed through the streets of Safad I have felt the centuries slip away like the sand which trickles through my fingers when I pick it up on the beach. To convey an impression of an Oriental ghetto in the sixteenth century I can think of no better way than to take the reader with me to Safad as it still survives.

Going from our hotel, and passing the 2,000-year-old olive-trees which stand near to the main entrance, we have barely left the narrow, crowded streets before we are lost in a maze of lanes and alleys zig-zagging down the mountain side. Whitewashed or brown and earthy-grey houses with sun-bleached red tiles stand huddled together, the street so steep that they appear to be built one on top of the other, and resemble when seen from above a flock of sheep. No two doors or windows are alike or symmetrical, and everything is low and narrow except for the grotesque balconies of fantastically wrought iron which bulge out from the walls, and the singular ornaments over the doors and gateways which resemble fossilized reptiles.

There among playing children and busy women go long-bearded men, rabbinical types of a past age, wearing long colourful velvet gowns and huge fur caps, and with long twisted earlocks, the *pajes*, dangling at their temples. Their mild eyes have a distant look as though oblivious of the street around them and seeing only things remote and otherworldly.

Proceeding on our way, we listen to remarkable stories. Here, we are told, lay the pool where, 300 years ago, a rabbi dived twenty-six times before writing down that most sacred symbol JHVH, which stands for *Hashem*, and is the name of God, the number twenty-six representing the value of the four letters of the symbol. Over there stood the apple-tree—the *Hakal Tapuhim* in Hebrew—where Isaac Luria, called Ari, the most renowned of all the pious men of Safad, went with his disciples every Friday afternoon, clad in white, to welcome the Sabbath Queen to their city. Almost one can hear the tones of the sabbath song *Leko Dodi*: 'Come, my beloved!' Written at Safad, the song was adapted into German by Heine and is sung every sabbath in countless synagogues all over the world. The returning queen is greeted, after six days of absence, with the joy of a bridegroom welcoming his bride.

The time to see Safad is on a day in spring, when a carpet of flowers covers the mountain side with red, blue, and cyclamen colours; not any day, but on *Lag Baomer*. And here we must pause to consider an ancient Jewish custom.

The word 'Omer' means 'sheaf' but is applied in Palestine to the season of the barley harvest, beginning on the second day of the Passover and lasting to the fifteenth, when the 'Festival of the Weeks' begins, the festival that was to become the Christian Whitsuntide. *Omer* is a time of sorrowing, when the Jews commemorate the martyrs who died for their faith. No beards or hair are cut at that time, no weddings are held, and music and dancing are banned. And *Lag* means thirty-three, that being the numerical value of the two consonants in the word. Thus *Lag Baomer* is the thirty-third day of *Omer*. That day is the one bright spot in this long and sad season, for it is the day which saw the end of an epidemic among Rabbi Akiba's disciples 1,800-1,900 years ago. There is general rejoicing on *Lag Baomer*. It is the wedding day *par excellence* and children sing and dance round bonfires.

Lag Baomer should be celebrated outside Safad. Some five miles away is another old town, Meiron; and the two towns,

SAFAD

each on its mountain-top, are almost within hailing distance. In Meiron in ancient times lived the celebrated rabbi Simeon bar Johai, the legendary author of the *Zohar*, the cabbalistic 'Bible'. He died on *Lag Baomer*, and he exacted from his disciples the promise that they would gather at his grave in Meiron on that day every year. For 1,800 years it has been an unbroken tradition to celebrate *Lag Baomer* there. It is that festival we will now attend.

The evening before, tens of thousands gather at Safad from all over the country, and a great procession carries banners and Torah rolls through the streets. Outside the town they enter cars and drive across to Meiron, the procession filling the whole route. By nightfall, vast crowds have assembled round Simeon bar Johai's grave, where they pray and dance amid indescribable scenes. Persons possessed by the Devil are led to the tomb, to beat their heads against the stone and drive out the evil spirit, and the sick are healed. While a silver moon shines on the mountains, bonfires are lit on every hill, the crowds sing and dance, the rabbis chant their prayers, and babies cry. It is a night when people believe in the old tradition that some priests who had fled from Jerusalem and its burning Temple after the destruction made their way to Safad where they kept up the sacrifices.

Safad is both a spiritual and a demonic town, a legendary city of deep shadows and brilliantly sunlit house-tops, a city of this world and yet above it. It stands now as it stood in the days of its greatness in the sixteenth century, which we will now consider.

Of the four holy cities of the Jews—Jerusalem, Hebron, Tiberias, and Safad—Safad is the one whose fame is most recent, but in the sixteenth century it exceeded that of Jerusalem itself. In the capital, though it was the holiest of them all, the Jews lived a miserable existence. Full of Christian monks and Moslem dervishes, it was a place of pilgrimage for every faith, but the Jews hid in corners. The old inhabitants were loth to share what little they had with newcomers, and the refugees from Spain found themselves ignored. They therefore turned to Safad, and made it great.

They brought energy and capital, and some of them became farmers, growing barley, wheat, olives, and figs. Most, however, went in for trade and the primitive industry of the time, especially weaving and clothes-making. There was room in Safad for every occupation except one, that of servant. All were humble men, and even the grandee was ready to do rough manual work, fetching water from the well and carrying goods home from the market. Such was their eagerness to help one another that they would resort to tricks in order to do so: like the famous teacher who, meeting a younger colleague, asked for a drink of water from his pitcher, and when the other put it down in order to pour him some out, snatched it up and carried it to his house for him.

In Safad at that time religion was not only in the air, it was in everything. Imagine a series of revivalist meetings prolonged for decades, with penitents flocking from all the four corners of the earth, and you have an impression of Safad as it was then. The principal object of its inhabitants was the worship of God, and it was with regret that they occasionally turned to such minor affairs as earning their living and raising money with which to pay their taxes. Their true occupation was prayer, and the three prayers a day that were prescribed were far from satisfying their needs. Many men would get up in the night and, dressed in black, would go to the synagogue to mourn the destruction of the Temple and confess their sins which delayed the coming of the Messiah. For years there was a man who used to knock on doors nightly, rousing the sleepers with the cry:

'My brothers of the house of Israel! Do you forget the holy Temple lies in ashes while you sleep? Rise! Let us worship the Lord our God, the King of grace.'

Then soon the synagogues would resound with the voices of men chanting the old prayers.

It need hardly be said that religious zeal like this sometimes led to excesses, and some of the stories clearly display pathological features. There is, for example, that of the unfortunate man, a sort of Jewish Faust, who succeeded by means of incantations in getting Satan himself into his power. This was a triumph beyond measure, since the destruction of the Devil is one of the prior conditions of the coming of the Messiah. Alas, the Evil One proved too cunning for the man. He begged his captor for the favour of a smell of incense, and in a weak moment the request was granted. Instantly Satan recovered his power and, now the stronger, forced the unlucky man to commit suicide and so gained his soul.

Safad will always be remembered by Jews, however, for its great men. No other town in their history since the destruction of the Temple has had such a brilliant succession of great men as this little hilltop town in Galilee, men widely diverse in gifts and character but united in one thing: their belief that religion was all. We will confine ourselves to the two greatest: Joseph Caro and Isaac Luria.

Joseph Caro was born in Spain, but was only four years old when Isabella expelled the Jews from her domains. His father, Ephraim, wandered with his family in many countries before arriving in Turkey and finding an asylum in Adrianopolis. There the highly gifted boy grew up and trained himself in the study of the Talmud. He was exceptionally well equipped for this study, having an extraordinary memory and a remarkably logical brain. These two gifts helped him to become an outstanding scholar, the vast amount of material which he read being critically analysed from beginning to end. To Caro, all that was worth knowing was in the Talmud. He brooded on its massive books, reading and pondering and reading them again until he knew them all by heart. He became the typical super-rabbi.

For more than thirty years he laboured on the work that was to make him one of the great lights of Judaism. His gigantic work was called *Beth Joseph* (House of Joseph), and in it he examined the whole Jewish Law in both the Bible and the Talmud. He did not finish the book until long after he had left Adrianopolis and had arrived in Safad, to become the head of one of the town's famous Talmudic schools.

An enormous scholarly work like *Beth Joseph*, of course, was unsuitable for ordinary people. But in the light of recent history, there was need of a popular guide to Jewish tradition. In the widely scattered countries inhabited by Jews traditions differed, and book-publishing was now disseminating Jewish knowledge, sometimes contradictory, in every country. Who, it was asked, was right? People who for a thousand years have been trained in logical thought look for clarity and system in all things, however small. Now there was confusion and endless dispute. All longed, therefore, for some authority that could speak *ex cathedra*—to use a Christian term.

Joseph Caro had the lucky idea of popularizing his great work, and the result was the *Shulchan Aruch* (The Table Prepared). He regarded this popular digest of his major work, the *Beth Joseph*, as no more than a by-product of it, but it arrived at the right moment, when it was needed. The *Shulchan Aruch* is one of those rare books which may be said to have influenced an entire people. It was fortunate that it came at a time when it could be spread by printing, and it rapidly reached the Jewish communities scattered throughout the world. Criticized at first, it was cherished all the more by those who welcomed it. When the Polish rabbi Moses Isserles adapted it to conditions in Poland its success was assured.

The *Shulchan Aruch* became the Jewish authority on all matters of life, as in many places it still is; to 'live by the *Shulchan Aruch*' is a motto among orthodox Jews. In it they find the code which guides them through the labyrinth of life. The title is very characteristic: the table has been prepared, the food laid out, and all that is now necessary is to sit down and eat. 'Be strong like the leopard, light as the eagle, swift as the stag, and mighty as the lion to do the will of thy Father, which is in Heaven,' reads the opening sentence. It is followed by rules governing all things, from the shoe that should be put on first in the morning and the manner of dressing, to the way a man should love his wife and educate his children. The book is a compendium on food and feasts, on dress, on marriage and divorce, on business and charity; it is an authority, universally recognized, which codifies life from the cradle to the grave.

At the same time it is a classic monument to the period of the ghetto. Death had the Jew in its grip. An avalanche of disasters threatened him. And yet he refused to die. His reaction was to protect himself behind a wall of law and tradition. It narrowed his outlook, and to the outsider he seemed like a fossil. But behind the wall he managed to survive, restricting his functions to the bare minimum like a hibernating animal. To the non-Jew the life prescribed by the *Shulchan Aruch* may seem a poor one; without it, the Jew might never have survived.

There is more in the story of Joseph Caro. This great legalist and logician was neither dry nor dusty; law was a shell which contained a rich kernel inside. He lived at Safad, and from that it follows that he was also a mystic, envisaging life on earth, like every other mystic, as a reflection of the true life that is in Heaven, everything here below being only a copy of the original. So, too, with the *Beth Joseph* and *Shulchan Aruch*. They were reflections of the Talmud, which was a revelation of the heavenly *Mishnah*.

There is a remarkable diary which Joseph Caro kept for fifty years, and which records his nightly conversations with this mystical and supernatural world, through a *maggid*, or messenger, who is none other than the heavenly *Mishnah* himself. In the dead of night when his studies were over, he would listen to the beloved's voice, as the *maggid* admonished him to asceticism, reproached him when he drank more than one glass of wine on the sabbath, rebuked him even for drinking too much water, bade him be chaste, never fall to anger or useless words, always to remember and grieve for his sins. His *maggid* would also help him with his books, both criticizing and praising them, and indeed Caro was convinced it was the real author.

To compare the *Shulchan Aruch* with the diary and to reflect on the fact that they are both from the same hand, is to wonder if this was a case of split personality, a Dr Jekyll and Mr Hyde. In the personality of Joseph Caro, however, opposite trends were joined. At Safad mysticism was an integral part of life. The admired prophet, the man whose shoe lace even Joseph Caro felt unworthy to unloose, was Isaac Luria.

Isaac Luria's parents had come from Germany and so were Ashkenazi Jews, for which reason his disciples named him Ashkenazi Rabbi Isaac. As was customary, they abbreviated the title to the three initials, calling him Ari. In Hebrew the word *Ari* means 'lion', and it was a name he well deserved, just as his disciples were known as the lion's whelps.

Isaac Luria was born in 1534 in Jerusalem, and legend has it that before his birth the prophet Elijah told his father of the great future which awaited his son:

'The Most High has sent me to announce that a son shall be born to you. You shall call him Isaac. He shall liberate Israel from the power of evil and deliver many men from the transmigrations of the soul, and through him the message of the Cabbala shall be revealed to the world.'

The boy turned out to be wondrously gifted, and by the time he was eight none of the scholars of Jerusalem could debate the Talmud with him. When his father died, his mother took him to Cairo, where she had a rich and distinguished uncle. He adopted the boy and provided him with the finest teacher in the city, and so enabled him to continue his brilliant career. When Isaac was fifteen, the uncle gave him his daughter in marriage. The turning-point in the boy's life had come.

One day in the synagogue he saw a stranger saying his prayers from a book Isaac had not seen before. His curiosity aroused, he tried to follow by looking over the stranger's shoulder. He then discovered that it spoke of the secrets of faith in a way he had never known. Unabashed, he began to question the man, and shyly the man stammered that he was a *Marano* in exile. In fact he did not understand a word of the Hebrew book, but merely pretended to be praying from it because everyone else in the synagogue intoned prayers from a book. Luria asked if he could buy the book; and the upshot was that the man let him have it for a good price.

It turned out to be the Zohar, the sacred book of the Cabbala, that Isaac was now to become acquainted with. With the fanatical enthusiasm characteristic of everything he undertook, he applied himself to the study of it. And there the meditative youth found a light which the Talmud had never given him. Withdrawing from everything that had occupied him, he took up his abode in a lonely hut on the banks of the Nile. This solitary life lasted for seven years. His family visited him only on the sabbath, and he seldom spoke and then only in Hebrew. On the six weekdays he remained alone, praying, watching by night, and carrying out frequent ritual ablutions.

Such a life easily makes its man visionary; and Isaac often fell into a trance. He believed that the prophet Elijah visited him and bore him off to eternity, where he had long talks with devout men of the past and was initiated into the deepest mysteries. This was the Isaac Luria who came to Safad and settled there for life.

He found men of like minds there. The devout in Safad had three steps to ascend: the Bible, the Talmud, and the Cabbala. The last of these was the highest. The best time for studying the Cabbala was the midnight hour or the sabbath, when it was peaceful, and when the mind is known to be most receptive to deep mysteries. Then they experienced what the eye has not seen and the ear never hears. Isaac Luria became the greatest of Safad's many mystics; everyone bowed to the young man's authority and desired only to belong to the lion's whelps.

Luria must have been something of a superman. Even if we allow for preposterous exaggerations in the tales told of him, it is possible to discern a personality of quite exceptional stature. Friends looked upon him as one of the supernatural beings sent on rare occasions by Providence for the salvation of mortals. Their real home is in Heaven, and they are here on earth until such time as their mission has been accomplished. His face—it is said—shone; his thoughts were pure and healthy. And he could do things which others could not do, such as reading palms, and had only to look at a person's face in order to know what lay behind it. It is part of the teachings of mysticism that sin and passion set their mark on a face and disturb the image of God. Here is one of the stories about Isaac Luria which enable us to divine a little of the mental atmosphere that prevailed in Safad in his time.

One day he looked shrewdly at one of his friends, a big cloth merchant, and said:

'Thou shalt not covet thy neighbour's goods.'

Appalled, the man hurried home. He did not think that he

had taken anything from anyone; but when the master suggested such a sin he felt forced to test himself. Calling all his workpeople together, he asked if any among them felt cheated by him. No one had any complaint. But unable to forget the master's piercing gaze, he continued to question them. Finally, he took out a bag of money and scattered it on the table, asking each to take what he considered due to him. No one touched the money. For some time they all stood round the table in silence.

At long last a woman stretched out her hand and took a farthing.

The merchant then went to tell Ari what had occurred. But he had hardly opened his lips to speak when the master smilingly said:

'The mark of your sin is gone.' He then went on to say that the man should remember that the woman who had taken the coin was his best worker. She ought to earn a little more than the rest.

'How could a mere farthing mark my face when I never thought of denying her her right?' the merchant asked in astonishment.

To which Luria replied:

'In Heaven they are very particular about such things.'

Ari not only knew the living, he saw the souls of the dead as they roamed about and took up their abode in stones or animals. He saw their spirits and heard them whisper in running water, in swaying branches, in birdsong, in the crackling of flames. To him, every mystical nook and corner was as well known as the streets of Safad.

With his disciples he would often go to Meiron, to converse and pray at the tomb of Simeon bar Johai, and every Friday afternoon, as we have already seen, they left the city to welcome in the sabbath. On that day they all dressed in white, and Isaac Luria's mantle had four edges, one for each of the four letters in the name of God.

On one such Friday, just before the sabbath, he suddenly asked his friends:

'Will you go with me to Jerusalem and keep the sabbath there?'

They gazed at him in bewilderment, for, as they said, it

was many miles to the holy city, and only a few minutes before the sabbath.

In despair the master cried:

'Woe unto us, unworthy creatures, who do not believe in miracles! I have seen the Messiah on His way to Jerusalem. Had you but believed, the hour of redemption would have been come.'

Men such as Isaac Luria do not live long, and he was only thirty-eight when he died. To his friends he seemed like Enoch in the Old Testament, who had walked with God and was no more, for God had taken him. He had written nothing, and had forbidden his friends to take notes of what he said. But after his death his closest friend, Chayyim Vital, wrote his biography. That has been read—and is still read—all over the world.

Experience shows that national disasters create fertile soil for mysticism, and the Jews have experienced disaster like no other people. The two episodes of the destruction of Jerusalem and the massacres of the Crusades left waves of mysticism in their wake; the Spanish Jews, too, had experienced an upheaval, and in their exile they were like trees uprooted and transplanted in another soil.

In such minds there will always be nostalgic currents. Surely now, men will think, the cup is full? Surely now, the end must be in sight? Surely now, at long last, the Messiah is at hand? They knew from the Zohar that the great redemption that was to come depended on the religious deeds of the pious. If they prayed and repented, if they scaled the heights of holiness and devoted themselves to contemplation, then their endeavours would reach up to Heaven and set the eternal processes in motion. He who believes can influence the will of God.

The medieval Cabbala speculated on the origins of the earth, and on the way in which the visible world flows from the everlasting God and will always return to its source. Isaac Luria, however, looked, not to the beginning of history, but to its ultimate end. The old Cabbala was a philosophical work, but Luria's Cabbala, the Cabbala of Safad, has been rightly called 'the practical Cabbala'. Increasingly, it became psychological in influence, permeating and activating the religious emotions.

Some of the strange ideas of Isaac Luria have already been hinted at: his belief in the transmigration of souls and the presence of the spirits of the dead in trees, stones, and animals. One step more and the end would have been the magic and sorcery of superstition. Many, in fact, took that fatal step, and they ended in the delusion and despair which followed the Cabbala like a shadow.

But the mysticism of Safad had other and more positive aspects. The lion's whelps went out into the world and spread the news of the holy Ari; and among other countries, they went to Poland. Later on we shall consider the next great calamity which befell the Jews, in the ghettos of Poland. Before then, however, the sparks which fell from the beacon lit in Safad took fire and created the movement called Hassidism.

V

ITALY

One day in the spring of 1524, all life in the streets of Rome came to a sudden halt. As if to order, everybody stopped and stared in the same direction. In the residential capital of the Popes processions of foreign emissaries were a common sight, but this one was unique.

Attended by a magnificently clad suite and a large escort of armed followers, a man came riding a dappled horse from the alley-ways of the ghetto. He was a strange figure: a wizened dwarf, emaciated by continual fasting, he had jet-black hair and a complexion shading from brown to black, a sign that his ancestors included Negroes besides Arabs. He wore long, flowing clothes in the Oriental fashion, with a sword which rattled at his side as he rode, and he sat proud and upright. In spite of his incongruously small size, he looked every inch the warrior. A wave of whispering inquiry passed through the crowd, and the well-informed were able to tell that he was David Rubeni, a Jew from one of the remote and unknown lands of the Orient.

As the procession arrived at the gates of the Vatican a red-cloaked cardinal advanced to meet him, and delivered an address of welcome in studied Hebrew, since he was one of a fair number of people who in those days were familiar with the language of the Old Testament. Immediately afterwards he escorted the little Jew to an audience with the heir to St Peter; namely, Pope Clement the Seventh. For a long time the two men conferred in private; and the interview must have ended favourably for the Jew, for in the weeks that followed, the Jewish community in Rome laid all its riches at his feet. What was the meaning of this remarkable visit?

A few months earlier David Rubeni had arrived at Venice by ship from Egypt, and had made straight for the ghetto in order to report his mission. It appeared that he was a member of the tribe of Reuben (which explained his name), and that he had come from Arabia, where his brother Joseph ruled the desert kingdom of Habor and where he was its commander in chief. He had been sent by King Joseph to inform the West that he intended to launch an attack upon the Turks, who had conquered the Holy Land seven years before, in order to liberate Jerusalem. The king had the men he needed for the campaign but lacked the modern arms; and David had come to negotiate with the Pope and the kings of Christendom in the hope of obtaining these.

David Rubeni found a deep response both among Jews and among Christians. Since time immemorial Jewish myth and legend had been busy with the ten tribes of the old Northern kingdom which had been lost when the Assyrian king had devastated Samaria and carried off its people into exile. It was a subject of which the imagination never grew tired. There was a tradition that they inhabited a region to the east, beyond the River Sambation. But that river was impassable; for though it contained no water, its bed carried a stream of stones which flowed with the swiftness of arrows, except for a period beginning two hours before the sabbath and lasting until it was over, when it lay completely still. Adventurous Jews had gone on long journeys to find this mysterious river. Now this remarkable stranger had brought news of the romantic land that lay on the other side of it. Speculation had given way to fact.

The Pope, too, was interested. He had recently suffered some severe setbacks. For one thing, the Church of Rome had almost lost half of Europe to the Lutheran Reformation, and, for another, the Emperor, Charles the Fifth, was pursuing a ruthless policy of extortion against His Holiness. Thus the Pope found himself between the devil and the deep blue sea; and in such a situation even a pope will clutch at a straw. Possibly he could restore Rome's failing prestige by leading a successful new Crusade and recapturing Jerusalem for Christendom.

The upshot, at any rate, was that David Rubeni embarked

ITALY

on a papal ship, which flew the Jewish flag, and sailed for Portugal, carrying in his pocket a strong recommendation from the Pope to King Juan the Third. Juan received the Jewish emissary at the summer residence of the Portuguese kings at Almerim; and as in Rome, Rubeni conducted himself in style at the court, flying a white silk banner on which were embroidered the ten commandments. Along with the letter from the Pope, he handed King Juan despatches from Portuguese captains which confirmed his accounts of the Jewish kingdom in Arabia.

The king fully appreciated the value of dealing a blow at the Turks; for in their recent conquest of Egypt they had cut an important Portuguese trade route through the Red Sea to the spice islands of the Orient. He accordingly promised to furnish Rubeni with both guns and warships.

David Rubeni must undoubtedly have been an astute diplomatist. The situation forced him to talk with two tongues. To the Christian potentates he emphasized the help which Christendom would gain from having a Jewish army at war with the infidel; while to the Jews he stressed his mission's Messianic importance. This ambivalence was eventually to cost him his life.

There was almost a disaster in Poland. Seeing a Jew accorded such high honours, the miserable *Maranos* found new hope. This man, they thought, must be the Messiah, and they rallied to his banner. In some towns they openly revolted.

They also provided David Rubeni with his greatest disciple and at the same time his most troublesome problem: namely, Salomo Malko. Baptized as Diego Pirez, this young zealot had experienced since childhood the *Marano's* conflicting attitudes to the Christianity he was forced to profess and the Judaism he believed in at heart. A gifted young man, he was already well launched on a legal career when David Rubeni appeared to agitate his emotional spirit. He at once circumcized himself, changed his name, and, while still weak and feverish after the operation, presented himself as Rubeni's disciple, talking loudly and excitedly of Messianic visions.

Rubeni, frightened by the man's almost manic condition, and realizing that he could ruin everything, exhorted him to go away; and taking the exhortation as a hint from Heaven, Molko went to the Orient, where he spent his days in wandering from place to place. In Salonica he met Joseph Caro, and perhaps it was Molko who suggested that Caro should go to Safad. At any rate, he deeply impressed Caro, and introduced him to mysticism.

While in Salonica he heard of the disaster that had taken place in Rome. The Emperor, leading his mercenaries across the Alps, had captured the city, which had been sacked and had suffered damage the like of which it had not seen since the ravages of the Vandals. Molko interpreted this as a sign from God. Edom, or Esau (that is to say, the Church), had been overthrown. The event must presage the coming of the Messiah; and he hurried to Rome in order to be present at the Latter Day.

There he stationed himself by the bridge facing the papal palace, among beggars and cripples; for there was an old tradition which said that the Messiah would come that way. Excited ideas rushed through his brain; and he imagined the great figure of the Messiah standing on the white peaks of Hermon, handing him the book of Edom's destiny. For thirty days he fasted, preaching with fervent eloquence of the things which impended. The whole city talked of him, and he was summoned before the Pope, whom he warned of three cataclysms that would usher in the Latter Day: a flood which would devastate Rome, an earthquake in Portugal, and a comet that would flash across the sky. The Pope was greatly impressed and dropped Molko a warning that the Inquisition was watching him; and he took the hint and went to Venice.

In Venice he met Rubeni, who had felt that Portugal was getting too hot for him. All the king's promises of arms had proved to be nothing more than talk, and the *Maranos* endangered his presence. He now lived in princely state in one of the Venetian palaces, though his star was waning. Molko's, however, was waxing fast; for the three cataclysms he had prophesied had actually taken place.

Returning post-haste to Rome, he had long interviews with the Pope. Whether the troubled Pope was in fact impressed by Molko's eloquence and prophesies, or whether he merely saw him as a tool with which to further his own plans, can-

ITALY

not be known; but he certainly provided him with a letter of protection against the Inquisition.

However, that did not prevent the Inquisition from investigating Molko's past; and with the help of informers it succeeded in preferring such incriminating evidence against this lapsed *Marano* that even the Pope could not save him from sentence of death. With all the customary ceremony, Molko was burnt at the stake in the Piazza dei Fiori in Rome.

Yet to everybody's astonishment the heretic was seen to enter the Vatican as usual the next day! The Pope had saved him and had caused another man, who resembled Molko, to be burnt in his stead. But it followed that he could not remain in Rome; and under papal escort he returned to Venice and was reunited with David Rubeni.

The romantic story is approaching its tragic close. Before the end, however, the two visionaries were again to astonish the world; for they announced their intention to attend the Parliament at Regensburg and there meet the Emperor. Their friends, realizing the inevitable outcome of appealing to the pious, silent, and at the same time ruthless Emperor, tried to dissuade them; but nothing could stop them. They set out on their journey, bearing a flag embroidered with the letters MKBJ, which are the Hebrew initials of the motto: Who among the mighty is like unto the Lord?

It was a foregone conclusion. The Emperor remained unmoved by the two men and their promises of Jewish support in the struggle against the infidel; and showing more respect for the Inquisition than the Pope, he had them put in irons and dragged by horses when with his retinue he travelled to Italy.

In Mantua, Salomo Molko was again sentenced to be burnt at the stake. As he stood with the faggots piled about him, a messenger arrived from the Emperor with an offer of pardon if he would repent of his lapse. Molko's reply was:

'My only regret is that in my youth I confessed to your faith.'

At that the pyre was lit and Salomo Molko achieved the martyr's death his soul had so ardently desired; the dream of *kiddush hashem* (the sanctifying of the name) had come to pass. A few years later David Rubeni followed him to the stake in a Spanish city.

The incredible careers of these two men exemplify the interlocking of Messianic hopes and mystic dreams with political aspirations. Nostalgic fanaticism, cool speculation, and diplomatic intrigue were all intermixed. For a few brief moments the great hope flickered and then was once more extinguished in the impenetrable darkness of despair.

For nearly as long as memory can tell, Italy has sheltered Jews in every city and every state. There were Jewish settlements in Rome long before the Christian era, and at least as far back as the time of Pompey. It was Pompey who initiated the permanent connection between Israel and Rome when he took Jerusalem and, sweeping the horrified priests aside, entered the Holy of Holies. He took Jews into captivity, and some of those who were afterwards liberated rose to high positions in society. Caesar, who liked the Jews, was magnanimous to them; and after his murder they mourned him for a week and wrote lamentations in his honour. Augustus, too, was friendly to them.

In those remote times the Jews did not inhabit ghettos but could buy houses in any part of the capital. Even so, they preferred to live near to one another, and a special Jewish quarter grew up. A long time later, they were forced to live there, and it became the ghetto. An air of mystery clung to Jews in the time of the Empire. They were reputed to command the gift of prophesy, to be familiar with strange medicines, and also to be masters of the secret arts of love. Many a noble Roman made his way to the Jewish quarter to buy remedies for ailments physical or mental.

Jewish princes also rose to power at the Imperial court. Archelaus, Antipas, and Salome, all were trained under the Emperor before taking up their high offices at home. They were not famous, as a rule, for their virtues. Ugly rumours circulated about Agrippa, the grandson of Herod the Great, an adventurer and fortune-seeker who became the bosom friend of a later emperor, the depraved Caligula. His daughter, the beautiful and corrupt Berenice, also played a dazzling role in Rome. Her incestuous relations with her brother, the younger Agrippa, were a public scandal. Yet when Titus took Jerusalem she became his mistress and lived with him in the royal palace, though she never succeeded in getting herself made empress. Not even Titus dared to crown a Jewess.

Throughout the Middle Ages Italy was the country, after Spain, where conditions were most tolerable for Jews. The people of that sunlit country did not take religion quite so earnestly as did the people of France and Germany, the crusading spirit never got quite the same hold.

Italy was a land of great contrasts. The spirit of the Middle Ages in its sublimest form is expressed in *The Divine Comedy* of Dante. Dante was on good terms with a Jewish philosopher, and it is an amusing fact that the pawnbrokers (who were usually Jews) are represented in the *Inferno* as Christians. At the same time, Italy was the land of Machiavelli, the man who represented infamy, cruelty, and lying as the virtues of statesmen. Where such contrasts existed, Jews could always find a refuge. Again, perpetual unrest in Italy, with insurrection, revolution, and war, split the country into many small independent states and cities, and their Jewish policies were not always the same. Thus Jews that were expelled from one place could easily go to another. The intolerance of the Church tended to increase with distance from Rome, and most Popes, at any rate, were formally tolerant in their attitude to the Jews. Several papal edicts opposed the charges of ritual murder, and Ferdinand of Spain had almost to force the Pope of that time into setting up the Inquisition.

Jewish thought was actively engaged in the Renaissance. One of the great names of the Renaissance period, Pico della Mirandola, found vital inspiration in Jewish studies; and absorbing the entire knowledge of his times, this spirited genius assimilated it all into a strange philosophical system. The sources of true wisdom he found in the Orient, in the sacred traditions of Judaism and Christianity, but the solution to the mystery of life itself he saw in the mysticism of the Cabbala. He was the man who formulated the celebrated thesis that philosophy seeks after the truth, theology finds it, and religion holds it. We shall see later on that there were connections between Pico della Mirandola and the German

Reuchlin, who in his turn was to have a deep influence on the early Reformation.

The picture that we get of the Jews at the close of the Middle Ages is a flickering and uncertain one. It is necessary to bear that in mind if we are to understand the amazing careers of David Rubeni and Salomo Molko. In the end both were crushed. The horizon was beginning to darken, and night in all its gloom lay ahead.

It was the beginning of the Counter-Reformation.

When in 1555 Pietro Caraffa succeeded to the throne of St Peter as Paul the Fourth, there were some who said that Satan himself had come to reign in Christ's name. His election was a source of dismay to all, including cardinals, who could not understand how such a fanatic had gained so many votes.

Caraffa came of a family of Neopolitan nobles, and it was in his native city that he achieved his first success. As Archbishop of Naples he conducted the campaign against the young Evangelical movement with all the fiery energy of a southern fanatic; and as Pope, holding the full powers of the Church in his vigorous hands, he continued the operations with uncompromising ruthlessness.

Paul the Fourth was the inquisitor on the papal throne, and the Inquisition was this pale ascetic's only joy. Lenient to other crimes, in cases of deviation from clerical doctrine, be they never so trivial, he was strict in the extreme. The slightest suspicion of heresy brought the Inquisition into play, and its punishments were dire. Even princes and bishops were fed 'with bread of affliction and with water of affliction' and ended their days at the stake. To this fanatic, Charles the Fifth and his family were the Devil's brood; for had not the Emperor held synods and diets that had been attended by Luther and other heretics? But for him, the Evangelical movement would have been stifled at birth.

It need hardly be added that this Pope was also bigoted. There was an occasion when he humiliated Michelangelo by commanding one of the master's pupils to drape some of his nudes. Michelangelo's reply was:

'Tell His Holiness that he should rather apply himself to bettering the world. A work of art is easily worsened.'

ITALY

Paul the Fourth never employed spiritual means, but confessed that the pyres and prisons of the Inquisition were his only reliable aid. With them he crushed the rising Evangelical movement of Italy. What was left of the flock that had been overtaken by the Reformation had to be saved at all costs.

Reaction spread its sinister shadow over the countries where the spirit of the late Renaissance still lingered on, and the new era was dominated by the Society of Jesus. In the Middle Ages the Church's shock troops had been the Dominican friars; in the Counter-Reformation they were the Jesuits. The Church of Rome put its house in order systematically and with a thoroughness that had never been known before. The popes were no longer the liberal patrons of literature, science, and the arts. Those now elected were men to whom the Church's power, spiritual and temporal, was the prime consideration, and who were prepared to enforce the canonical laws down to the last comma.

Paul the Fourth was the prime mover in this relentless campaign, both before and after his election. To serve his purpose he devised two major instruments: first, in 1542, the notorious Sanctum Officium, the supreme tribunal of the Inquisition; and, secondly, the Index Librorum Prohibitorum, or index of prohibited books, the papal censorship that was to prevent the spread of free thought promoted by the introduction of the printing press.

To begin with, the Inquisition was directed against heretics only; that is to say, against errant Christians. Soon, however, its arm extended beyond the Church, and the first victims among 'unbelievers' were the Jews; not without reason, for Rome feared them. We shall see later on the part which they played in the early years of the Reformation.

The Inquisition stopped at nothing in its efforts to suppress the Jews, resorting, among other means, to informers: Jews who had been bought over. None was more dangerous; for, brought up in the Jewish faith, they were far more familiar with the Torah and the Talmud than were the theologians of the Inquisition, and they soon became experts in the practice of wresting out of their context passages which, given the right amount of ill-will, could be construed as offensive to the Christian doctrine or to Christ.

In every period of Jewish persecution there are these tragic figures, the converts turned traitor. They present psychological problems; they were men for whom things had gone wrong. Some of them had lacked religious stamina, and others had met with disappointments; the chain of disasters which had overwhelmed Judaism had robbed them of their faith. No doubt, also, there were some who quite simply were for sale. Common to all was their anxious need to justify themselves in their own eyes. Their names have been quickly forgotten and were never worth remembering; but frequently they came of famous families and possessed considerable education and learning.

Men like these put weapons into the Inquisition's hands; and soon the first blow was struck. In the autumn of 1553, actually on the Jewish New Year's Day, a vast quantity of Hebrew books was destroyed by burning at a great *auto-da-fé* in the Piazza dei Fiori, where, later on, Giordano Bruno was to die. The Roman example was catching; and Jewish books were burnt in a large number of Italian towns and cities.

One means of Jewish self-defence was to introduce a similar censorship. Strict measures were resorted to in order to ensure that no book was published in Hebrew without prior examination by a specially appointed censor to prevent the inclusion of objectionable matter. This measure was of course abused in its turn. Censorship in any form becomes sooner or later a weapon directed against freedom of thought. It was to make the atmosphere of the ghetto even more confined than it had been before.

These, however, were only the first of the events initiated by the Inquisition and Paul the Fourth.

The crucial blow fell on July 12, 1555, the day on which Pope Paul issued the bull of *Cum nimis absurdum*. It is a milestone in the long record of man's inhumanity to man; and like all papal decrees it takes its name from the words by which it is introduced. The following translation attempts to preserve the tortuous style that is characteristic of them:

'Whereas it seemeth absurd and outrageous that Jews, being by God condemned for their guilt to everlasting slavery, should enjoy our Christian love and tolerance and, rewarding this our indulgence with ingratitude, instead of submission should aggressively seek power; and whereas we are informed that such is their shamelessness that in Rome, as elsewhere within the domains of the Holy Roman Church, they take up their abode among Christians, and indeed in the immediate proximity of churches, without outward sign of their identity, and that they also rent houses in respectable streets, purchase and acquire property, keep Christian servants and nurses in their houses, and in other ways trample Christian honour under foot; be it known that we find ourselves compelled to have recourse to the undermentioned measures . . .'

Then follow fifteen detailed regulations in which the papal Grand Inquisitor revives the anti-Jewish legislation of the Middle Ages and makes new additions to it. These are some of the most important provisions:

Jews were to live separately from Christians in a prescribed street or locality, marked off from the rest of the city by a wall containing only one gate. Holders of property outside this quarter were to sell it forthwith, and no Jew was to own house property anywhere. There was to be only one synagogue in a town; any others were to be destroyed. Every Jew was to wear the badge of shame, consisting of a saffron-yellow hat or, in the case of women, a veil. It was forbidden to keep Christian servants or to have dealings with Christians. The courtesy title of *Signor* was to be denied to them. Jewish doctors were forbidden to treat Christian patients. Jews were not to trade in grain or other vital commodities, but were to be restricted to the buying and selling of old clothing and other second-hand goods. All personal and local privileges were abolished.

Such severe regulations had existed in the past, but had been local or temporary in character, and little respected. Now they were to be fully enforced, and any attempt at their evasion would be subject to the strictest penalties.

The bull was enforced with ruthless severity. A wall was erected round the Jewish quarter in Rome with astonishing speed, the Jews being, of course, required to pay for it. The unlucky owners of houses outside it, having to sell them at short notice, found the situation exploited by the buyers, with the result that they got no more than a fifth of their value. The excess synagogues were demolished—two being permitted in Rome—but the Jews still had to pay tax on those destroyed.

The bitterest humiliation was that they were forced to build a *Casa dei Catacumeni*, or house of catacombs, inside the ghetto. It was a Christian conversion centre, where monks taught Jews the Christian faith, and where attendance was compulsory. The ghetto gates were to be closed and opened at exactly prescribed times. The only door remaining open day and night was the one which led to the house of catacombs.

Christians as well as Jews lived in perpetual fear of Paul the Fourth. Fortunately, his reign lasted for only five years. When it was reported that he lay dying the news spread like wildfire through the city. Crowds stormed the Inquisition's prisons and freed the inmates, who could scarcely believe their own eyes. Others tore down the Pope's coat of arms and overturned his statue on the Capitol. A wit crowned it with a yellow Jewish hat.

But Paul the Fourth had established the ghetto, and it survived him by centuries. It is for that that his name is still remembered.

The Rome ghetto lay—and still lies—by the Isola Tiberina, facing the Quattro Capi bridge. From the lofty arch of this bridge there is a view of the small, congested houses where the washing flutters from innumerable lines. The Jews lived nowhere in Europe under such wretched conditions as they did in Rome. The ghetto was low-lying and every spring the narrow streets were flooded. With the melting of the snow in the mountains and the closing of the river's mouth by the west wind the Tiber would overflow its banks, and the ghetto would then resemble a Noah's ark, with the water washing high in the streets. When it receded it would leave a layer of stinking mud, an ideal breeding-ground for malarial mosquitoes. All manner of epidemics raged in the overcrowded streets, and 800 of the 4,000 inhabitants died in epidemics in 1656.

The main entrance to the ghetto was at the Piazza Giudea, or Jewish Square, and from there the Via Rua, the only true street, ran to the small Piazza delle Scuole, where the synagogue stood, and where there was a spring fed from the Alban Hills. For the rest, the ghetto was a network of narrow, dank alleys and courtyards; a warren swarming with penniless dark-skinned and talkative people who went in perpetual fear of insult and were tireless in their efforts to earn a living.

It was brought home to the Jews of Rome that they lived in the centre of the Catholic world, and—a further affront, because it reminded them of their great national disaster—they were forced to pay homage to each newly-elected Pope at the Arch of Titus, though there they drew the line, refusing to pass under the arch. At the arch they would hand the Torah to the new Pope, who would look at it and return it, with the words:

'We confirm the Law, but condemn the Jewish people and their interpretation of it.'

Pope Leo the Tenth, who otherwise was one of the liberal popes, allowed the roll to fall on the ground, and the Jews had to bend and kiss his foot.

The Roman Carnival was an occasion for licentious humour, of which the Jews were the first victims. To begin with it was comparatively harmless; twelve Jews had to run a race from St Peter's Square to the Castel San' Angelo, under the direction of the Pope's physician, a baptized Jew, and escorted by hundreds of pressed Jews carrying olive branches and papal banners.

Before long, however, the races became exhibitions of sheer cruelty. Jews had to run the length of the Corso, wearing loin cloths, and soldiers, riding behind them, would hurry them on. A jubilantly yelling crowd of spectators would line the street and the Holy Father, seated on a balcony, got great amusement from the spectacle. Before the start, the runners would be forced to overeat, and there was more amusement when they had to stop and vomit. Occasionally, one of them would die of a stroke.

The ghetto at Rome was only one of many. Nearly every town and city had one. Let us try to form a general impression of the Italian ghettos.

From a distance the ghetto seemed as if built against the side of a hill. This was because the allotted area was too confined for the number of inhabitants, and any extensions had to take the form of new storeys built on the already rickety houses. The houses got increasingly taller, and came to resemble small skyscrapers.

Such a practice could sometimes be costly; and it was not uncommon for a house in the ghetto to collapse. This, unfortunately, would most often occur during a celebration, when many more people were assembled on one of the floors than the house could bear. Thus more than one happy wedding feast ended in tragedy. Once, no fewer than sixty-five people, including the bride, were crushed to death.

Large fires were in those days unavoidable, but when they occurred in a ghetto the effects would be more than usually serious; for the houses were so high and the streets so narrow that it was impossible to get at the site of the fire with the primitive fire-fighting equipment then available. The entire ghetto could become a smoking ruin in a matter of hours.

In many towns the ghetto consisted of a single street, but in large cities it was a maze of narrow alleys, a town within the town, the houses being often built so close together that it was possible to pass from street to street without setting foot on the road. There was always a *piazza,* however, which was the scene of the market and, in the early spring, of the festival of the *Purim.* Jews are a cleanly people, as their religion requires them to be; but cleanliness in the congested conditions of the ghetto was almost impossible. As a result, the frequent epidemics were particularly virulent there.

As the streets were thick with people, it was not surprising that they all had to shout in order to make themselves heard. The noise of the ghetto became a by-word, the phrase *fare un ghetto* meaning the same as a 'din'. The noise did not grow less as people accustomed themselves to speaking in

ITALY

the highest descant. Their language was Italian mixed with many Hebrew words, and in time a special Italian-Jewish dialect developed that was mid-way between Ladino and Yiddish.

A remarkable legal code developed from the overcrowding. As already mentioned, Jews could not own property; all the houses of the ghetto, therefore, belonged to Christians. In view of the chronic shortage of housing, a grasping landlord held a strong position and could evict a tenant for someone who offered to pay a higher rent. The inhabitants therefore protected themselves by means of the old Jewish law of property, the *Hassakah*, which they adapted to the conditions. It was prohibited, under threat of severe penalty, to bid against another or occupy a house from which a tenant had been evicted. Provided that a man paid his rent when it fell due he had security of possession. Tenancy was passed on from father to son, or was given in dowry. By an amusing mixture of Latin and Hebrew, this arrangement was called *jus gazaga*, the word *gazaga* being derived from *Hassakah*, in which the Hebrew letter 'h' (*het*) is pronounced like the guttural German 'ch', in Italian 'g'. This *jus gazaga* was recognized by the civic authorities and is a fine testimony to Jewish solidarity.

Outside the ghetto it was not easy to tell Jews from Christians. The Italian Jews were descended from people who had lived in the country for 1,500 years, and it took a good eye to detect that their lips perhaps were a little thicker and their mouths rather larger than the rest. They were indistinguishable by their dress, and most Jewish men had cut their beards and were clean-shaven.

For this reason the Church feared mental contamination from the ghetto, and for this reason insisted on absolute segregation. After nightfall when the gate had been locked, a wall divided the two people; and woe to the Jew discovered in the town outside, or the Christian who had failed to get out in time. The law which prescribed yellow hats for men and veils for women was strictly enforced. Originally the colour had been red, but a shortsighted cardinal had one day greeted a Jew in his red hat as a prince of the Church, and in order to avoid a repetition of the *faux pas* the colour had been changed to yellow.

It could be costly to venture outside the ghetto without the yellow hat, and a reward was offered to anybody who apprehended such a person. The hat also had to have the prescribed cut; if it did not, anyone could snatch it from the wearer's head and take it to the police, who paid him a cash reward for his vigilance. Only very exceptionally, as in the case of large merchants or celebrated physicians, could persons be exempted from wearing the hat. In time, many Jews came to regard it as a mark of honour, so that when, in a more tolerant period, they were allowed to discard it many proudly continued wearing it.

The bitterest humiliation was the obligation to pay tax to the house of catacombs, where the Church laboured to persuade them of the superiority of the Christian faith; but the Church held them under observation in every respect. A Jew who persuaded a waverer to remain true to his fathers' religion risked public flogging. Among the Christian population there was a widespread belief that a person who converted a Jew had all his sins remitted and was sure of Paradise. An abandoned sinner might suddenly seize a Jewish child in the street and baptize it in water from the gutter, in order to be saved. What is incredible, however, is that the Church recognized such a baptism and ordered the child to be taken from its parents and brought up in a convent. A man also had to curb his tongue. There was a Jew who turned away a priest who wanted to baptize his child, saying, in a lighthearted moment, that the child should only be baptized if the Pope stood godfather. His remark cost him his child, for the Pope did stand godfather. Jews were obliged to attend regular conversion sermons in the house of catacombs; and before they entered, their ears were examined for cottonwool. The vergers, the *fattori*, were responsible for seeing that they did not fall asleep during the sermon, using pointed sticks.

Students had a free hand with Jews, and in university towns it was their privilege to be the first to snowball them in winter, though the Jews could buy themselves free with a large supply of sweets and paper for the coming year. Every year on St Catherine's Day the students of Pisa would pick out the fattest Jew and weigh him, and the ghetto would then have to pay his weight in confectionery.

Yet for all their pinpricking, the Italians remained Italians, by nature friendly and compassionate. There were no large-scale persecutions in Italy. Jews and Christians would on rare occasions eat and drink together, and there are accounts of love affairs between the two, though these were savagely punished if discovered. For example, the mistress of a Roman aristocrat was buried alive when she was discovered to be a Jewess.

Economic activities were strictly limited, and besides house property a Jew could not own, or farm, land. Medicine, an old and distinguished Jewish profession, could, with rare exceptions, be practised only inside the wall. The craft guilds were also closed to Jews, though they could occasionally obtain work as artisans, especially in trades which combined manual skill with art. There were Jews who made water clocks, or playing-cards. Book-binding was a Jewish craft, and Jewish goldsmiths excelled in filigree work with precious metals. Above all there were Jewish printers, for printing was a trade which, more than any other, involved the use of brain as well as hand.

All these were, however, exceptions; and apart from the old Jewish occupations of banking and pawnbroking, there was nothing else but the trade in cast-off clothing and other second-hand goods, though this was a large business. Cheap, ready-made clothing being then unknown, the poor had to wear the discarded clothing of the rich; consequently, a man who traded in old clothes was more important than he is today, and was in fact a necessary middleman. He also supplied work for Jewish tailors; there would be stacks of old clothes awaiting repair in the ghetto, and at the beginning of the eighteenth century three-quarters of all the tailors in Rome were Jews. Men and women could be seen on a summer's day by the hundred, working with needle and scissors outside their doors. The constant close work made many of them shortsighted and some went blind; but Jewish women especially made excellent menders and it was said that their repairs were invisible. These people became adept at evading the law against dealing in new clothes, for it was easy to make new clothes look second-hand with the help of a tear.

The junk trade also reached a high level of efficiency, as Jews often took expensive things in pawn, and when they were unredeemed would sell them. Nothing was too large or too small to deal in, and one might see famous pictures by Titian or Veronese, as well as superb carpets and jewels. A nobleman wanting to buy high-quality articles would often find what he wanted in the ghetto.

At the same time, rich second-hand dealers were exceptions, and a far more common occupation was that of restoring old mattresses, which was left to Jews. They would take the mattresses and empty out the wool, which would after many years of use often be caked, and they would be called in to beat and clean mattresses in the sun after a death.

Mattress repairers were known for their coughing and wheezing, and many died of infection.

Sunshine and shadow fell on the ghetto, but there was more shadow than sunshine. Yet, strange to say, those who were victims of the system did not find it so bad as it seems to us now, looking back on it across the centuries. Though they bitterly resented it when it was forced upon them, they soon discovered that the surrounding walls also had their use in keeping out enemies. The gates were therefore locked on both sides. Segregation was humiliating, yet it proved to be a means of preserving Jewish culture and individuality, and, paradoxical though it may seem, there were cities in Italy where the establishment of the ghetto was an occasion for celebration.

Any account of the Italian ghetto would be incomplete without mention of Venice. In this city where the ghetto got its name the Jews stood out in prestige as well as in the number of its remarkable men.

'We live in the city of cities.'

It is a sentence which occurs more than once in letters from Venetian Jews in the ghetto period.

'The institutions of Venice are divine, and God has

ITALY

promised through His prophet to preserve this most sacred Republic.'

The superlatives indicate the Jewish devotion to the city of the Doges.

In Venice indeed the Jews lived a far freer life than in any other Italian city; though high walls surrounded the ghetto there as elsewhere, the segregation was nothing like as complete.

The many Jews who passed through this important centre from all parts of the known world broke down the barriers of Jewish isolation. Jewish merchants came there from other cities in Italy as well as from the Levant and from Amsterdam and Poland, and the Italian-Jewish dialect mingled both with Ladino and Yiddish and with the elusive Ashekanazi Hebrew. In the streets went turbanned Jews from Levantine ports, escaped *Maranos* from Spain and Portugal, and pilgrims from Poland on their way to the Holy Land, taking their ancestors' coffins for burial on the Mount of Olives at Jerusalem.

The Venetian Jews had a reputation for good looks. 'The man are handsome with fine features, the woman as beautiful as any I have ever seen,' a traveller recorded in his diary. They closely resembled their Italian neighbours, and in fact it could be difficult to tell the difference between the picture of a Venetian patrician and that of a merchant from the ghetto.

The financial standing of the Jews in the Venetian ghetto was well above the contemporary average, and indeed some of them were merchants on a big scale, with connections in distant countries which they had not been slow to exploit. Their standards of living, in spite of the restrictions and regulations, were relatively high, and they developed various specialized occupations. Their international contacts, for example, enabled them to act as spies, and there were few patricians residing in the palaces along the Grand Canal who did not have Jews in their confidential service. It was a Venetian Jew who discovered invisible ink.

Life in the ghetto paralleled in a striking way the general life of Venice, both in its virtues and in its vices, and there were in fact many links which passed through the ghetto wall. The lively musical activities that went on in the ghetto were closely watched from outside, and Christian priests and monks would often attend the synagogues to hear the sermons preached by rabbis, just as long-bearded rabbis could be seen in Christian churches. The funeral of a prominent Jew would often be attended by many Christians.

It is no wonder that the Venetian ghetto was regarded as the best and that it enjoyed great prestige among other Jews, and yet there were intellectual differences which could sometimes lead to clashes. The German and Polish Jews who at one time or another had found a refuge in Venice were strictly orthodox and not free from philistinism, and they were continually at odds with the more aesthetic Venetians. Sometimes this internal dissension would be concentrated in a single person, resulting in a career so complex and so full of tension that it was probably without an equal outside Venice.

It is such a man as this that we now have to consider. His name was Leone de Modena, and he can best be characterized as the *luftmensch* of all times.

The word *luftmensch* is Yiddish and it was first coined in a Russian or Polish ghetto some time in the nineteenth century, but the type is as old as the ghetto itself. It stands for a person who is so high up in the air (*luft*) that his roots can never reach the ground. Men such as this were the inevitable product of the ghetto, where the streets were packed with people and there were more tailors than there were caftans to make, more shopkeepers than customers with the money to buy. Where competition was so keen the prizes went to those who were quick-thinking and resourceful.

The *luftmensch* became a common phenomenon in the ghetto, as exemplified in the busy little man hurrying through the streets full of airy ideas, always chasing after the object of his dreams but never succeeding in catching up with the fleeting opportunity, and yet refusing to give in, for ever courting his inconstant *mazl*, the luck which resembled a coy and unresponsive mistress. Not a day-dreamer entirely, he was the incorrigible optimist who was not to be put down by adversity but was always hoping against hope and for ever laying new plans. Something of a poet, a little of an adventurer, as a Jew he was first and foremost a philosopher, and generally an honest man. From bitter experience he knew the meaning of the words in the Talmud that 'the food is short and the road long', and the ghetto had neither shortened the road nor increased the amount of food. The possession he never lacked was children, a large family being considered a blessing. Heinrich Heine, himself a Jew, called him a 'famillionaire'.

Leone de Modena was a classical *luftmensch*.

He was born in 1571 in the Ghetto Vecchio in Venice, where he was to spend the whole of his long and eventful life. His family was descended, in the Middle Ages, from French-Jewish refugees, and many of his ancestors had attained to high position, Leone's grandfather, Mordecai, for example, having been invested with the order of the Golden Fleece by the Emperor Charles the Fifth. As the name indicates, his father had lived at Modena, but he had later escaped to Venice. A wealthy man, he had lost all he possessed before his son's education was complete.

Leone deserved the best education the times could provide, and one had to go far to find an infant prodigy the like of him. At the age of two and a half he read the prophets in the synagogue, and at thirteen he wrote a book in which he attacked card-playing, though by a strange irony, card-playing was to become the incurable vice of his later years. It was lucky that a boy could not publish books under his own name but only under a pseudonym, or he might later have been confronted with his own words.

This was the only piece of luck that he had, however, his whole life long, for misfortune invariably dogged his footsteps. He nearly died when an accident befell his mother before he was born, and at the age of two he fell into a bathtub and would have drowned if his mother had not entered the room at the last moment. If there were any diseases about, he got them, from smallpox to tapeworms. He nearly died as a result of the latter, though not from the disease itself but from the treatment his father had learnt from an old woman.

While he lived, his father made every sacrifice in order to better him, in spite of the loss of his fortune. Leone of course learnt all the Jewish disciplines, and he was also skilled in

Latin, mathematics, natural science, philosophy, and even such frivolous subjects, for an orthodox Jew, as music, singing, and dancing. At the death of his favourite teacher the boy, then only thirteen, composed a funeral oration that was so ingenious that by a change in the emphasis it said the same thing in Hebrew and Italian.

Bad luck kept on dogging his footsteps. Soon after his father had lost his money he died. His fiancée died the day before their marriage; and when forced by the family into marrying her sister the result was a life of domestic quarrels.

He achieved only one success that was to last him for the rest of his life, his success as a preacher. When this gifted and eloquent man spoke there was wild excitement, and Christians as well as Jews would flock to hear him. Foreign ambassadors, Venetian patricians, princes of the blood, even monks, priests and bishops listened eagerly to his words.

It was necessary, however, to earn a living, for the family, in spite of the domestic disagreements, continued to grow. As a *luftmensch* he was continually devising new means of making money: he gave lessons in the various languages he had mastered; was scribe, typesetter, and proof-reader, as well as legal adviser; composed epitaphs for tombstones, translated documents, wrote a succession of books, and tried his hand at writing plays in Italian; and in addition to all this he engaged in business. In one of his bitter moments he listed no fewer than twenty-six occupations, discreetly concealing the fact that in addition he had dealt in charms and spells and had dabbled in alchemy. As for the last-named, his primitive laboratory one night blew up and nearly killed him.

Leone de Modena became notorious for gambling at cards, a great vice at the time which had also spread to the ghetto. Having written a book against it, he should have been forewarned, but he became hopelessly involved in the vice and consoled himself with the reflection that it must have been written in his stars and that consequently there was no use in resisting it. The wheel of fortune always turned against Leone, so that whenever he seemed to be winning, his luck would change and he would lose in the end. The occasional small winnings went no way to covering his losses, and repeatedly he found himself on the verge of bankruptcy. When things were at their worst he would promise to turn over a new leaf and for a few months he would stop gambling, only to fall for the temptation again later. Speaking once of the sum of 500 ducats which he had won, he dispassionately remarked:

'They went the way they had come, taking more with them.'

When rebuked by the elders for his bad example, Leone would draw upon his theological reserves to find excuses, and on one occasion he claimed that among the 248 commandments there was none which said 'Thou shalt not play cards'.

His home life obviously suffered as a result of his improvidence, and his quarrels with his wife, who would grow hysterical, were a common topic of conversation in the ghetto. She had rheumatism; but he would say that though her limbs were stiff, the same was not true of her tongue.

It is a testimony to the liberalism of the ghetto in Venice that such a man could for so long maintain his reputation as a preacher and writer. What gave him stature was the conflict in his mind between faith and doubt, a fact which has since become clear. Outwardly he advocated orthodoxy, and it was he who caused Uriel da Costa to be cast out as a heretic. Yet a manuscript found in 1852 shows that at heart he agreed with da Costa, and that he, too, had profound doubts about the Talmud.

This manuscript, ostensibly written by an old sceptic, was in fact his own work, though he furnished it with an epilogue which refuted it, and which he bombastically headed 'The Lion's Roar'—an allusion to his own name. In fact, for the roar of a lion it is very meek, the doubt carrying far more conviction than the polemical reply.

The personality of Leone de Modena, composed of the conflicting elements of enlightenment and superstition, orthodoxy and scepticism, together with his slackness of character and his constant ill luck, are memorials to an age. He was the ghetto's despair and its joy.

But in fact Leone de Modena was a *luftmensch*. He deserves a poet who would penetrate into the complexities of his mind and follow him on his tortuous paths. In him there is the material for a great and tragic poem on the ghetto's *luftmensch*.

VI

GERMANY

It sounds incredible and yet is none the less true that there were Jews in western Germany before the Germans lived there. When the Romans founded the veteran colony of Colonia Agripinensis—afterwards Cologne—about the year 50 A.D. the Rhineland was Gallic, not Teutonic. It is probable that there were Jews in this first Cologne, though there is no proof of it. But it is certain that there was an organized Jewish community in Cologne at the beginning of the fourth century B.C., for their rights are laid down in an edict issued by the Emperor Constantine in the year 321.

It was not until 150 years later that the Teutons crossed the Rhine and settled in the old Roman province, and so Germanized it. It is amusing to reflect that a man who in the fourth century arrived in Cologne and spoke only German would have had difficulty in making himself understood, but would have found it easier to do so with Hebrew. When, twenty-five years ago, the Nazis crushed the Jews of Germany they did so on the ground that they threatened the nation's purity; but it is not the Jews who were the most foreign element in Germany, in the Rhineland at least.

It can be both amusing and surprising to analyse old allegations about the Jews, which did not die even with Hitler but which still live on in murky corners. There is, for example, the anti-semitic belief that since Jews are Asians they should stay out of Europe. Yet even the name of Europe derives from Asia; and what is more, from Palestine. Europa was a Semitic girl, the daughter of the King of Phoenicia, whom Zeus in the form of a bull carried off to Crete.

A crucial period in Jewish history is marked by the

Crusades. The appalling persecutions which followed in their wake left a trail of blood and fire, struck at the roots of Jewish culture and prosperity, and sapped Jewish courage. The evil passions they evoked have never altogether died down; the repeated accusations of ritual murder, the absurd suspicions that Jews were the cause of the Black Death in the fourteenth century, the tales of well-poisoning—these inflamed them again and again. If a city or a country was overwhelmed by some disaster the Jews were blamed. Did they not set cities on fire, call in the enemy, encourage heresy? Through the streets would go the answering cry of 'Down with the Jews!'

The confusion of disturbances and tumults which in Germany attended the massacres and expulsions of Jews towards the close of the Middle Ages is indescribable. Ancient communities were overthrown one after another; and though families and individuals would survive in pockets here and there, it was only in two large cities in Germany—Worms and Frankfurt on Main—that important communities managed to hold out. All the rest were destroyed.

The Emperor did what he could to save them, since the Jews were his personal property, his *Kammerknechte*, or house servants, as he put it; for, as the head of the Holy Roman Empire, he regarded himself as the rightful heir of Titus, who had acquired them through his capture of Jerusalem. This odd legal sophistry was maintained chiefly in order to enable the Emperor to fleece them through 'protective' taxation. Some protection was, however, given: it pays to save the hen that lays the golden eggs.

But the Emperor could not allay their fears, and dread hung heavily and at all times over their heads, keeping them awake at night, stifling their breathing almost. They would huddle together on dark nights in their corners, the words of an ancient biblical curse echoing in their minds: 'And among these nations shalt thou find no ease, neither shall the sole of thy foot have rest . . . And thy life shall hang in doubt before thee . . . In the morning thou shalt say, Would God it were even! and at even thou shalt say, Would God it were morning!' Through the night would fly the news that now this community, now that, or those, had been overwhelmed. The fourteenth century saw the destruction of 350 of their

GERMANY

communities in Germany, the members of them being murdered, burnt at the stake, strangled or buried alive.

The survivors would seize the staffs that had been their faithful companions down the ages and take to the roads in flight. Germany had nothing for them but a grave, and they wanted to live. The stream flowed east, to the cities of eastern Germany and especially Poland.

They had lost their possessions; the fruits of generations of labour and thrift had all been stolen or destroyed. But they took with them two things which none could steal from them: their Book and their language.

The Book had been given them from on high many centuries earlier, and they had read and re-read its ancient scrolls, poring over every chapter, weighing and deliberating on every one of its 647,319 letters, each of which had been paid for in lives. That Book they clung to.

That the German Jews survived at all is a striking proof that 'man doth not live by bread alone, but by every word that proceedeth out of the mouth of the Lord'. Later we shall see how they guarded their Book.

The Yiddish language which they had learnt to speak in Germany, and which the Ashkenazi Jews took with them to other countries and later other continents, was destined to be the bearer of a distinctive culture, and it is still spoken by millions of people today.

In centuries long past when the Old Testament was written the Jews had spoken Hebrew. While they remained safe in their homeland, at first in the great kingdom of David and afterwards in the two smaller kingdoms of the south and north, the kingdoms of Judah and Israel, Hebrew was both the language of the Bible and the national and colloquial language.

With the exile a remarkable development took place in the linguistic field. In Babylon, in the period of their early exile and captivity, they of course learnt to speak the local tongue; when they returned home to Jerusalem and rebuilt their Temple, therefore, they spoke, not Hebrew, but Aramaic, the language of the great Persian Empire. There are clear indications of this fact in the most recent books of the Old Testament, parts of Ezra and Daniel being in that language.

When the Jews were scattered in their second exile, they once more learnt to speak the language spoken by their neighbours; they became linguistically assimilated, in other words. In the centuries which followed the destruction of Jerusalem Aramaic came to rival Greek, then the great world language; but the Jewish community at Alexandria spoke the latter tongue almost exclusively. In Spain, the country of the *Three Rings*, they first spoke Arabic and later Spanish, and these were the languages used by the great Jewish philosophers and poets, whose works were thus accessible to all.

Yet they were determined never to lose themselves in their foreign environment, and in time they transformed the languages which they spoke, so that these came to express characteristically Jewish ideas and emotions. Slowly and imperceptibly, Jewish dialects developed almost into distinct languages, strikingly manifesting as they did so the ability of the Jewish character to survive.

To trace the long processes by which Jewish words and expressions which were of Hebrew origin were absorbed into other languages along with Hebrew formations and Hebraic characters is an interesting philological study. In Spain the result was Ladino, in Italy the special Italian-Jewish dialect that has already been mentioned.

It is remarkable that they should have taken these languages with them when disasters forced them to migrate or they were expelled. It would have been natural to suppose that they would have died out; but that was by no means the case; the Jews clung to them with great pertinacity. We have seen how the Spanish Jews continued to speak Ladino in Amsterdam; and it is a striking fact that in Istanbul and Salonika their descendants still speak it. For this reason, philologists wishing to study old Spanish dialects that have long since died out in Spain can go to the Balkans and find them still alive.

It is fairly common knowledge that modern German has its roots in Luther's translation of the Bible; but the roots of Yiddish go even farther back, right back to the German that was spoken in the Judengasse of Rhenish cities at the period when Cologne Cathedral was being planned. That medieval

GERMANY

German dialect is still preserved in Yiddish, and it is through Yiddish that it can chiefly be studied. But it is full of Jewish words and ideas taken over from Hebrew, and in course of time it evolved into a separate language.

Not for nothing, it calls itself *Mameloshen,* which is a characteristically Yiddish word made up of the German *Mama* (mother) and the Hebrew *loshaun* (language) and meaning therefore 'mother tongue'. The Yiddish for 'Hebrew', on the other hand, is *loshaun kaudesh,* which is formed from two Hebrew words and means 'the sacred language'—the language, that is, of the Bible and prayer.

The word 'Yiddish' is itself a contraction of *Jüdischdeutsch* or *Judendeutsch* ('Jewish-German'). It is a unique hybrid tongue which fully answers to its name, for it is written with Hebrew characters, is German in construction, and contains many Hebrew words, especially such as are connected with religion and its practice, or which express emotions, longings, sorrows and joys springing from the Jewish character. Untrammelled by pedantic rules of grammar, and loosely cohesive, it was well suited to the German Jews who fled to Poland, where they needed many new words and expressions that Yiddish was capable of absorbing. It continued to keep pace with developments and came in time to absorb Russian elements, with the result that today Yiddish is a strange mixture of German, Hebrew, Polish, and Russian, with elements taken from Greek, Latin, and the Romance languages. Finally, in New York it has taken in American words.

During the centuries of exile, Yiddish was the language of everyday Jewish life. It is not well suited to the expression of clear and abstract philosophical ideas; but it is a fine medium for expressing the thoughts and feelings of ordinary people in folk songs and tales. It also became the spoken language of those who lived behind the wall.

Most of the German Jews fled to Poland, but some stayed behind, and among these was one of the greatest inspirers of the Reformation.

We have seen, again and again, how the Church of Rome feared the Jews. It had good reason to fear them; for though their synagogues were grey and drab-looking, and bore the marks of much stone-throwing, they constituted a challenge to the Christian religion. Scattered throughout Christendom, they formed a network of small outposts which questioned its supremacy. They did not put out anti-Christian propaganda, and in fact Jews have very rarely tried to convert others to their faith; but the very existence of men who denied important aspects of Church doctrine was an encouragement to doubt and disbelief, since they showed that it was possible to remain outside the Church and yet face life and death with equanimity.

What is more, the Jews knew the Bible, like none others, in its original form, and could go beyond the Vulgate, which was the authorized Latin version, back to the basic Hebrew text. For thousands of years Jewish scholars had studied it and had written a vast amount of literature about it. They held both the treasure chest itself and the key to open it.

Some Christians understood this, and they found their way to the synagogue and sat at the feet, as it were, of Jewish theologians. The results were soon visible. The two great reforming movements of the Middle Ages, those of the Albigenses in the south of France and of John Huss in Bohemia, had their roots in the Bible studies inspired by Jewish theology. The Church was right in describing these as dangerous 'Judaizing' movements.

Rome mobilized all its forces against them, and succeeded in crushing them with the help of the stake. But the Reformation came when the soil had already been prepared. It proved too strong for Rome, and the great split in the Church became a reality. The Protestant leaders had found their weapons where their luckless predecessors had found them; they, too, had learnt from the rabbis. To take the most obvious example, Luther had studied the biblical commentaries of Nicolaus Lyra, a fourteenth-century Franciscan who had probably been a baptized Jew. Lyra's books are almost verbatim copies, with only a slight Christian gloss, of the commentaries of a celebrated medieval rabbi, Salomo ben Isak of Troyes, known as Rashi. The river can thus be traced back to its source, a fact which Luther's opponents were well aware of when they said:

GERMANY

'If Lyra had not played his lyre, Luther would never have danced.'

But before Luther had appeared on the scene there had been a dramatic debate on the books of the Talmud which had caused a great stir and had already blazed the trail that was to lead to the Reformation.

The story which follows tells how German obscurantists set off a chain reaction which in the end split the mighty Catholic Church. It was a movement which, had they guessed its results, they would not have started.

'Men of darkness' was the name which German humanists gave to those reactionary clerics, monks and priests, who thought that the Jewish persecutions did not go far enough, and that not only Jews but Jewish ideas should be rooted out, especially since the introduction of printing facilitated the spread of these infectious ideas throughout the world.

These men, the Church's watchdogs, were chiefly Dominicans, centred on Cologne, and their prior at the beginning of the sixteenth century was Jacob von Hoogstraten. It was he who started the movement when he decided to launch a theological campaign against the Jews. By breaching the wall which protected them it might be possible, he thought, to effect a series of mass baptisms on the Spanish pattern.

He found a willing tool with which to further his designs in one Johann Pfefferkorn, who as a seceded Jew was a highly dangerous opponent of his former co-religionists. Pfefferkorn's lapse was connected with none of the painful problems with which we have been concerned above; the truth was that in the Jewish community in Moravia from which he had come he had been dismissed from his post of ritual butcher and had been banished for burglary. He had then fled to Cologne, where he had had himself baptized—a familiar enough procedure with Jewish criminal elements. Taking him under their protection, the Dominicans there had given him the temporary post of attendant at one of their hospitals.

Pfefferkorn showed his gratitude by revealing some of the 'secrets' of the Talmud; namely, the passages alleged to ridicule Christianity. Making use of this material, the Inquisition at Cologne, in collusion with Pfefferkorn, then drafted a number of scurrilous pamphlets against the Jews, one of which, *Der Judenspiegel* (The Jewish Mirror), was published under Pfefferkorn's name. It demanded, not only that the Talmud should be confiscated and publicly burnt, but also that Jews should be forced to attend missionary sermons. Should they remain obdurate, they were to be expelled from Germany as thoroughly as they had been removed from Spain and Portugal.

The Dominicans did not stop at pamphlets but proceeded to direct action, and they laid their plans with great ingenuity. Kunigunde, the sister of the Emperor Maximilian, who was a devout nun, was won over to the scheme, and wrote to her brother commending it, Pfefferkorn being sent to the Emperor in Italy with the letter. There, in 1509, he got the authority to confiscate all Jewish books.

Believing in the value of striking while the iron was hot, Pfefferkorn and his masters hurried to the synagogue at Frankfurt with an official escort, and announced the Imperial command. The Jews had no alternative but to obey, but while surrendering their books, they despatched a messenger posthaste to the Emperor, complaining of this violation of their traditional religious liberty. As it turned out, the Church was divided on the issue, and enemies of the Dominicans, among them the powerful Archbishop of Mainz, supported the Jewish complaints. The Emperor thus found himself in an awkward dilemma, and not knowing how to get out of it, decided to play for time and resorted to that well-tried device, the appointment of a commission.

Instead of shelving the matter, however, the commission set things moving. Among its members was Johann Reuchlin, one of the finest and most dynamic figures of his day, whose name has already been mentioned.

At the time in question a man in his mid-fifties, Reuchlin was, next to Erasmus of Rotterdam, the most celebrated humanist of his day. Twice, with the Duke of Württemberg, he had visited Italy and there come to a turning-point in his life; for at Florence he had met Pico della Mirandola, who had drawn his attention to the Cabbala and led him to study Hebrew. With a Jewish physician as his teacher he had engrossed himself in the language and had introduced it as a subject for study among Christians. One of his pupils, Philipp Schwarzerd, a young relative who later took the name of Melanchton, was to be Luther's chief associate at the Reformation.

Reuchlin, filled with enthusiasm for 'the sacred language', wrote a Hebrew grammar for the use of his students, and he also noted traces of Christian doctrine in the Cabbala. While he valued Jewish culture, however, it never affected his Christian faith and he longed for the conversion of the Jews, not by force, but by the 'path of grace', as he expressed it. Johann Reuchlin was one of the few early believers in tolerance, and he had the courage—which in those times was necessary—to put his theories into practice.

Pfefferkorn's agitation naturally aroused deep detestation in Reuchlin, a fact which he did not conceal, but which he expressed in the memorandum that he drafted in the commission and afterwards had printed and distributed, and which is headed: *Whether it is godly, useful, and praiseworthy in the Christian Church to burn Jewish writings.* Among other things, he says that many Jewish books are of great use in the study of the Scriptures, and he pronounces strongly in favour of the Cabbala. As to the Talmud, he confesses that he has not gone deep enough into this vast collection of books, but adds that those who would have the Talmud burnt no doubt understood it even less than he did, and asks, with a sure polemical touch, what one would say of an ignorant person who would burn books on mathematics because he did not understand them. Further, he argues that Jewish books are of value to Christian theologians, and that disagreements should be settled by spiritual weapons, and not by suppressing opponents by brute force. The Emperor agreed with Reuchlin and ordered that the confiscated books should be returned to their owners.

Reuchlin's memorandum, however, raised a storm of protest which swept through the academic world of Europe. Pamphlets were published for and against it and the question was debated by the students and professors of every university. As in the Dreyfus case 400 years later, Europe was divided into two opposing camps, humanists against churchmen. Neither Pfefferkorn nor the Dominicans of Cologne tempered their abuse, and they accused Reuchlin of having written his book with 'ink of gold', by which they meant he had been bribed. He was ready with a reply:

'This baptized Pfefferkorn says that we are forbidden by the Divinity to have dealings with Jews. That is false.' On the contrary, a Christian should love the Jew like a neighbour. That alone is right.'

It was during this violent feud that Erasmus of Rotterdam made his famous ironical remark:

'If it is Christian to hate Jews, then we are all very good Christians indeed.'

Then suddenly the course of the debate took a new turn and the sound of laughter was heard in all the university cities of Europe. The occasion was the publication of the *Epistolae Obscurorum Virorum*, a book which purported to be the correspondence of some monks with their superiors in Cologne. Written in an elegant scholastic Latin and carrying the papal imprimatur—which was, of course, false—it was couched in such innocent terms that at first it was believed to be a serious contribution to the dispute by the monks and the Inquisition.

On a closer reading, however, it was found to have a double meaning, and in fact it was a pungent satire on the decadent monastic life, containing bold exposures of monkish ignorance, fanaticism, sensuality, and love of food and wine. It was an attack on the Inquisition and indeed Rome itself, written in a style which, evoking at first smiles, soon gave rise to loud peals of laughter, and to suspicions that the Holy Roman Church was full of ignorance and corruption.

This dispute about the Talmud formed the prelude to the Reformation. In a way, Luther began where Reuchlin had left off, and without Luther the dispute would have been no more than one of many between churchmen and humanists. At the same time, the genius and the religious inspiration of Luther appealed to minds which had been made receptive by the publications and debates of the Reuchlin issue. From this point of view, it is important that the dispute ended in Rome's disavowal of Reuchlin. That was as late as 1520, by which time the Reformation was in full progress and could no longer be checked.

GERMANY

It was not the walls of Judaism but the ancient bastions of the Catholic Church which began to crumble. Without the Reuchlin dispute about the Jewish books, it is safe to assume that instead of the Diet of Worms Luther would have appeared before the Inquisition and would have been burnt at the stake. The Reformation would, of course, have come even without Luther, but it would have come in a different way.

A fervent hope animated the German ghetto when Luther hurled defiance at the Church of Rome. His revolt caused an upheaval which shook the Catholic Church in its ancient foundations; and whenever that has happened the Jews have seen intimations of the approach of the Messianic age. Luther has himself described how two Jews visited him after he had nailed his ninety-five theses on the church door at Wittenberg in an attempt to win him over to their faith.

Luther suffered the fate of a heretic and felt what it was like to be persecuted by the 'Roman pagans'. In those years of struggle when the fate of the Reformation still hung in the balance he sympathized with the people who throughout history have suffered most at the hands of Catholic fanatics.

In 1523 Luther wrote his book *That Our Lord Jesus Christ was a Born Jew*, in which he opposed the medieval concept of the Jews as the murderers of Christ and called them 'brothers of Jesus in the flesh'. Luther was a man who never minced his words, and on this occasion he had this to say about Jew-baiters:

'Our fools, popes, bishops, sophists, and monks have behaved in such a way to the Jews that any good Christian would have rather been a Jew. If I had been a Jew I would rather have been a pig than a Christian. The Saviour's blood relations, His brothers and cousins, whom God honoured like none others, and in whom He confided the Holy Scriptures, these they have treated like dogs.'

And he went on to say:

'If the Apostles, who also were Jews, had behaved to us

gentiles as we have behaved to the Jews we should never have been made Christians.'

But Luther's generosity to the Jews was not of long duration. To tell the truth, it was not chiefly for love of justice and the sacred cause of freedom of belief that he set out to better their condition, but rather in order to win them for his faith. Probably he believed that the purified Christianity that he preached, and that was inspired by the Bible, which the Jews had first possessed, would lead them in large numbers into his fold. What inspired him was missionary zeal more than love of the Jews. While it is true that the ideas of the Reformation contained the seeds of religious liberty and tolerance, it was to be a long time before they would spring into life and break through the hard crust which enclosed them.

Like Mohammed nearly a thousand years earlier, Luther was to learn that the Jews as a people cling obstinately to their ancestral faith.

When he realized that his gospel had no appeal for them he changed his attitude; so totally that there must have been some underlying personal crisis. Otherwise it would be psychologically inexplicable that a believer like Luther, whom mountains never stopped, could be driven to such contrary lengths. Such a crisis cannot be established in any detail four hundred years later, but there is other evidence that Luther as he grew older bore the bitter marks of hard struggle and disappointment.

As regards his attitude to the Jews, it was as if the cloak of the reformer fell aside, revealing in its appalling nakedness the figure of the one-time monk, whose traditional, deep-rooted hatred of the Jews was made glaringly manifest. It is like a pathological phenomenon we might call *judaeophobia*; and to a member of the Church which bears his name it is deeply humiliating to reflect on its leader's fall on so vital an issue. For fall it was; a renunciation not only of the ideas of his youth but of the Master whose gospel he preached. Painful though it is, we must trace the development in Luther's attitude to the Jews.

In the *Table-talks* and *On the Jews and their Lies*, Luther says that the hearts of Jews are as devilishly hard as sticks and stones and cannot be moved. He does not hesitate to repeat all the medieval charges of well-poisoning, ritual murder, and of practising the black arts, and he adds the accusation of conspiring with the sworn enemies of Europe, the Turks, and of spying for them. They deserved the severest of punishments. Their synagogues should be razed to the ground, their houses burnt down (like gipsies they could live in tents), their sacred books confiscated; the rabbis should be prohibited from teaching them; they should be employed on only the roughest and heaviest of work; rich Jews should be deprived of their money, which should be devoted to conducting missions among them. If all these measures proved of no avail, then it was the duty of the Christian authorities to drive them from their territories like dogs. Bitterly opposed to the Catholics though he was, Luther praised Ferdinand the Catholic of Spain for his expulsion of the Jews. He seems to have seen the eternal Jew as a diabolical figure, filled with hatred of Christ and the Christians, mocking by his mere existence the curse which hangs for ever over his head.

Luther's last words about the Jews were:

'In short, they are everlasting devils, condemned to Hell.'

Of course Luther's writings became in time an inexhaustible arsenal of anti-Semitic propaganda; but his harsh words also had immediate consequences for the Jews. In the numerous religious wars which followed in the wake of the Reformation they found themselves between hammer and anvil. The Protestants gave them no quarter and suspected them of secretly siding with the Catholics. The Catholics, for their part, declared that the entire accursed Reformation could be traced back to Jewish influence. Consequently, the Lutheran Reformation brought no relief at all to the German Jews. Their fortunes were as hard as before. The leaden sky hung lower than ever over the ghetto.

Frankfurt on Main had Germany's and perhaps the world's most famous and most talked-of ghetto. It was not only famous for the men who emanated from it and the influence it wielded well outside its confines, it was typical of the ghettos. To study its life is to become familiar with German ghettos in general.

The Jews of Frankfurt could trace their history as far back as the twelfth century. Like Jews everywhere in Germany they were the Emperor's 'servants' and it was his duty to protect them. In 1349, however, he sold his rights in the Frankfurt Jews to the city Corporation for a large sum, though the city obtained no lasting benefit from their possession, since the year 1349 was one of the worst in Jewish history. It was in that year that the Black Death broke out, bringing appalling disasters. Every Jew in Frankfurt was murdered, and every house was burnt down. Thus there were no Frankfurt Jews among those countless refugees who fled to Poland.

It was another ten years before there were Jews again in Frankfurt. Survivors of scattered ghettos in various parts of Germany found shelter there, but no security. Every three months they had to apply for permission to stay there, and pay for it. Though at first they could live where they liked in the city, in 1460 they had to give up their houses and move into a ghetto, called the Judengasse, owing to their presumption in living close to churches, which was condemned as profanation; for a Jew to see the body of Christ or listen to the singing of Christian hymns was regarded as infamous. The Judengasse of Frankfurt is thus nearly a hundred years older than the ghetto in Rome.

It was built on a drained moat which surrounded the old town wall, and where there was a gap in the wall a new one was built, so that the Judengasse was walled in completely. There were three gates, one at each end of the street and one in the middle, and these were locked at night, and watchmen posted there. Bitterly recalling their captivity in Biblical times, the Jews called the Judengasse New Egypt. We happen to possess some descriptions of the Judengasse by Christian eye-witnesses. One of them wrote a letter in which he said:

'Imagine a long narrow street shut in between tall houses five or six storeys high. Picture these houses with back buildings and, where there is room, back buildings to back buildings. The courtyards are so hemmed in that the daylight never reaches the bottom of them, and every nook and corner of a house is utilized for tiny rooms. The occupants feel lucky when they can go out and get a breath of 'fresh' air in the dank and dirty street. Every inch of space in front of the houses is full all day long of men and women who sit there working, for to work inside is impossible. The visitor is struck by the pale and sickly appearances of those who live in the Judengasse. The gates are kept closed on Sundays and Christian holidays, when the inhabitants are like prisoners confined to their cells.'

It was a condition attaching to residence permits that the number of inhabitants must never exceed 3,000; in other words, the Jews of Frankfurt were prohibited from increasing their numbers beyond a fixed limit. Probably this limit was not always kept, and we may estimate that the population fluctuated between 2,500 and 4,000. Disease and early mortality, however, were factors which inevitably helped to keep the numbers within the prescribed limits.

To accommodate these 3,000 people there were 190 houses, and overcrowding was intense. The only way of increasing the accommodation was to build upwards; and so storey after storey was built on top of the ramshackle houses, the upper parts of which overhung the streets and almost touched one another. In these narrow, dismal, and tortuous lanes and alleys all was grey, drab, and dirty. There were no trees, and no flowers could grow there. It was as if the wind which came blowing in to the city turned aside when it reached these thoroughfares, begrudging them its whiff of fresh air. Down in the street it was scarcely possible to see the blue sky and drifting clouds, and no ray of sunshine ever reached the thick layer of dirt which accumulated and overlaid the alleys and yards. Diseases spread freely and epidemics found a ready breeding-ground. The men slunk through the street with pallid faces and the good-looking women faded all too soon; of ten children that were born, seven died. In the ghetto secrets were impossible, and everyone knew everything about everybody else; where people constantly rubbed shoulders with one another, gossip quickly spread from one end of the street to the other. It is not surprising that the Judengasse had its full share of nervous complaints.

There was one characteristic feature of the street scene: hanging from every house was a sign which bore a painted figure indicating the name. There would be pictures of animals, an eagle, a lion, or a wild duck; of fruit, such as an apple or a pear; of trees or branches; or of utensils, such as a pair of tongs, a step-ladder, or a cup. Sometimes people would take their names from these signs; and one of the names which originated in the Judengasse was in due course to become world-famous: namely, that of the family whose house carried a plain red sign, and who therefore called themselves Rothschild.

Jews who ventured outside the Judengasse were made to feel that they were inferior people. Urchins would shout catcalls after them, or try to knock their hats off, while adults would cross the road to avoid them, saying that they smelt. A Jew who had an errand at the Town Hall had to enter by the back door, except on one day of the year, New Year's Day, when Frankfurt expected a deputation from the Judengasse to present the city fathers with a precious gift of spices, as they humbly returned thanks for the privileges they were allowed to enjoy.

To earn a living was a constant problem to the Jews, for in Germany they were excluded from every respectable occupation. They could neither acquire fixed property, nor farm land, nor belong to the guilds. They were forbidden to offer their goods for sale from behind counters in the public market, or even to sell clothes they had made themselves. There remained the mutual trading in the Judengasse. But no community can live by shaving one another; they had to go outside to obtain goods and resell them. For that reason, many Frankfurt Jews became pedlars and hawkers of cheap wares.

This apparent dead-end had, however, one exit: the old Jewish business of money-lending, which also opened a roundabout way to business in quality goods. Of course Jews only lent money on pledge and a creditor was always entitled to sell unredeemed pledges. Thus arose a Jewish trade that was to become important. Jewish pawnbrokers were able to sell not only household articles but goods of real value, including costly apparel, furniture, and jewels. As time passed, many a house in the Judengasse developed into a storehouse where every conceivable object could be bought, even cheaply; for as a rule goods could only be pawned for a fraction of their real value. No wonder that the Jews became objects of hatred and envy with the Christian merchants of Frankfurt because of the competition they created.

The city's hatred and contempt could be read on the big bridge which crossed the Main. There, in the town sign, was the picture of a boy who was alleged to have been murdered by Jews. It was away back in Catholic times and the monks had declared him a saint. The boy was shown bleeding from many wounds, and below him a Jew was being trampled on by a pig.

Among the more serious manifestations of this hatred there was a book, published in Frankfurt, which was written by a theological professor of Heidelberg, one Johan Eisenmenger. Eisenmenger's book is a compendium of anti-Semitism, compiled from many passages drawn from the Talmud and later Jewish literature. The title is so long that anyone reading it aloud must pause more than once for breath. Here it is:

Jewry unmasked: or a true and full account of how the stiff-necked Jews most dreadfully dishonour and disgrace the Holy Trinity, the New Testament, the Evangelists and the Apostles, damning all Christendom in the extreme, together with many another unknown or unfamiliar delusion of Jewish theology and religion and absurd fables, all carefully and most diligently culled from their own books and now written down for the true instruction of all good Christians.

The Jews of Frankfurt, well aware of the damage which such a book could do to them, offered the author 12,000 florins to stop its sale and destroy the remaining copies. When he demanded 30,000, they appealed to the Emperor, who made an order banning further reprintings in the Empire. By this time Eisenmenger was dead—from chagrin at losing so much money, it has been said—but his heirs, wishing to profit from it, submitted the book to the King of Prussia. This primitive and pedantic man was so taken by it that he ordered the printing of a new edition at his own risk and expense; and as the Emperor's ban also applied to Prussia, it was printed at Königsberg, which lay just outside. Things went as expected: Eisenmenger's book was to prove an arsenal in which Jew-baiters everywhere could find new weapons or refurbish old ones. It also supplied those authorities who adopted stern measures against Jews with a semblance of moral justification.

In August, 1614, a storm burst on the Jews of Frankfurt. A lower middle-class group of small artisans and shopkeepers had long agitated among the city's poor to break the power of the oligarchic rich. They were unprincipled demagogues and they won the support of the masses by pandering to their crude emotions, including anti-Semitism. Their leader was one Vincentz Fettmilch, a baker, who boasted that he was a new Haman—a successor to the notorious Jew-baiter in the book of Esther. He succeeded in inflaming the rabble to make an assault on the ghetto, and they advanced to an attack on the locked gates of the Judengasse, to the cry of 'Raid the Jews!'

To their surprise, they were pelted with stones, and forced to retreat with broken heads. The Jews had expected the attack and had made their preparations; while the women and children had gathered in safety in the burial ground and at the far end of the Judengasse, the men, after having fasted and prayed, had got out their weapons.

Though the first attack had failed, Fettmilch did not give in; he and his mob found a weak spot in the wall and managed to break through into the street beyond. There was hand-to-hand fighting, with killed and wounded on both sides, but the attackers proved too strong for the Jews and they were forced to withdraw to the burial ground, from where they heard the jubilant cries of the looters. The following day they managed to obtain some river craft, and all the survivors sailed away from Frankfurt, to find a temporary refuge in neighbouring towns, where their fellow-Jews shared their confined accommodation with them.

There was a sequel to the affair; for the Emperor had recourse to the legal apparatus of the Empire, and, depriving Frankfurt of its rights over the Jews it had so poorly protected, made them again his 'servants'. Fettmilch was out-

GERMANY

lawed throughout the Empire and, with six other ringleaders, was eventually caught and beheaded. Their heads were exposed outside the city gates.

Two years later the Jews returned to Frankfurt and were accorded a ceremonial reception. Over the three gates of the Judengasse signs were set up which bore the inscription: 'Under the protection of His Imperial Majesty and the Holy Roman Empire'. Every year from then on the Frankfurt Jews celebrated the day of their return, and the memory of the violent events and their happy ending still lives on, though the walls of the ghetto have long since crumbled away.

The Frankfurt Jews were the victims of a further disaster later on. By 1711 the population had exceeded the prescribed limits and the authorities could no longer stop its growth. At a conservative estimate, 8,000 people were then living in the Judengasse, and as there were still only 190 houses the overcrowding was appalling. The disaster which many of the ghettos experienced then befell it.

The great fire of the Frankfurt ghetto broke out in the chief rabbi's house almost in the centre, on January 14, 1711. When the clouds of smoke were seen to rise from the Jewish quarter the Christian authorities despatched their fire-fighters; but knowing from experience that these men were among the worst of looters, the Jews kept their gates locked, and the entire ghetto was burnt to the ground. The new ghetto when it was built was as confined as the old one had been, and the 190 old houses were replaced by the same number of new ones.

Towards the close of the ghetto period Frankfurt's most famous citizen, then a young man, became acquainted with Jewish living conditions in his city. The young man was Goethe. In his autobiography, *Dichtung und Wahrheit*, he writes vividly of his impressions; and we will conclude this sketch of Frankfurt's Judengasse with the great poet's own words. He paints a picture of the dirty crowded street, the sound of a strange and alien tongue, and the general air of cheerlessness that he perceived when he passed by its gates. And he goes on to say:

'It was a long time before I ventured alone through the gate;

and when at length I got out again I knew that it would be a long time before I returned. It was almost impossible to escape from the intolerable badgering of those tireless and persistent peddlars. And my youthful mind vaguely recalled the tales I had heard of Jewish cruelty to Christian children. Yet they remain God's chosen people, with a history going back to the earliest times. In spite of everything they are human beings, enterprising and helpful; and one must admire the persistency with which they cling to their customs and traditions.'

And with a youthful touch he adds:

'What is more, the girls are pretty and have no objection to a little attention and friendliness from a Christian boy when he meets them.'

In the free city of Hamburg at the mouth of the Rhine Spanish Jews found a refuge at an early date; we have already visited the city in company with Uriel da Costa. Hamburg was a world trading centre and it allowed Jewish merchants to trade there freely. Their ability and extensive connections soon provided a powerful stimulus to trade.

Jews of Hamburg were the first merchants to trade with overseas countries, importing tobacco, cotton, sugar, and spices, and they played a leading part in founding the Hamburg banking business. One of them, whose name, Rodrigo de Castro, indicates his Spanish origin, was rewarded for his public services by the granting of Senate permission to buy a house of his own, a rare distinction for those days. Another well-known Hamburg Jew and large-scale merchant was Diego Texeira, who lent large sums to King Christian the Fourth of Denmark, and whose son became banker and financial adviser to Queen Christina of Sweden.

The first Jews to settle in Hamburg were Sephardi; but with the disastrous turn in the fortunes of the Polish Jews at the end of the Thirty Years War considerable numbers of Ashkenazi fled to western Europe and many of them settled in Hamburg either as small tradesmen and artisans or, more especially, as jewellers and pawnbrokers. Though less firmly established than the Sephardi merchants, many of them in time became prosperous.

Neighbouring on Hamburg was the city of Altona, which was the frontier town of the Danish monarchy, and one of the places where King Christian had half-opened the door of his realm to 'Portuguese of the Hebrew religion', as they were called at that time. Under Christian's son, Frederik the Third, Altona was to prove important to the Hamburg Jews; for when the demonstrations against them by the mob grew too violent they had only to cross the Elbe and obtain 'the protection of the just and pious King Frederik'. In fact for some years they lived there, the men crossing into Hamburg every morning to their shops and offices, and paying a guilder a month for the right to do so; and returning in the evening to their wives, who would 'thank God for their safe return'. With the outbreak of war in Denmark in 1657 and the capture of Altona by the Swedes the Jews moved back to Hamburg, where conditions had grown quieter in the meantime.

In one of these 'Hamburger' homes in Altona was born a girl who was afterwards to become well known as Glüeckel von Hameln. She wrote an autobiography which as a human document of the times is outstanding, and which was unusual in having been written by a woman, and what is more a Jewish woman. This remarkable book, which is in Yiddish, provides a vivid picture not only of her own varied fortunes, but of Jewish life in general in the seventeenth century.

Glüeckel was married at the age of fourteen to Chaim von Hameln; and though they met for the first time at the wedding, the marriage was to turn out a very happy one. She wrote that 'the great loving God had brought them together and guided them exceedingly', and she calls her husband 'the crown of my head'. Chaim, a jeweller, was an industrious and enterprising man who worked far more than his feeble strength could support, and he was furthermore a devout man who fasted on Mondays and Thursdays and who observed the daily prayers and read the Torah. While praying he refused to be disturbed, and for that reason lost many a good piece of business. But that could not be helped; for God came first and business second. Above all, he strove to behave justly to all men, the devout man being, to Judaism, a just man, and justice more important than praying and fasting.

Glückel herself was devout, in the Jewish way. 'The Almighty is just', she says, 'and what we may believe to be misfortune He will turn for the best. We erring men and women do not know what serves us best. The world is a stormy sea, full of temptations in which we easily drown; but the Torah is the lifebelt thrown to us in the deep by the great and merciful God, that we may seize it and be saved.' For thousands of years Jews have believed 'that the way to salvation has been laid down for us in the beloved Torah'.

All her life long Glückel von Hameln had her hands full of work. She gave birth to twelve children and, surviving her husband by thirty-five years, bore the burdens of family and business on her own shoulders. She made long journeys to the markets in the heat of summer and the bitter cold of winter, and at home she stood in her shop the whole day long. One of her journeys took her to Copenhagen, where her son Joseph married the daughter of the founder of that city's Jewish community, Meyer Stadthagen, called Goldschmidt.

She finally married again, this time a respected man from Metz; but unhappily, a year or two later, he lost both his own fortune and hers. The ruined man died of grief; and Glückel, who had always had means, was left in solitude and want. But she never complained of her harsh fate; 'it would be better of me to praise and show gratitude to merciful God for all his loving-kindness to me,' she said.

After the Thirty Years War Absolutism made rapid strides in the various German lands. The Emperor's authority fell below zero level; the several States were in actual fact independent and aspired to centralized rule on the French pattern. Many of these authoritarian princes found their officials in the Judengasse, realizing that Jews were often both intelligent and adroit. In war a Jew could look after the Army's finances, in peace he knew how to raise big loans; there was always a Jew ready to procure money and materials for new ventures, or jewels for the prince's latest mistress.

Thus most German countries soon had their *Hofjuden*: Jews who were in the prince's personal service and who possessed the requisite financial knowledge and political skill. These 'Court Jews' were fully assimilated. They talked, behaved, and dressed like other courtiers, kept luxurious establishments, and of course were exempted both from living in the Judengasse and from wearing the badge of Jewry, as well as from the payment of taxes. Yet they remained Jews at heart, a fact which was made plain when they took the part of their persecuted fellows. The careers of some of these men were dramatic, their fall more sudden than their rise to the peak of power and glory.

A famous example of such a man was Joseph Süss Oppenheimer, who was known as Jew Süss. His father was a Court Jew and he therefore grew up in a rich world that was far removed from that of the ghetto. He naturally followed in his father's footsteps, was handsome and intelligent, and was irresistibly attracted to the beautiful women and rich men of the Court. He succeeded in winning the trust and friendship of Karl Alexander, a young prince of Württemberg, and when the prince unexpectedly succeeded to the throne became his confidential adviser.

Süss had now achieved his ambition, and on the duke's behalf held absolute power, administering the finances as it pleased him, introducing new monopolies, and founding banks and factories. Many of his projects and reforms were undoubtedly beneficial, but they naturally gained him many enemies and jealous rivals. He was also careless, living in unlimited luxury, and—Jew though he was—having amorous affairs with ladies-in-waiting. There were some who declared that he had got the duke in his power with the help of the black arts. Süss, realizing the risks he ran, decided at this point to retire from the stage with his new-won gains. Hardly had he received the permission to do so, when the duke had a stroke and died. Süss was gaoled, confessed under torture to the seven deadly sins, and was sentenced to death. Before executing him they did what they could to convert him to Christianity, but without success: Süss declared that he would die a Jew. And with a great display of ceremony he was hanged from a tall gallows in sight of the crowd. His death cry, the Jewish confession, 'Hear Israel: the Lord our God, the Lord is One', was drowned in their shouts of joy as they saw the hated tyrant meet his pitiable end.

The Court Jews were exceptions, but in due course another special class of Jews developed. They were the 'protected' or 'tolerated' Jews, who were generally fine craftsmen: engravers, goldsmiths, and artists. For certain limited periods they enjoyed special privileges and were free from the restrictions which continued to apply to ordinary Jews.

Court Jews and tolerated Jews were few in number; yet they foreshadowed an emancipation that could be sighted on the far horizon. An act of much greater significance was Prussia's decision to admit Jewish refugees. The life which awaited them there was hard, subject to degrading abuse, ridicule, and rigid supervision; but Berlin soon became a leading centre of European Jewry.

It was Berlin that was to provide the setting for the life of Moses Mendelsschn, the man who caused the walls of the ghetto to begin crumbling. His story, however, is one that belongs to the next book in this series.

VII

POLAND

King Popiel of Poland was dead and his end, according to the legends, had been gruesome: a swarm of mice had worried him to death in the royal palace on Lake Goplo. Now, at Kruszwica, his subjects had gathered to elect a successor to the vacant throne; but though they argued one way and another for days on end they could not agree. In the end, they decided to allow fate to decide. Accordingly, four guards were posted on the bridge which led into the city across the river, with instructions to stop the first person who crossed at dawn the following morning. That man should be their new king.

It so happened that the man was Abraham, a Jew. The guards welcomed him and escorted him into the city, where the assembly duly acknowledged him as their sovereign. Abraham, however, unexpectedly declined the honour, declaring that he had no desire to become king. But being pressed by the assembly, who said that he must accept the crown because fate had so ordained it, he asked for a day in which to think the matter over. He then withdrew into a room in the palace so as to be alone with his God, giving strict orders that he was not to be disturbed.

The day went by and then the night. Yet another day and another night passed, and still Abraham had failed to appear. By the morning of the third day the people were getting near to the end of their patience, and a peasant called Piast cried:

'Brothers, we cannot go on like this. The country must have a leader. If Abraham refuses to come out by himself I must force him to.'

So raising his axe he began to pound on the door where

Abraham was closeted. Abraham, however, suddenly appeared on a balcony, and ordered the assembled people to take Piast for their king.

'He is wise enough to see that the country cannot remain without a king, and he is brave enough to defy my order for the good of his country. Give him the crown, and in time you will thank God and Abraham for the choice.'

That is how Poland got Piast for King. From him descended its earliest dynasty, which included many brave and chivalrous rulers.

Of course little remains of such a legend when it is subjected to the test of historical research; but no doubt it contains a grain of truth, and it is interesting that the chief protagonist of such an old Polish legend should be a Jew, for it suggests that there were Jews in Poland at a very early date.

Where the first Jews in eastern Europe came from is unknown; such remote times are veiled in the mists of legend. But one thing is certain: Jews lived in that part of eastern Europe which is now under Soviet control as far back as the early Roman Empire. It has been established by archaeological finds that there were Jewish settlements in the Cimmerian Bosporus, what we now know as the Crimea, in the first century of the Christian era. They spoke Greek, and their numbers soon increased, as new immigrants arrived from Babylon and the Eastern Roman Empire, driven north by the ruthless Byzantine Church.

It was also in eastern Europe that an historic development took place when, after the fall of Jesusalem, the Jewish kingdom of the Khazars flourished at the foot of the Caucasus Mountains, as I have related in my book *The Three Rings*. The capital, Itil, at the mouth of the Volga, prospered for several centuries until it was eventually overthrown by warlike tribes from Russia.

Among the Khazars Judaism had prevailed in rivalry with both the Church and Islam. With the conquerors of the Khazars the Jews challenged the other religions once more; only this time they lost. An old chronicle relates that King Vladimir of Kiev wished to renounce his faith and find a new one. As the Khazar king, Bulan, had once done, Vladimir invited spokesmen for the three great religions to a contest for his own and his people's souls. On that occasion a memorable exchange took place between the king and the Jews.

The Jews said to King Vladimir:

'We know that the Christians have preached to you. They believe in a man whom we have crucified. But we believe in the one true God, the God of Abraham, Isaac, and Jacob.'

The king asked them:

'What is your law?' and the answer was:

'We have ourselves circumcized, do not eat pork, and keep the sabbath.'

'And where is your homeland?' the king then asked.

'In Jerusalem.'

'Do you dwell in Jerusalem?'

'No,' they had to reply: 'God became angry with our forefathers and for our sins scattered us across the earth. Our country he gave to the Christians.'

At which King Vladimir settled the matter with these words:

'How dare you teach others when you yourselves have been cast off by God and scattered before the winds? Would you call down the same disaster on my head?'

A ruler like King Vladimir could not possibly be inspired by the religion of a conquered people. The destruction of Judeah and the collapse of the Khazar kingdom were clear proofs of Judaism's inferiority. The king chose the religion of the people who ruled the world. The details of this conversation also derive from old legend, but are typical of the pagan attitude to the Jews. We will now look at the facts.

In 1054 Christendom split into two parts, West Roman and East Roman Catholicism, centred respectively on Rome and Byzantium. The Russian princes chose Byzantium, but Poland received its Christianity from the west and so became Roman Catholic. This created a deep and never healed rift between the two Slav neighbours, which was also reflected in their Jewish policies. The Byzantine Church was always severe, and employed harsh means to convert the Jews. The rulers in Moscow prohibited foreigners and unbelievers (and by the latter they meant Jews) from setting foot on their sacred soil. Poland, on the other hand, had long been open to

Jews. Perhaps, too, the first Polish Jews came from the east. At any rate there are eminent scholars who suggest that the Mongol features of the so-called Eastern Jews go right back to the celebrated days of the old Khazar kingdom.

The Slav groups which in time coalesced to form the kingdom of Poland inhabited a broad belt of territory which extended from the Baltic to the Black Sea. At its greatest extension it was a thousand miles in length and in breadth, greater than east and west Germany, Switzerland, and Italy put together. But it was loosely connected, and even at its greatest Poland had to contend with rivals in all directions, while its princes and nobles clung jealously to their privileges and guarded their traditional independence of the monarchy.

This was the Poland to which the Jews of Germany fled. We have seen in an earlier chapter how they left their homes in order to escape from the terrors and the uncertainty of the Crusading period. Germany now held only bitter memories; perhaps a future awaited them in Poland. And so they came, at times fleeing panic-stricken by the thousand, in quieter periods arriving in a steady flow, hoping to find a better life than they had known in the old country. These anxious exiles could have no inkling that they and their children would create, in Poland, one of the greatest Jewish communities the world has ever known. All that lay hidden in the future; but in this and the following chapters we shall consider what it was they accomplished.

Poland lay dreaming in its mighty forests, waiting for the Jews and their achievement which it so greatly needed. In Poland there were only two classes, the upper and the very low. The upper class consisted of the nobility, comprising chiefly the *voyvoder*, or provincial governors, and the *szlachta*, or landowners. The lower class was made up of the vast proletariat of serfs, whom their lords kept in the most abject poverty. There was no middle class of tradesmen; there lay the vacant place which awaited the Jews.

Furthermore, most of the nobles liked an easy and carefree life, spending their money freely. The result of this is indicated by the old Polish saying about the impoverished nobleman's dog, which, when sitting in the middle of its master's estate, had to rest its tail on his neighbour's land. But poor or rich, the nobleman was loth to defile his escutcheon with anything so common as an honest living. If the nobles, then, were spenders, there had to be collectors and earners; and there lay the opening for the Jewish merchants and artisans. In this spendthrift country there were plenty of opportunities for a thrifty, hard-working, and purposeful people.

They were helped by one further factor. In religion the Poles were tolerant, a fact which is proved by the language they spoke, for at that time it did not contain the word 'heretic', only 'dissident'. The Inquisition was late in acquiring the scope it desired under the banner of the White Eagle. In short, the Jews had found in Poland a land of opportunity.

There is early evidence of Jewish settlement there, and finds of bracteates bearing Hebraic letters indicate that they had obtained the right to mint their own coins. It is probable that they also had other privileges at an early date, and were responsible for financial transactions on behalf of the royal and ducal families. It is a notable fact that the only important document which has survived from those times is a charter that was granted to the Jews.

Duke Boleslav issued his famous *privilegium libertatis* to the Poles of Great Poland in 1264. With its thirty-seven articles it laid the first legal foundation of the proud edifice which the Polish Jews were to build.

'Human labour of which there are no witnesses and no evidence soon passes out of mind. Accordingly, we, Prince Boleslav, of Great Poland, declare to generations now and to come that we hereby invest all Jews who dwell in our lands with these statutes and privileges.'

With these solemn words the duke introduced the charter which not only granted the Jews legal protection but which in certain respects made them a privileged class. In the first place, it gave them judicial self-government, disputes between Jews being placed under the jurisdiction of the synagogue, in certain cases directly under the king. Next, Jews and Christians were placed on an equal footing in trade and money-lending. There was no restriction on the interest allowed on loans. Jews were allowed unrestricted freedom of movement in the duke's domains, and were exempted from special taxes. It is interesting to note how this magnanimous prince protected Jewish institutions. For example, he ordered their funeral rites to be respected; their synagogue was declared inviolate, and no Jew could be brought before a court on the sabbath. Where Jews were charged with ritual murder there had to be three Jewish as well as three Christian witnesses, and a unanimous verdict by all six before sentence could be passed. The accuser who could not prove his case suffered the same fate as a man who was proved guilty.

The taking of oaths between Christian and Jew being an uncertain affair, this, too, was strictly regulated by the charter. The Jew had to stand on a chair facing the east, wearing his shroud or his white prayer shawl with the four tassels, together with the large Jewish fur cap. He had to pronounce the oath clearly and loudly, and was fined if he stammered three times. It was a solemnly worded oath which contained passages like this:

'So help me God, Creator of heaven and earth, air and mist, mountain and valley, flowers and grass, I am innocent of the charges brought against me by this Christian man; and if I am guilty, may I be struck down by the poison and leprosy which Elisha cured in Naman and which fell on Gehazi. If I am guilty, may the fires of heaven consume me and the evil sickness and disease come upon me. If my oath be false or impure and untrue, may Adonai the Almighty cast me out and the Devil seize me and lead me to eternal damnation. Amen!'

Jews were not alone in migrating eastward into Poland, and in fact were only one element in a general movement that was to upset the balance of Europe and lead to the *Drang nach Osten*, the colonization of the east by the Germans. In the time of Charlemagne the eastern frontiers of Germany were the Elbe and Saale rivers. This was followed by a period of vigorous expansion, a typical example of which was the growth of the Hanseatic League. The prosperous middle classes of Germany began to look around for means of expansion, and they found it in the east. By the close of the Middle Ages there were three German spearheads extending, respectively, to the Baltic, Cracow, and Transylvania, the

POLAND

Slavs holding out only in the Czech and Polish regions. The Polish rulers welcomed the German settlers for the same reason as they welcomed the Jews; and the self-government which they accorded to the Jews followed the pattern of the Teutonic, or, as it was later called, Magdeburg Law. German towns, many of them actually Jewish, grew up in the middle of the Polish forests, and were organized in guilds.

The Germans rather naturally regarded the Jews as rivals. Both were merchants and artisans, and both were able and industrious. The Germans, however, had the support of the Catholic Church, which taught its members the Good Friday prayer of *Oremus et pro perfidis Judaeis* (Let us also pray for the infidel Jews), and German merchants and artisans excluded Jews from membership of their guilds. The struggle was not only for souls but also for markets. It was no new phenomenon; what was new in Poland was that the Jews were not altogether at the mercy of their rivals, but had powerful allies, especially in the monarchy.

The greatest of the Polish kings was known colloquially as 'King of the peasants and Jews'. He was King Casimir Vielkim, or Casimir the Great, who reigned in the middle of the fourteenth century, and with whom began, not only Poland's short-lived Golden Age, but also the history of the Jews in Poland. In his strong hands the kingdom was united and to some extent reorganized on western lines, and it was said that 'he inherited a Poland of wood and left it a country of stone'. That was one of the reasons why he called in German and Jewish settlers.

Casimir gave his Jewish subjects free and liberal conditions; taking Boleslav's charter, he extended it to every province and improved upon its privileges. He allowed Jews to settle where they liked and granted them unrestricted freedom of trade in imports and exports, money-lending, and property-owning. While in nearly every country in Europe the Jews were subject to arbitrary action and the whims of rulers and city corporations, in Poland they lived in peace.

Peace meant social prosperity and wealth. Their ships carried cargoes on the rivers. They dressed like knights, wearing golden chains, bearing swords, and doing war service on equal terms with the aristocracy. They farmed taxes, minted coinage, and controlled the production of alcohol and of salt. The king's physician was a Jew. King Casimir's positive approach was the result of his assessment of their importance in reinvigorating the economy.

Malicious tongues said, however, that there were personal reasons for his patronage. It was stated that he loved Esther, the daughter of a Jewish carpenter, and that he had built a castle for her near Cracow, and had had two sons and two daughters by her, the daughters being educated in their mother's religion, the sons, Pelka and Niemerz, the founders of distinguished Polish families, as Christians. After the king's death Esther was murdered by rivals. Once again this is a romantic story in which truth and legend are inextricably mixed.

From the time of King Casimir we have the first certain evidence of Jewish settlement in some of those cities which afterwards became Jewish centres: namely, Cracow, the capital, Lemberg, and Posnan. There were no ghettos; yet following old custom the Jews congregated in their own quarters which in time came to resemble voluntary ghettos. Rich Jews, and there were rich Jews in those days, lived outside these districts. In Cracow the credit system was controlled by Jewish capital and a Jew, Lewko, was private banker to the king; he also administered the great salt works and had purchased the right of minting coinage. In view of Lewko's outstanding position, the middle classes alleged that he possessed a magic ring which enabled him to dominate the king.

Powerful and benevolent though he was, the king was unable to prevent the rioting which broke out against the Jews at the time of the Black Death. We have already seen how the Jews fled to Poland after the plague in Germany, and the spiritual contagion went with them, especially in the provinces adjacent to Germany. As a Polish chronicler tersely observes: 'The Jews of Germany and well into Poland were exterminated, some by the sword, others at the stake.' Down to the Second World War hymns of mourning were sung in Polish synagogues in memory of those grim years. In this war, Polish Jewry was virtually wiped out. There are no longer any songs of mourning in Polish synagogues, for the synagogues have ceased to exist and those who sang the hymns are all dead.

In the centuries after Casimir Polish Jewry continued to flourish and numbered at its peak nearly a million persons. But as always in Jewish history, the shadow fell heaviest when the light was brightest.

The charges of ritual murder with which it all began came faster and faster. In the course of one prosecution a Polish churchman put forward a legal argument which deserves to be remembered for its deliberate malice. For the meal of the Passover, the *Seder*, he said, the Jews had to drink red wine, which in Hebrew is called *jajin adom*. The word *adom*, meaning 'red', was the same as Edom, the name of Esau's descendants, which the rabbis gave to Christendom or the Church. Thus it was obvious that the Jews used Christian blood. The idea is perfectly absurd; but the Jews felt the effects of it and were not amused.

This is one example of what happened. In Cracow the prosperity of the Jews had long been a thorn in the flesh of both the citizens and the Church. Many Christians, moreover, were in debt to Jewish bankers. They had heard of how, in Germany, a way had been found of annulling debts and pledges by killing the creditors. In order to reap one must sow; and so they started a whispering campaign. From mouth to mouth the rumour went that the Jews counterfeited money; a culprit was found, and was burnt at the stake with a crown of his own coining on his head. It was also alleged that Jews had stoned a priest as he was carrying a crucifix through the street; and, finally, that another Christian child had been murdered and its blood used for the *mazot*.

In the end the city was a whirl of excitement and a howling mob attacked Jewish houses, looting and murdering to their hearts' content. This was the capital city, however, and the king was in residence. He took firm measures and sent troops to stop the disturbances. Peace and order seemed to be reasserted. An hour or so later, however, the tocsin, rung by unknown hands, sounded from the Town Hall, and now the rabble felt sure that they had a free hand. In a few minutes the streets of the Jewish quarter were in tumult; and when some of the inhabitants sought refuge in the church of St Ann, the mob set fire to it and they were burnt to death.

Once more the king was forced to interfere, and the culprits were afterwards sentenced and punished. But he could not bring the dead back to life.

There were other occasions on which the Church exploited ignorance and superstition in order to damage the Jews, and the following is only one of many. It was rumoured in Posnan that some Jews had bribed a poor woman, a Christian, to steal from a church three hosts; which they were alleged to have mocked, impaled, and thrown into a pit, but which had miraculously reappeared as butterflies and complained of their treatment to a shepherd. A search being made, the three hosts were found in the pit, and solemnly reinstated in the church, where they afterwards worked miracles.

The usual course was followed. The rabbis and thirteen other members of the Jewish community in Posnan were hauled before the court, together with the unfortunate woman. After extreme torture on the rack, they all confessed and were duly burnt at the stake. A few years later, King Jagello ceremonially laid the foundation stone of a church and monastery on the spot where the body of Christ had been found, and the place became an object of pilgrimage.

The Christians thus achieved all their aims: the citizens of Posnan struck at their rivals; the pious monks helped the dogma of the Lord's body to attain new renown, and into the bargain ensured an abundant revenue in the future.

There was a period in the fifteenth century when the Polish Jews suddenly found themselves face to face with disaster. It was the period of the Hussite movement that was endangering the unity of the Church, whose vigilance was intensified to the utmost. At that precise time the Polish Church had an archbishop of the most rigid orthodoxy, a man of great gifts, who wore the red hat of a cardinal. While he had held office in Poland he had been its virtual ruler. The one point on which he did not control the king was in relation to Jewish policy.

The crown of Poland was again borne by a Casimir, the Fourth. This Casimir, too, held a protecting hand over the Jews. What is more, he issued a statute that was clearly aimed at the clergy and ran contrary to the decisions of a Church council. As so often before, it concerned the accusations of ritual murder: he decreed that in such cases only the man convicted of the crime should be punished, and not his fellows. Christians, nobles or ordinary citizens, who nevertheless did violence to Jews should have their property confiscated, their lives being dependent on royal clemency.

This was too much for the archbishop and he summoned outside aid. The instrument he needed was at hand. Johan of Capistrano, a Franciscan monk from Italy, was on a missionary journey through Italy and Germany, campaigning against Hussites and Jews. This man was a stiff-necked character with a dash of fanaticism, a prime hater of heretics, a grim example of how religious zeal can consume a man's soul. It was the Jews he hated with the greatest intensity, and in Germany they had called him 'the scourge of the Jews'.

Johan of Capistrano happened to arrive at a psychological moment, when Casimir was equipping an army to fight the Teutonic Knights in what was then called Pommerellen and is now west Prussia. The fanatical legate made his ceremonial entry into Cracow with the whole city out to welcome him, and, wasting no time, went straight to the palace square, where, in a speech animated with zealous indignation, he inveighed against the Jews, declaring that the capital was full of them, and that, 'to the detriment and ignominy of the faith', they also occupied high places. Boldly he warned the king that he would be defeated in battle unless he mended his ways:

'Beware, O king, lest the punishment of God descend upon you if you disregard my warning!'

The king went to war, and actually lost the first battles. Plainly, this was the punishment of God, and he accordingly gave way. The Jews were deprived of their privileges and were even commanded to wear the badge of Jewry, a thing never before seen in Poland. Criers went through the country proclaiming the new order.

The clerical triumph was, however, short-lived, and once more in this strange country of Poland the Jewish luck turned. The archbishop died suddenly and the papal legate was recalled because of the capture of Constantinople and consequent urgent business elsewhere. What is more, after his initial setbacks the king was victorious. The following year, he restored the Jewish privileges, and all was as it had been before.

In the final century of the Middle Ages Jewish immigration into Poland grew into a mass movement. Thousands of refugees from Germany, Austria, and Bohemia sought refuge in the country they had heard so highly praised. These new settlers were active people and every branch of social life soon displayed the results of their enterprise. In Poland and Lithuania, which had entered into personal union, the king leased his estates to Jews and granted them the right to trade in grain, cattle, alcohol, and dairy products. The nobles followed his example. The arrangement brought great advantages to them; for both the Crown and the aristocracy had their revenues collected conveniently and efficiently, and other huge sums accrued to them through the Jews. In spite of canonical prohibitions, the real administrators of the national finances were Jews. They were well paid for their work and gained privileged positions; they also enjoyed freedom from taxation, and they were under the king's and the aristocracy's direct protection. Poland began to resemble Spain in the Middle Ages.

The Jews of Poland, however, were living on the edge of a volcano. As we have already seen, the first rumblings had occurred earlier on, and during the Reformation the menace grew stronger.

Poland is always thought of as a Catholic country, yet there have been times when it almost went Protestant. Each wave of the Reformation—Hussite, Lutheran, Calvinist—passed through Poland like a storm, nearly sweeping the Catholic Church aside. There, as in other countries, the Catholics accused the Jews of inspiring the heresy.

It was only under King Zygmunt, or Sigismund, of the Swedish house of Vasa, that the Church finally weathered the storms. Sigismund threw himself for good or ill into the arms of the Catholic bishops; and though the Reformers contemptuously called him 'the Jesuit king', it was a title he was proud of. Aware of its danger, the Church through the

Jesuits succeeded in persuading the king to appoint only Catholics of the nobility to public office; and in 1598 the papal nuncio was able to report to Rome:

'Not long ago heresy seemed to be forcing the Church out of the country; now we are bearing heresy to the grave.'

A chain of Jesuit colleges was built up. It was an ominous sign; and several events presaged the catastrophe that was slowly but surely approaching. All things were conspiring to form an ill-fated pattern that sooner or later was to spell disaster.

First, the Jewish element was rapidly expanding through large-scale immigration. Where Jews are few in number, there they seem to escape interference. There they supply a useful ingredient in social life, their skill and industry find scope and opportunities, and envy is held in check. No sooner, however, are there many of them than they become too many. Their mutual fellowship and solidarity tend to make others feel that they are being deprived of the opportunities that by rights are theirs. Bitterness and jealousy find fertile soil and are sedulously cultivated.

In Poland there were many converging factors. The impoverished landowners found themselves in debt to Jewish creditors, and enterprising German burghers viewed them as rivals. Above all, Jews farmed rents and taxes for the Crown and the nobility. It was a system which had its advantages for the latter, because it meant that they could be sure of the money being collected. But the Jews who did the collecting, often with a stern hand, found themselves objects of hatred. The exploited peasants never saw their landlords, but they knew and hated their tools, the Jewish stewards and bailiffs. Granted such a soil, the Church when it sowed its suspicions of ritual murder and heresy had ample opportunities.

The tragedy came in due course. But before we review it we must consider the life and the faith of the Jews of Poland during the centuries of their greatness, when Jews in every corner of the Dispersal pointed proudly to the land where the Third Temple was erected.

VIII

THE THIRD TEMPLE

THE ancient city of Lublin is an important centre in the region which, 400 years ago, was known as Little Poland. It stands perched on a high plateau overlooking an extensive plain and first impressions are of solid walls and massive towers, and of the royal palace and chapel rising high above the surrounding houses. But it was neither the fortifications nor the castle which made Lublin famous all over Europe, it was the great fair.

Merchants from far and wide came for the opening of the fair at Candlemas, on the 2nd of February, and the well-stacked stalls offered a choice of cloth from Germany, Italy, and France, linen from the Rhineland, Flanders, and France, silk and velvet from France and Italy, spices from the Orient, furs from Lithuania, and salt from the mines of Galicia. Germans, Frenchmen, Italians, Turks, Tartars, and Armenians, all displayed their wares for barter. At the Lublin fair East met West.

There were also, of course, many Jews, since Candlemas falls at the same time as their festival of Purim, and they came from every Polish settlement—in Great Poland, Little Poland, Galicia, Volhynia, Podolia, and Lithuania—as well as from remote centres across the Dnieper in the Ukraine, wearing their bulging sheepskin coats and black cloth caps, or silk caftans and large round fur hats, called *streimels*, which form the costume of Polish Jews even today. Their stalls would be piled with goods of their own make, including textiles and silks, wooden and metal ware, clothing and footwear, necessaries and luxuries, besides, of course, religious objects like phylacteries and prayer shawls, silver crowns and plates for the synagogue Torah, and bulky volumes of the Talmud, printed at Lublin, or in Cracow or Venice. Every aspect of Jewish life in Poland was reflected at the Lublin fair.

To the seeing eye it was obvious how well the Polish Jews had fared in contrast to their depressed kinsmen in the confined ghettos of western Europe. In Poland they were free to trade, worked in their own workshops like other artisans, were allowed both to own and to farm land and fell forests, worked salt mines, rented estates, operated mills and managed inns, or acted as bankers for the Crown and the nobility.

Many visiting Jewish merchants were quick to appreciate the opportunities which Lublin provided and to settle there, so that in a short time the city had become one of the largest and richest Jewish centres in Poland. It did not occur without friction. German merchants in Lublin felt the effects of the competition and there was dissension between Jews and Christians, leading to complaints and legal proceedings. The king had constantly to intervene in order to restore peace, but he continued to allow the Jews all necessary privileges. In time a Jewish quarter, a sort of voluntary ghetto, grew up at the foot of the castle hill, consisting of a collection of handsome and substantial houses, synagogues, schools and colleges, a hospital and a guest house.

Lublin was an economic centre of Poland, and thus in time it became the Jewish capital and seat of the *Va'ad Arba Arazot*, or Council of the Four Lands. And here we must pause to consider a phenomenon that is unique in the history of the Jews in exile.

We have already seen how in the Middle Ages the king of Poland granted self-government to the Jews in civil and religious affairs. Under the edict of Sigismund Augustus, the last king of the Jagello dynasty, in 1551, this was exercised through the *Va'ad Arba Arazot*, which had the authority both of a Government department and a Supreme Court, being independent of the civil courts and responsible solely to the Crown. It was the Magna Carta of the Polish Jews. In the Council of the Four Lands the Jews saw a renascence of the Sanhedrin of Jerusalem after a lapse of 1,500 years.

The concept of a national minority, so self-evident today, was formerly unknown. Social life was based on the estates, the privileged or unprivileged classes of the nobility, clergy, and peasantry, each of which administered its own affairs. The Jews, whom we should now regard as a national minority, lived mainly in the towns, yet were excluded from the urban middle class which was organized in guilds and companies, to which Jews could not belong. The Jews constituted a community within the community, an estate or class apart from the burghers who managed their own affairs and had their own legal machinery. Their separate character was emphasized by the fact that they lived in a separate quarter, even when not obliged to do so.

In Spain a local Jewish community was called an *aljama*, and in Poland a *kahal*, which is Hebrew for 'religious community'. There were hundreds of *kahal* in Poland, distributed throughout every region, and each one of them was like a cell in the social body of Jewry.

A *kahal* was democratically constituted, the officials being elected by its members. There were many officials: four *rashim*, or elders, at the top, five *tobim*, or assistants, fourteen councillors, and the rabbis who also functioned as *dayanim*, or judges. Besides these there were many who had other special duties, such as administering the synagogue, governing the school, running welfare institutions and the market, auditing accounts, levying and collecting taxes, and acting as guardians of the law. The Polish Jews were alert people with wide-ranging interests. So each *kahal* had a network of societies and fraternities which had charge of charities and of cultural affairs such as education and Talmudic studies, and which organized sick nursing, burial, the ransoming of prisoners (soon to become important), and Jewish craft guilds. The *kahal*'s elected council did not confine itself to administration and judicial matters, it also passed laws, *takanoth*, which regulated the religious life, family affairs, and occupations of the community.

This is where Lublin comes in again. It was not only in order to buy and sell that Jews gathered in their thousands at the great Lublin fair; they had many other errands. Delegates from a remote *kahal* would come there to look for a new rabbi, or to invite a famous *maggid*, or preacher, to visit them and preach in their synagogue. Fathers appeared with their sons in order to enrol them in Lublin's celebrated *yeshiva*, or Talmud school, and among the victors in the *yeshiva*'s Talmudic debates there would be those who wanted a son-in-law for their daughter at home. Polish Jews would rather their daughters married scholars than rich men, knowledge to them being the true riches. There would also be occasions when rabbis and laymen from various districts would gather to discuss problems and difficulties. Something can always be learnt from others, and one can get new impulses and ideas by seeing one's own affairs in the light of others'. In time it became the custom for the principal local communities to choose representatives whom they sent to Lublin to negotiate and to keep abreast of the times.

The Crown became aware of these facts and the Government soon realized that they could exploit them. In the past, royal agents had collected Jewish taxes through each *kahal*, but the procedure was involved and uncertain. It was found to be much easier if the Jewish community as a whole organized this complicated business, and the Jews for their part were no less willing to do so, since the arrangement made them independent of other local authorities, which could be hostile, while it also offered them the self-government which no Jewish community had possessed since the fall of Judea. That was the background to the famous edict of 1551. Neither the *exilarches* of Babylon, at the period when the Talmud had been compiled, nor the Jews of Spain had enjoyed such independence.

The 'four lands' were Great Poland, Little Poland, Podolia, and Volhynia, which were the four provinces of Poland proper. (The grand duchy of Lithuania was granted a similar arrangement.) The Council became a Jewish parliament, a central democratic authority which welded the Polish Jews into a nation. It had thirty members, forty laymen and six rabbis, who were elected from the principal *kahal*, and to be represented on the Council was regarded as a great local honour. The Council met at Lublin during the spring fair, and at Jaroslav in Galicia for a summer session. Day-to-day affairs were administered by a standing committee, and the Council could be convened for an extraordinary session in the event of an emergency.

Its primary object was to levy the Crown taxes, collect them, and pay them into the Treasury at Cracow; but it also levied special Jewish taxes to cover joint expenditure, and in addition it formed a legislative body which promulgated its own *takanoth* and governed all Jewish affairs in Poland. Knowing the ease with which jealousy was provoked by ostentation, it urged moderation in dress and general habits. It regulated contacts with Christian neighbours, mediated in commercial disputes, laid down general rules of policy on moral and religious matters, organized education, made grants, censored books before printing, and was the Supreme Court to which judgments of the local *dayanim* could be referred.

No 'toothless' body, the council had the means to enforce its decisions, notably in the case of excommunication. As a general rule, the threat of this appalling punishment was sufficient to bring the recalcitrant to heel.

Finally, the council kept a vigilant watch on the Government. When the Polish parliament, the *Sejm*, assembled in Warsaw, the council sent an agent, called the *shtadlan*, who handled Jewish interests and ensured that no unfair taxes were levied or traditional rights and privileges interfered with. In short, the edict of 1551 was in line with modern constitutions and formed a true basic law of the Jews.

There is an old Latin saw that 'Poland is the nobleman's Heaven, the citizen's purgatory, the peasant's hell—and the Jew's Paradise'. It was not altogether wrong, though the word 'Paradise' must be taken with a grain of salt. The fanaticism of the Catholic Church and the zealous guarding of guild and company rights against Jewish competition made the paradisal conditions rather problematic. There were rich Jews, it is true, but they were few and far between. Yet Moses Isserles, a famous Jewish rabbi of whom we shall hear more later, was right when he wrote to a friend in Germany:

'If you come to Poland you will be better off than you are now. You may have to be content with dry bread, but you will be able to eat it without fear.'

He spoke the truth. In the rest of Europe Jews lived precariously and in perpetual fear, and were forced into the

THE THIRD TEMPLE

disreputable businesses of lending money and dealing in junk. The Jews of Poland had greater security and far more scope. At the same time, rich Jews were few and far between and the general level was solidly middle class. That, however, has always provided a good foundation for cultural development; and just when the conditions were ripe book-printing was introduced. Ordinary people could now read as never before, and a stream of Hebrew books flowed into the homes of Polish Jews and were read.

Yet it would be wrong to suppose that Polish Jewry formed a parallel to the earlier Spanish community in culture, and in fact there was a great difference between them. The Spanish Jews had been in touch with the world at large; they read the Greek and Latin classics, they kept abreast of the rich civilization of the Arabs, and they paved the way for the influx of both classical and later culture into Europe. They were a vital influence on the Renaissance. It may even be claimed that they laid the foundations of modern European civilization, without which Europe might not have become what it is today.

The culture of the Polish Jews, on the other hand, was wholly Jewish and inward-looking; Europe knew nothing of them and gained nothing from them. Yet the entire Jewish community of Poland lived by it, and though it was of a high level it was neither sophisticated nor exclusive, but truly democratic. There is perhaps no better place in which to study Jewry in all its variety of light and shade than in Poland during those happy years which preceded the great disasters. There is no wonder that Jews all over the world looked to Poland and called its Jewish community the Third Temple. In ancient days the Jews had first honoured the temple of Solomon and later the so-called Second Temple. In Poland what they saw was a temple, not of stone, but of the human spirit.

It was a wholly religious culture, with no place for secular scholarship; and indeed those who read secular literature were suspect, as constituting a potential danger to the faith. Within this limit, important though it may be, Polish-Jewish culture reached an outstandingly high level, and, what is more, it was enjoyed by all. It would have been difficult in those days to find a Polish Jew who was illiterate, and this in itself is a remarkable enough fact in an age when few other ordinary people could either read or write.

The Jews have always given a high place to learning. As the Talmud says:

'He who has knowledge has everything, but he who lacks knowledge lacks everything.'

There was none more despised than the *Am Ha'aretz*, or man from the country; that is to say, the ignorant man. Thus education has always been considered important and Jews have sent their children to school since time immemorial. This was one further feature that was conspicuous. There was a pagan philosopher who once in days of old was asked the easiest way of getting rid of the Jews. He replied:

'Go round and look at their schools. For as long as the voices of children can be clearly heard there, nobody will touch a hair of the Jew's head. "The voice is the voice of Jacob, but the hand is the hand of Esau." While the voice of Jacob is heard in the schools, the hand of Esau will be powerless against them.'

In Poland education began at home while the children were small, and both boys and girls learnt the prayers by heart. While they spoke Yiddish, the prayers and benedictions (*berakot*) were said in Hebrew. In this there is a sound educational principle, for a child of three or four does not understand a prayer even in the colloquial tongue; religious feeling is something that comes later. The Hebrew prayers, however, sink into the mind, where in due course they germinate.

A boy was taken to school, when he was five, at the feast of Pentecost, which commemorates the giving of the Law on Mount Sinai, and which coincides with Whitsun. The first day at school was a never-forgotten occasion. Dressed in his best clothes, he would be accompanied by a respected member of the community, and on arrival at the school, or *heder* (the word means 'room'), he would be solemnly welcomed by the teacher, who would present him with a tablet bearing the Hebrew alphabet, from *aleph* to *tau*, and back again from *tau* to *aleph*. The tablet would be smeared with honey, and the boy would lick it off as he learnt the letters, thus learning from the start that God's word is sweet. Later on he would receive a cake on which would be inscribed some verses from the Psalms and the Prophets, and would be allowed to eat it when he learnt to say the verses.

Then would begin the more serious work. The class would learn to read and write, and would learn the Bible in Hebrew by heart by reciting it in chorus. As there are 5,648 verses in the Bible, they would have to work hard. There were no other subjects; not even history and geography were taught, though the Old Testament is so rich and varied that no boy would suffer from lack of mental nourishment when the Bible was brought to life for him.

The *heder* was always a happy school, where there was plenty of freedom and entertainment. In many ways it resembled a modern school, run on lines advocated by progressive educationists. The following instruction to a teacher in an old Polish *heder*, differently phrased, could almost have been devised today:

'Teach the boy in a pleasant manner. Begin by rewarding him; give him fruit, sugar, honey, then small coins, if he works hard. Later you can go on to reward him with any clothing he may want. Always adapt the rewards to his age and intelligence. When he grows bigger you can tell him he may make a good marriage with a large dowry if only he studies well, and may even become a rabbi. Never force him with punishments but lead him on until one day he realizes that he is studying because it is the will of God.'

This kindly way of teaching has always been customary with the Jews. A teacher may still lay a few sweets or a couple of small coins beside the book a little boy has been studying hard, as he says:

'An angel has dropped those from Heaven because you have worked hard.'

The ablest boys advance from the *heder* to the *yeshiva*, or Talmudic school. Ever since Rabbi Johanan ben Zaccai founded the first *yeshiva* at Jabneh in Palestine after the destruction of Jerusalem (as I have related in *The Son of a Star*) Talmudic education has been the spiritual backbone of

Jewry. Wherever the Jews went they took the Talmud and studied it in their *yeshiva*. Metaphorically, it may be said that the *yeshiva* is a plant that derives from Palestine. The Jews got it to grow vigorously by the rivers of Babylon, and it opened into large colourful blooms in Spain. It stood transplanting to the wintry cities of Poland, and perhaps there it bore its finest fruit. Famous *yeshiva* grew up in Lublin, in Cracow and in Lemberg. These 'vineyards of the Lord', as the rabbis called them, were tended in Poland by gardeners who had both love and understanding.

'Eat bread and salt, drink a little water with it, sleep on the bare ground, live a life full of hardship, and pay attention to learning!'

That was the precept for thousands of students who left home and settled near to one of the famous *yeshiva* in order to get an education. They worked hard at their studies by day and by night, and they were hospitably given food and a lodging, for it was a good deed to open one's home to a student of the Talmud. Eventually, these students became teachers; but it was characteristic of Polish Jews that scholars did not form a class apart from the ordinary people. In fact, in Poland every Jew was a student. Though a man might earn his living during the day, study of the Talmud was his real work. There was not a home where the Torah and the Talmud did not lie on the table, to be read and studied and reflected upon. Incredibly long passages would be learnt by heart, and the problems raised by them were constantly debated.

The Polish Jews fostered some outstanding teachers, one of whom, Moses Isserles, the *rosh yeshiva*, or head of the Talmudic academy, of Cracow, has already been mentioned. In his day he was famous and respected not only in Poland but in all Europe, from where he would receive requests to settle problems on which scholars could not agree. His reputation reached extraordinary heights, and he was known as the new Moses Maimonides. The epitaph on his tomb was the same as that on the famous tomb at Tiberias: From Moses to Moses there was none like Moses.

His name is now remembered in two connections: he pioneered the *pilpul*, a remarkable system of interpretation, to which we shall presently return; and he adapted the *Shulhan Aruk*, the book by Joseph Caro of Safad, making it a corner-stone of Polish-Jewish theology.

His friend and theological opponent, Salomo Luria, made his own *yeshiva*, in Volhynia, famous. An avowed antagonist of the *pilpul* who leant towards mysticism, Luria was one of the rather numerous rabbis who engrossed themselves in the Zohar and the work of Isaac Luria, as we have seen in the chapter on Safad. In this absorption in Cabbalistic studies he was not alone. Ordinary people held a mystic belief in the early coming of the Messiah, and their mysticism and Messianic visions were in time to find full expression. That, however, we shall consider in due course. For the present, let us look at the extraordinary study of the Talmud which gave Polish Jewry its distinctive character.

In the long centuries of exile the Talmud was a protective wall, at first against the influences of paganism, and later against the Christian Church and State. It was the Talmud which welded the Jews into a people animated by the spirit. Its unique religious discipline imbued them with the strength to resist and to survive calamities that would have engulfed other people. The hard shell of the Talmud kept national unity alive and the kernel of Judaism intact wherever the Jews might be living.

The Torah may be likened to an inner defence and the Talmud to an outer one. In countless debates and precepts the extent of the Law and the rules of conduct have been so sharply drawn and to such an extent that they embrace every aspect of a Jew's life, private as well as public. This severe discipline fortified him against alien religions and their dissipating cultures and customs. The Talmud could not help but be restrictive; encompassing the Jew in a network of precepts, rules and rituals, it trained him to such a degree of self-discipline that all his actions, and indeed his every physiological function, had to be fitted into the pattern. It set out to sanctify his whole life, down to the smallest everyday act; and of course there was always a danger that the means adopted to that end might become an end in itself, and the religious consciousness be degraded to the level of a narrow and formalistic piety.

The danger became a pressing one in Poland, and we come now to the period of the notorious system of interpretation known as the *pilpul*. The name *pilpul* means a 'strong spice', such as pepper. That food had to be spiced in order to give it flavour was known to every Jew, and there is a Jewish saying that 'a grain of pepper is better than a basket of sweet vegetables'. The word was extended to mean the interpretation of the Talmud.

Originally, a Talmudic teacher had to have two qualifications: he had to be widely read, and he had to have understanding. In time, however, understanding acquired priority over learning. Talmudic students, even in the old centre of ancient Babylon, delighted in debating, especially in the academy of Pumpadita, and they trained themselves not only in understanding as such, but also in casuistic interpretations of unimportant details in the Talmud, their exegesis thus coming to resemble strong pepper, or *pilpul*. With a fervour that was worthy of a better cause, both teachers and students degenerated, through their debates, into sophists and quibblers, engaged constantly in ravelling and unravelling conundrums. It became the height of intellectual prowess to build up artificial concordances between entirely disparate subjects, and to link wholly unrelated texts to form a single meaning. As this accomplishment was developed to an increasingly abnormal degree it was considered commonplace or childish to suppose that a passage meant just what it said. Only the scholar parading his vast understanding by means of *pilpul* carried any influence.

This method of interpreting the Talmud became common practice in Poland. It was not only useless, it was ridiculous. At the same time, it trained students to a pitch of intellectual keenness that has had few equals.

It is well-nigh impossible to appreciate this aberration unless one has been trained, and trained thoroughly from childhood, in Jewish thought. I have tried hard to find examples of *pilpul* that would be intelligible to the ordinary reader, but I have found none that would not require lengthy explanation. To understand Polish Jewry without at least a little knowledge of the system would, however, be impossible, and so I have chosen to quote a somewhat caustic satire of it. It is several hundred years later than the period we are considering, when *pilpul* flourished, but for that reason is perhaps even easier to appreciate.

The story in question illustrates what in Yiddish is called *lernen* (to learn), but the system is the same as *pilpul*. Here is the story.

Rabbi Chaim Meerschaum was a great wool merchant, but he was an even greater Talmud scholar. An infant prodigy in the *heder*, at the *yeshida* he was regarded as *harif*, or understanding, and in time he became a great *lamdan*, which means a scholar who has penetrated to the deepest secrets of the Talmud. If the Talmud is likened to the sea, then Rabbi Chaim was the expert sailor who knew every submerged reef and was acquainted with all the hazards of the ocean. Whenever he had a spare hour and for most of the night he used to study the Talmud, for he knew that it had not only to be read and interpreted, it had also to be 'learnt'. Behind the obvious meaning of every word in it there was a multitude of deeper meanings, to be found only by persistent search. Not one word was superfluous and every letter had a purpose. To discover that was the art of the *lamdan*. When Rabbi Chaim taught the Talmud he used to say:

'You see, when the Talmud was written paper and ink were rare and expensive, and so nothing but what was necessary was written.'

Rabbi Chaim had an only child, a daughter. She attended the *heder*, but, as it would have been a waste of money to educate a girl further, she read whatever fell into her hands. One day Rabbi Chaim came upon her reading the poems of Goethe, and he asked her to read one to him. So she read the famous ballad *Der Erlkönig* (The Erl King).

Who rides there so late through the night dark and drear?
The father it is, with his infant so dear;
He holdeth the boy tightly clasp'd in his arm,
He holdeth him safely, he keepeth him warm.[1]

[1] Translation by E. A. Bowring, in Bohn's Library.

At this point her father shouted:
'Stop!'
'Did I make a mistake?' she asked frightened.
'No, but you must understand what you are reading.'
'Understand? I read it distinctly, and I emphasized the right words,' the girl objected.
'Understand and understand!' her father replied. 'It is not simply a matter of hearing the words; you must reflect on them and grasp their deeper meaning. You must *lernen*, my child; that is the point. Now I will show you how to *lernen* such a poem.

'How does Goethe begin? With a *kashe*, a question: "Who rides there so late?" He wishes to know who rides by night. And what answer does he get?'

'The father with his child,' sighed the daughter.

'Yes, but if the question is really "*who rides?*" and the answer is "the father", then Goethe is a big question himself, because he knows the answer before asking. If he knows that it is the father riding with his child, why does he ask "Who rides"?'

And he went on in a droning voice:

'When a similar question is asked in the Talmud, the Talmud has an immediate answer ready: In itself the question is superfluous; it is only asked in order to sharpen the student's wits. The fact is that the reader must always, even in the simplest of cases, sense difficulties and so consider the matter from all sides, penetrate deeply into it, because he may chance to overlook the real difficulties. Thus we might well answer our question, Why does Goethe ask who rides, etc.?, when he knows it is the father, with this Talmudic rule. But it would not suffice. The Talmud only employs this reply in an emergency case and prefers to evade it. It must only be used when there is no other reply to give. No, we must look for a better answer; and indeed there is one, if we decide to apply another Talmudic procedure to Goethe's poem.

'Now the question is not "*Who rides?*" but "Who rides *so late and at night?*" It is one of the rules of the Talmud that a journey should be arranged so as to begin at dawn and end before nightfall. The day is man's friend, and the Bible says that it is good but that the night is our enemy. Goethe's question thus gives support to this point in the Talmud, and it follows that the emphasis should be on "late" and "at night". But unfortunately we immediately encounter a fresh obstacle. Where in the whole poem do we get an answer to this question? If the question had been, as we first supposed, "Who rides?" then the answer would have followed in the next line: "The father". But if the question is "Who rides so late?" then the answer is lacking and the sentence "It is the father" becomes superfluous. For of what concern is it to us whether it is the father riding with his child, or the grandfather with his father? The question is immaterial. For the reply should not say "Who rides?" but "Who rides *at night?*"

'But perhaps we can still proceed by this route. Remember that it is not forbidden to ride by night, only that it is advisable not to do so; moreover, there are cases when one should travel by night, in the case, say, of a *mitzwah*, an errand pleasing to God. The only reason for not travelling by night is that it can be dangerous, but one who travels on a devout errand is protected by God. Thus we may answer Goethe's question of why the man is riding so late at night with the explanation that he is carrying out a *mitzwah*, and is hurrying on during the night because he knows that he need not fear any danger. A *rajah*, a proof that this assumption is true, is given in the fact that he has a child in his arms. If he is indeed engaged on a *mitzwah* then the carrying of a child has its own special reason. Doubtless it is a boy, at an age when he is to be instructed in the manner of keeping the Law and is being taken to attend the rites. But no, there, too, we come to an impasse, for there is not a word in the entire poem about a *mitzwah*; and it is a firm rule that, though one may suggest or hint at minor matters, the main point should be made fully clear. Consequently, the question still remains open: "Why does the man ride *so late and at night?*"

'We must look for a third explanation. It is possible, you see, that the rider may either be an *Am Ha'aretz*, an ignorant person who does not know the Law or the Talmud, and so is unaware of the advice against travelling by night, or he is a rash man who ignores the advice. If this were the case, however, it would be improper to frame a *kashe* like this: "Why does he ride by night?" and substantiate it in statements by our wise men. Thus we arrive at the contrary view that the rider spoken of by Goethe was a *hakam*, a Talmudic scholar. This being the case, we have no need to have recourse to a passage in the Talmud which does not contain a direct prohibition, but can cite one which does. In fact, there is a passage in the Talmud which says that a scholar should not go out in the dark *by himself*. We have now got a step further. If we assume that our rider is a *hakam*, then Goethe's question is justified: "Why does he ride so late through night and wind?" or "Why is it that a Talmudic scholar ventures to ride alone at night?" For now comes the answer: It is a father with his child: he is not really alone, but is carrying his child!

'At this point, however, we must ask an important question: Is it sufficient to have a child; or should a Talmudic scholar choose an adult as his companion when travelling at night? In order to answer this question we must first examine the reason why a scholar cannot go by himself at night. Two factors can here be considered: either the solitary scholar exposes himself to attack by evil spirits, who are particularly eager to attack and injure scholars, or the solitude by night is suspicious. A person who is alone is an easier prey to passion, and seeks out places that are unworthy when he knows he is unobserved. In company he would fear betrayal.

'With regard to the former possibility, it is obvious on a closer inspection that the prohibition against a Talmudic scholar riding alone at night is not lifted because he has a child with him. The spirits would scarcely take any notice of the child. On the contrary, the child's presence suggests that the other supposition is the correct one; for a child may easily betray the rider, perhaps more readily than an adult.

'So now at last we are able to see what Goethe is trying to teach us in this poem. When he asks: "Who rides there so late through the night dark and drear?" what he means to say is: "How dare a Talmudic scholar ride at night by himself?" And the reply given by Goethe is that in fact he is not, for he is carrying a child.

'Yet at the same time as he suggests this interpretation Goethe in fact puts the opposite explanation into the child's mouth: namely, that it is because of the spirits that he has the child with him:

"Look, father, the Erl-King is close by our side!"

To which the father, advancing the contrary interpretation, objects:

"My son, 'tis the mist rising over the plain."'

'And so we get two opposing views. The father declares that the reason for the prohibition against travelling at night alone is the danger of suspicion; whereas the child advances the opposite opinion, that it is because of the spirits that he is taking the child. But the father is stubborn, and Goethe makes him say that spirits are non-existent: "My son, 'tis the mist." Being of the opinion, however, that the child's view is the right one, Goethe of course allows that to prevail, by causing the Erl-King to kill the child:

The father gallops, with terror half wild,
He grasps in his arms the poor shuddering child;
He reaches his courtyard, with toil and with dread,—
The child in his arms finds he motionless, dead.

'At last,' Rabbi Chaim concluded, breathless but content after his long lecture, 'we know what Goethe wishes to say. You see, my child, one must be able to *lernen*. Now that I have explained Goethe's poem for you it has taken on quite a different *ponim*, another meaning.'

In which respect Rabbi Chaim was unquestionably nearer to the truth than he imagined.

After the wild flights of Rabbi Chaim it is a relief to come down to earth and see the effects of the Talmud on the ordinary life of Jews in a Polish city. They were evident at all times of the day and all the year round; nothing was too great or too small but the Talmud affected it. To go into every aspect of that life is clearly impossible, and so I will take a typical example. It has to do with the sabbath, the eagerly awaited seventh day. Everyone who wished to observe it in the right way and avoid breaking any of its traditions—and who did not?—had to be conversant with the strange idea of *Erub*.

The meaning of *erub* is 'blending', or 'fusing'. It was laid down in Exodus that no person should leave his house on the seventh day. How was that commandment to be interpreted? How solve the practical problems which arose from it? The subject was endlessly debated, and a solution was found by the application of *erub*.

For instance, it might be necessary to move a certain thing from one place to another, even on a sabbath. In such a case a distinction was made between different kinds of places (called *reshuyot*), a place belonging to an individual (or *reshut hayadid*) and a public place, or square. Traditionally interpreted, the commandment in Exodus does not apply to the removal of an object so long as it takes place on private ground. But it is forbidden to move anything from a private to a public place, or in a public place to move it more than eight feet. Supposing, however, that it is necessary to move an object off one's own ground?

It is possible, in such a case, to relax the commandment by the use of different forms of *erub*. For example, a public place can be turned into a private one by the act of stretching a rope from one house to another, or by driving stakes into the ground, and imagining that they represent a wall. If, however, the houses in the square are owned by different individuals there is a further complication, and the arrangement mentioned is not enough.

Fortunately, in this case another *erub* can be applied. The various owners can form an association, contributing as their membership fee a pot of food which is set out in the square so that all can share in it. This done, it is permissible to move objects at will.

There is yet a third *erub*, whereby the commandment against leaving the sabbath is interpreted to mean 4,000 feet from it, which is the length of a sabbath mile. Supposing, however, that a person has to go further than 4,000 feet? That can always be arranged by putting a plate of food, symbolizing a home, just inside the limit. If it is necessary to

THE THIRD TEMPLE

go yet another 4,000 feet, it is only necessary to put down another plate of food.

To imagine that these sophistries are part of a vanished age would be a mistake. I have seen people in Mea Shearim, the rigidly orthodox quarter of the Israeli sector of Jerusalem, stretching ropes in this way on a Friday evening. There the old Jewry of Poland lives on. The men wear long earlocks and large foxskin hats, and the Law, especially as it applies to the sabbath, is enforced so rigidly that on occasion it has brought the whole of Jerusalem to the verge of revolution.

The procedures I have described may appear absurd, but they are—and were in the Poland of 300-400 years ago—deadly serious; and eccentric though they may seem to us, they are at least an attempt to bring the will of God down to earth.

Many more absurdities connected with the sabbath commandment could be mentioned, yet in spite of them the sabbath is the focus of all that is grand in Judaism. The Polish Jews both loved their sabbath and knew how to celebrate it. Let us see how they did it.

It is the sabbath that has kept Israel, rather than Israel that has kept the sabbath, a Jewish writer has said. From earliest times it was the first of many Jewish festivals, and it was the only one that was included in the commandments: remember the sabbath day, to keep it holy. Ancient books describe the blessings bestowed by the sabbath both on the individual and the people in general. A Jew returning from the synagogue on a Friday evening is accompanied, it is said, by two angels, a good and a bad angel. If on his arrival home he finds the lights lit and the house radiant with the sabbath joy, then the good angel blesses his house, saying:

'May this home be always a seat of happiness!'

And the bad angel has reluctantly to say: 'Amen!'

But if the lights are out and the house dismal, then the bad angel curses it, saying:

'May this house never know the joys of the sabbath day!'

And the good angel weeps, and reluctantly responds: 'Amen!'

There are, it is said, two Jews, the weekday Jew and the

sabbath Jew, and they can be as different as night and day. On a sabbath the Jew was supposed to receive an extra soul, his *Neshamah Yeterah*, which, arriving on Friday evening, stayed until the end of the sabbath. It was obvious that that is what happened, for his mind was miraculously transformed and his face would beam with delight.

According to the Talmud, God said to Moses on Mount Sinai:

'In my treasure-house is a precious gift which I wish to give to Israel. Go and announce this glad news.'

The sabbath indeed is a precious gift, one which brings a foretaste of the heavenly bliss, and accordingly the Polish Jew gave it all his affection. He regarded it as a charming bride, a lovely princess, a gracious queen, greeting her on the Friday evening with psalms and welcoming her to the synagogue and his house. As we have seen, the pious mystics of Safad left their gates on a Friday evening in order to receive the sabbath.

The sabbath goes back to the Creation, for we are told on the first page of the Bible that God created the world in six days and rested on the seventh. Man must do as God did. To work on six days is to glorify the dignity of labour; but to rest on the seventh is to be elevated to a higher sphere. In fact, the sabbath is a symbol, serving as a perpetual reminder of the covenant between God and His people. It is greater even than the circumcision; for though that, too, is a symbol of the covenant, it is given to an infant as an involuntary mark of his origin, while to celebrate the sabbath is an act of personal volition, and consequently a testimony to a Jew's chosen and deliberate faith in the God he was taught to believe in.

In the home the sabbath duties always rested on the shoulders of the wife, and they had much to bear. The Yiddish *Mamme*, indeed, was the rock on which a house was founded. She is still celebrated in song and legend, and if these are any criterion she lived up to the ideal wife as described in the last chapter of Proverbs: 'She will do him good and not evil all the days of her life; her candle goeth not out by night; she riseth also while it is yet night; she layeth her hands to the spindle, and her hands hold the distaff.' The husband was fully conscious of what he owed to her. The husband in the Talmud calls her 'My house'. An epitaph inscribed by one man on his wife's grave takes the form of an acrostic based on his name, thus indicating that he was laid with her in the grave.

The whole moral atmosphere was clean and healthy, in sex as in other respects; once again in marked contrast to the surroundings, where promiscuity was common. Great men had concubines, and ordinary people saw nothing objectionable in this. At the great conclaves of Church leaders at Basle and Constance there were hundreds of loose women in attendance and the *morbus gallicus* was spread by them there. As for this, it is characteristic that the Jews were never suspected of carrying venereal disease. There was talk of 'Jewish stench', but that was a disease to be cured by baptism. They also suffered from haemorrhoids, which was the complaint inflicted by the Lord on the Philistines when they had violated the ark of the covenant.

To return to the sabbath and the Yiddish *Mamme*: for her the sabbath began on the Thursday, for of course she had to make all the purchases and preparations. There were plenty of things to choose from, including many Jewish specialities: all those spiced and savoury dishes, with Yiddish names, that we call 'Jewish', and that derived from old Polish-Jewish recipes and were devised by inventive and hard-working housewives. The fragrant smells which issue today from Jewish houses on a Friday evening are a heritage from that period. Let us consider some of these strange-sounding dishes.

The *hors d'oeuvre* include *Gehackte Leber*, which is liver mixed with chopped onions and hard-boiled eggs. A popular dish is *Kreutsuppe*, a cabbage soup eaten with *Latkes*, which are thin potato pancakes, boiled in oil; another is *Blinses*, cabbage leaves stuffed with mincemeat or chopped liver, with a sauce of soaked honey-bread with a little sugar and a dash of lemon juice in it. *Putscha* is a sort of veal brawn; *Zimmes*, small pieces of meat mixed with carrots, a form of goulash. Above all, there is *Gefilte Fisch*, which is the meat of freshwater fish, removed and minced and then put into the fish's skin again and boiled. *Gefilte Fisch* is served cold the day after making, stiffened in the soup. The feature common to every dish is the spicing, an art passed on from mother to daughter; and it is that which dots the 'i'. A typical sabbath menu of eastern Europe would consist of soup with *Lockschen Kreplech*, chopped liver, and *Gefilte Fisch*. The meat dishes are commonly chicken or beef.

It was the husband who would go to market on a Friday morning to make the family purchases, which had to be ample; the poor would save all through the week in order to afford the sabbath dinner. What is more, Jews know that you do not grow poor by buying in for the sabbath; on the contrary, the man who spends more than he can really afford grows rich, if he buys for the sabbath. Many good examples of this were given, including the following:

Joseph lived in extreme poverty, but saved all he could in order to keep a rich sabbath and have plenty of food on the holy day. Consequently, he was known as 'he who honours the sabbath'. His neighbour was a Christian, and just as rich as Joseph was poor; but one day a soothsayer told him that he would lose all his riches, and they would become Joseph's. The warning kept him awake at nights; but at length he found a way of cheating his fate. Selling off all his valuables, he bought the costliest diamond in the world, and this he sewed into his turban, which he always wore. Now no one could take his riches from him. One day, however, there was a storm; and when he crossed a bridge his turban was blown into the river and sank to the bottom, the diamond with it. Though he himself was now poor, at least there was no chance that Joseph would win his wealth, and that was always a consolation. In fact, however, that is what happened.

One Friday afternoon a fisherman brought in his catch, which included a specially large fish. Nobody would buy it, however, so late on the Friday.

'Go and take it to poor Joseph and try him,' one of his companions suggested. 'Joseph is a poor man, but he never says no to a fish for the sabbath.'

Of course Joseph bought the fish; and of course when he opened it he found the diamond, and had won his rich neighbour's wealth. One day he met an unknown man, who it was afterwards realized was the prophet Elijah; for he had spoken words of wisdom to Joseph, among them these:

'The man who borrows money to honour the sabbath is repaid by the sabbath.'

While their husbands were at the market their wives were hard at work. Their day began early, for the house had to be spotless and the food ready in time. The Friday evening feast can be brought in straight from the oven; but the Saturday dinner is something of a problem, for how is it to be cooked when a fire may not be lit on the sabbath? Every little rule and precept had to be observed, including this one; and women would shudder to think of what happened to those who broke it. There was a scribe who sat down on Friday evening to write, and another sat beside him in order to help him. To write on a sabbath eve, when no one may put two letters together on paper! The end was dreadful. The helper's parchment ran out; and so he flayed the other and used his skin!

Fortunately, there was a way of getting the dinner cooked. The women simply stoked up the oven and left the pot on over night; and though the Saturday dinner is well cooked, the prolonged preparation gives it a savour all its own.

Back from the market, and having proudly displayed his purchases, the husband would help the busy womenfolk by chopping sticks, salting the fish, and attending to the oven.

Then late in the afternoon the house would begin to look the way it should on a sabbath. All worldly things such as money, needlework, and kitchen utensils would have been put away, that the mind might not be distracted by mundane things, and the table would have been laid with a gleaming white cloth, a reminder of the whiteness of manna in the wilderness, as 'white as hoar frost', as it says in the Bible. Candles, symbolical of joy, would have been lit, and on an intricately embroidered cloth there would be the two twisted loaves called *hallot*, a word which is the plural form of *hallah*, meaning the measure of dough taken in biblical times by the priest. The bread of the sabbath is white, wheaten bread, that of the weekday being brown, rye bread. The reason why there are two *hallot* is that in the wilderness the Israelites had a double measure of manna on Fridays, to last them over the sabbath.

It has always been a privilege of the wife to welcome in the sabbath, since it is the festival of the home and the housewife personifies the home. This she does by lighting the candles, and then covering her eyes with her hands and pronouncing a blessing. Then over his glass of wine the master of the house recites the *Kiddush* prayer and blesses his children. There are few things that a Jew remembers with such depth of feeling as when his father laid his hands on the heads of the children, saying to the boys:

'May God make thee like Ephraim and Manasseh!'

And to the girls:

'May God make thee like Leah and Rachel!'

The sabbath is a general day of rest, for men and beasts, master and servant. But it is not meant that they should do nothing on it at all. The sabbath has a spiritual purpose, designed to inspire, ennoble, and uplift the devout, and so a large part of the day is spent in the synagogue. In the period we are considering, each house in a community was visited before the service began by the attendant, who would invite the occupants to come by a special knock on the door: first a single rap, then a pause followed by a double rap, then another pause, and finally another rap. The meaning of this was the biblical injunction 'I will come and bless thee', which in Hebrew has the initial numerical values of 1-2-1.

The prayer leader had to be the first to arrive and the last to leave the synagogue; and he had to be of good character, humble, universally respected, married, in good voice, and able to read from the sacred books so that all could understand. His deportment was governed by many strange precepts. For instance, he was required to concentrate on the devotions and not look about him, to keep his stands still, and when placing them beneath his cloak to hold them over his heart, the right hand above the left. He was to read out the texts calmly and clearly, emphasizing them according to the rules of grammar, and pronouncing them one by one, 'as if counting money'.

The Torah is divided into fifty-four parts; there is one for every sabbath, the whole being completed in the course of a year. Attendance at the synagogue, however, was also a social occasion, when news was heard of births, betrothals, and deaths, and the father of a new-born child was required to read a passage from the Torah, just as the bridegroom did on the sabbath before his wedding, and the boy of fourteen when he became *Bar Mirzwah*, or confirmed.

In the homes the sabbath was a day of *joyful* rest, altogether different from the bleak Calvinist sabbath of the seventeenth century. Where possible there were visitors, for according to the Talmud 'to open one's doors for guests is of greater worth than to open them for God'. Teachers, for example, would invite their pupils. It was the custom for a guest to say grace at table, when he would take the opportunity to bless his hosts. Hosts as well as guests would be gay and happy, cracking jokes across the table, and enjoying the relaxation after the mental exertion of praying and listening to God's word in the synagogue, in addition to the other sabbath duties. There is to this day a particular charm in sitting, an interested listener, at a Jewish table on a sabbath.

The Jews have a characteristic many-sided gaiety, and one of its qualities is the ability to laugh, not only at others, but also at oneself. There is the story told by a Jew about his own manner of telling jokes:

It is well known that a Frenchman laughs at a joke three times: when he hears it, when he retells it, and when he finally sees the point. The German, on the other hand, laughs only once: when he hears the joke. This is because he is too arrogant to ask for an explanation, and would not laugh if he were given one, being incapable of understanding it because he has no sense of humour. Tell a Jew a joke, however, and he will interrupt you almost before you have begun, because he has already heard it. And almost before you are aware of the fact he is telling you your own joke, much better than you would have told it yourself.

This brings me to the story that I was telling to a Jewish friend when he interrupted me:

Old Isaac was prosecuted by his neighbour for borrowing a pitcher and not returning it, and he defended himself by saying:

'In the first place, I did not borrow the pitcher. In the

second place, it was broken when I received it. And in the third place, it was whole when I returned it.'

This was the humour of the ghetto, knowing itself and its own failings, and pointing its barb at itself. But it could also aim its shafts at others. I recall from the Hitler period a quick retort which in its origins goes right back to the Polish ghetto. It was in Berlin and an SS man snarled at a Jew:

'*Schweinhund!*'

To which the polite reply was:

'And I'm Cohen.'

The sabbath would draw to a close with alternating gravity and humour. The youngest son, on watch outside the house, would announce the moment when he could see three stars shining in the sky, and then all would know that the sabbath day was at an end.

In the house they would light the candle of *Havdalah*—a word which means 'separation', and signifies the separation of the sabbath from the weekday. The *Havdalah* candle is woven and has several wicks, for it must burn brightly in order to throw the light of the sabbath well forward into the coming week. Next a jar of spices would be passed from hand to hand, and each person would smell it, and so carry the fragrant spice of the sabbath with him into the ordinary day. Finally, the master of the house would say the prayer:

'Blessed be thou, the Lord our God, King of the world, who draweth a line between sacred and profane, between light and darkness, between Israel and other peoples, between the seventh day and the six days of the week.'

When the Amen has been spoken after the *Havdalah* prayer the sabbath is over. But already the thoughts of all are directed to the sabbath that is to come at the end of the six weekdays, and perhaps all are thinking of the old saying:

'When God hallowed the seventh day it complained and said: "Almighty God, every day of the week belongs to another day—Sunday to Monday, Tuesday to Wednesday, Thursday to Friday. I only stand alone and belong to none other." And God answered and said:

'I have prepared for thee a bridegroom, that is my people Israel. It is the bridegroom and thou art the bride!'

IX

DESTRUCTION

THE Ukraine is a land of wide plains situated between Poland and Russia and irrigated by the Dnieper and Dniester rivers. The capital is Kiev. Today the Ukraine is a part of the Soviet Union, but 300 years ago it was a dependency of the Polish-Ukrainian king. More important in the present connection than history and geography, however, is the complicated pattern of its population. The Ukraine was the converging point of three peoples—Poles, Russians, and Jews—and three religions—Roman Catholic, Greek Orthodox, and Jewish. As a further complicating factor there were three very different and sharply opposed social classes—landowners, serfs, and tenant farmers. The problems presented by this involved national, religious, and social pattern were wellnigh insoluble, and in the end the country fell to pieces. It was the Jews who paid the biggest price, as we shall now see, in the tragedy which destroyed the Third Temple.

The estates of the great Polish landowners were so vast that they could not be traversed in a single day. Feudalism still prevailed, and the *pan*, as the lord was called in Polish, had the power of life and death over his serfs, who lived in wretched huts, and whom he contemptuously called his *chlopy*, or slaves.

Far more serious, however, than the social cleavages were the national and religious differences. The Polish nobles were Roman Catholics, whereas the peasants were Greek Orthodox. The Poles therefore regarded Greek Orthodoxy as the inferior religion of an inferior people, who belonged to Asia rather than to Europe.

The landowners exploited their peasants to the utmost,

exacting every possible labour service from them and extorting their last penny in taxes. But they did not do so in person, for that would have been beneath their dignity. They were absentee landlords, and if they visited their estates at all they had no dealings with serfs; they employed agents and collected the profits through them.

That is where the third social and religious group—the Polish Jews—came into the picture. Many of these had been ousted from the cities by their German rivals, but in the country, and especially in the Ukraine, they found plenty of opportunities. They worked for the landowners and administered their estates, and before long Jews occupied nearly all the key positions in Ukrainian finance. They collected taxes and held leases in the corn trade and on mills, dairies, distilleries, and inns; and in the end they controlled the judicial system. In all directions the peasants saw Jews in profitable, and sometimes extraordinary, positions. For example, some of them had the lease of church keys, and so controlled baptisms and weddings, the officiating priest having to pay an admission.

The Ukrainian peasants came to look upon Jews as the representatives of the Polish authorities and landlords, whom they hated as they hated Roman Catholics. Those, however, they never saw; but they did see their agents, the Jews. They were regarded as the oppressors and extortioners. Furthermore, they were unbaptized heathen. On the day of reckoning their turn would come first!

The Ukrainian peasant was by no means the dumb creature his Polish masters would believe. Many became Cossacks, or were friendly to the Cossacks. The Cossacks instigated the great revolt that broke out in Poland and the Ukraine.

The word is Russian and means 'guerilla'. The original Cossacks lived in remote parts near the coast of the Black Sea and they included all manner of men, among them escaped convicts, deserted serfs, bankrupt or criminal nobles, in fact adventurers generally. The one absolute condition was membership of the Greek Orthodox Church.

A Cossack's life was wild and lawless. His only discipline was that of war, and he was perpetually at war. Though

DESTRUCTION

Cossacks did a certain amount of farming and fishing, they were chiefly soldiers, and when they had no cause of their own to fight for they fought as mercenaries for the Turks, Tartars, or Poles.

The true Cossacks inhabited the region beneath the Dnieper and were known as *Saporogs*, but there were also some who were less wild, and who lived in the Ukraine, where they were principally employed as fontier guards, and otherwise worked as peasants. When the Polish nobles had the idea of incorporating them among their ordinary serfs, these Cossacks looked to the wild hordes of the steppes who lived a free life and were independent both of feudal lords and of Jewish agents. Fired with the spirit of freedom, they looked forward to the day of their revenge. That day was not far off.

The year 1648 is memorable as the year of the Peace of Westphalia, which brought to an end the appalling Thirty Years' War. In the Ukraine it was a year of bloodshed. A *hetman*—that is to say, a Cossock headman, one of the *Saporogs*—had a crime to avenge. His village had been attacked by Poles, who had molested his family and kept him in prolonged captivity. His name was Bogdan Chmielnicki, and it is a name remembered in Jewish history for the horrors with which it is associated.

Chmielnicki had scarcely escaped when he raised the flag of revolution and declared a holy war on the Polish *pans* and their Jewish stewards. An alliance was formed with a Tartar headman in the Crimea, and the combined armies of Cossacks and Tartars advanced against the borders of the Ukraine. A small Polish army which tried to intercept them was defeated. Thereupon the peasants of the entire Ukraine rose and, leaving homes and fields, banded themselves together and attacked the manors, killing everyone they found there, especially the hated Jewish agents, except for the few who adhered to the Orthodox faith. The whole of the Ukraine was in revolt, and the priests did all they could to pour fuel on the flames.

The accounts of those terrible weeks seem incredible, and yet are fully anthenticated. Cossacks at one place cut the throats of a hundred Jews, and after flaying the corpses threw them to the dogs. Some were buried alive, babies were transfixed with daggers to their mothers' breasts; pregnant women were ripped open and their unborn babies torn from their wombs; other women had rats thrust into their bodies. The wretches who endeavoured to defend themselves had their arms cut off. Hundreds of women were raped before the eyes of their chained husbands. Babies were roasted on spears and the flesh thrust into their mothers' mouths.

Compared to the Cossacks the Tartars seemed merciful; and so, facing attack from two sides, the Jews generally surrendered to them. They were content to add the handsomest women to their harems, and would spare the rest to sell them as slaves in Constantinople. To ransom prisoners was a Jewish duty, but the numbers expanded so rapidly that the Jews of Turkey could no longer meet the costs without help, and relief actions were organized in Italy, Amsterdam, and London.

The Cossack revolt brought Poland to the edge of collapse, and one disaster followed on the heels of another. The king died during the war and Parliament could not agree on a successor; so for six months the country suffered all the disabilities of an interregnum, as both internal and external rivals struggled for power. During all this time terror reigned in the Ukraine and in large areas of Poland itself. Two towns there will always be remembered in Jewish history.

The town of Nemirov lies to the east of the River Bug, and there a few thousand Ukrainian Jews had taken refuge from their open villages. It was a walled city and all were resolved on defending it to the last. Realizing that its capture would be difficult, Chmielnicki fell back on a ruse: he disguised a detachment of Cossacks as Polish cavalrymen and despatched them to the city bearing Polish flags. Welcoming this unexpected 'relief', the Jews joyfully opened the gates and let down the drawbridge; and in a few seconds their joy was turned into horror.

There, too, there were indescribable scenes of violence, which included rape, murder, and the drowning of children in wells. Sparing the best-looking women, the Cossacks dragged them off to the church, where a priest married them.

DESTRUCTION

At least one of these women, however, proved too clever for her husband. Resolved in no circumstances to outlive the shame, she succeeded in convincing him that she had the magic power to resist bullets.

'Try,' she said. 'No bullet can hurt me.'

And so she went to the death that she so bitterly desired.

The town of Tulczyn lay to the west of the Bug, over on the Polish side, and it too was fortified. There 1,500 Jews and 600 Poles had taken refuge. The city was invested by a large force of Cossacks and peasants under a leader known as 'Hooknose', a man whose ugliness of feature was matched by a brutal character. The besieged Jews and Poles had sworn undying loyalty and were determined to hold out till the end, and indeed they fought long and bravely.

Once again the Cossacks employed trickery: making secret contact with the Polish nobles in the city, they offered them a safe conduct if they would open the gates. The Poles did not hesitate to break their oath; but the Jews managed to get wind of the treachery, and, three to one, as they were, were on the point of despatching their betrayers when a rabbi intervened.

'It is better,' he said, 'that we ourselves should perish; for if we touch these traitors we shall expose our fellows in Poland to reprisals, and may imperil all our exiled people.'

When they entered Tulczyn, the Cossacks rounded up all the Jews in the park, set up a flag, and announced:

'All those who wish to be baptized will come forward to the flag, and will then escape with their lives.'

None of the 1,500 made a move; and all were slain.

The fate of Nemirov and Tulczyn is typical of what took place wherever the Cossacks advanced. Streams of panic-stricken Poles and Jews fled through Volhynia and Galicia, and the Polish nobles mostly failed in their duty. The armies organized by those few who did what they could to stem the tide were overthrown; and Poland lay open to the eastern foe.

Chmielnicki reached the gates of Lemberg; and there, for the first time, he met with determined resistance, as the city refused to surrender. From that moment the tide of terror began to turn. The Sejm in Warsaw, bringing its intrigues at long last to an end, elected Jan Casimir as king. Immediately, he opened negotiations with Chmielnicki and signed a truce.

But it did not bring peace; the parties could not agree on the terms, and war broke out anew.

King Casimir saw clearly that he could not rely on his aristocracy, and so he applied all his energies to building up a popular army. One of its regiments consisted entirely of Jews. It was a huge army which entered the field in the summer of 1649, but in arms and training it was inferior; and when it clashed with the no less numerous army of Cossacks and Tartars the fortunes of war seemed once more to smile on the enemy. Chmielnicki's Cossack hordes forged an iron ring of cavalry and lances round Casimir's army, and the Cossack leader appeared to hold the crown of Poland in his hand. In his extremity, however, the king managed to buy over the Tartars; and Chmielnicki was ignominiously defeated.

At long last the proud *hetman* was forced to make peace. But the price he demanded was high. The greater part of the Ukraine was declared autonomous and surrended to the Cossacks and the Orthodox Church. Moreover, the treaty expressly stated that no Jews or Jesuits would be tolerated in this region. The document is one of the very few which link Jews and Jesuits together.

The Polish Jews had still to drain the cup to its dregs. The years that followed were an interlude in a tragedy not yet complete. But it left them a little breathing-space in which to take stock of what they had lost, and to some extent time for healing the wounds that had been left by the war. They made good use of this period. Refugees returned to their ruined homes; those who had been forcibly baptized reverted to Judaism; lost children were traced and abducted women were ransomed.

Chmielnicki, however, remained unbeaten, and he was now looking to the east, to Moscow, the capital of the new Russia. Following negotiations between them, it was suddenly announced, by Chmielnicki and the Czar, that the eastern Ukraine and Russia had formed a union. No sooner was this a fact than the Czar at once laid claim to the western Ukraine; and once more the Cossacks were at war, this time in alliance with the Muscovites. Under the battle cry of 'For Russia and Orthodoxy!' the combined armies stormed through the luckless country and cut it in two, Casimir, a

DESTRUCTION

pious and sincere man but hardly dynamic, failing to hold them off.

Worse was to come. Suddenly and without warning, Charles the Tenth of Sweden landed in Pomerania with an army of 30,000 veterans of the Thirty Years' War. Poland was an easy prey and the Polish nobles went over to him by the thousand. In a few months he had occupied both Great Poland and Little Poland. His path blazed for him by treachery, cowardice, and intrigue, he raised the blue-and-yellow flag of Sweden over Warsaw, Posnan, and Cracow.

The Jews, who were neither Poles, Russians, nor Swedes, endeavoured to remain neutral. When the Swedish army of occupation imposed heavy war taxes on them they raised the money and paid them; it was all they could do. At the same time, the new Swedish masters treated them humanely, and they, in turn, were loyal to them. For this they were to pay a terrible price when the Swedes had left.

The departure came earlier than anyone could have foreseen; for Charles soon realized that his victory was as tenuous as it had been cheap. What happened was what has so often happened in Poland's turbulent history: the Poles, in the hour of their country's greatest need, rose and waged a war of liberation against both the Swedes and the Russians. Suddenly, the Swedes found themselves surrounded by bitter enemies, and the small army of occupation was unable to hold its extensive conquests. In open battle the Swedish king by swift manoeuvre and bold strokes had always defeated his Polish adversaries; but now all his victories were of little use and the situation began to look black indeed. So, seizing the opportunity presented by a foolish declaration of war by the King of Denmark, he pulled out of Poland and hurried off to Denmark, to conduct a campaign which narrowly won for him the Danish crown.

The Jews now paid dearly for their loyalty to the Swedes. In 1648 they had felt the lash of the Orthodox Cossacks, and now they were to taste the revenge of the Polish Catholics. Scores of their settlements, accused of collaboration with the Swedes, were wiped out. Once more, women were raped, children slaughtered, and men mutilated, while babies were left to die of starvation at their mothers' breasts. As a further refinement, alcohol was poured over the faces of the victims and set alight.

This account must be confined to the large and rich settlement at Lublin, the one we have already examined in the days of its prosperity. Lublin was occupied in turn by Poles, Cossacks, Swedes, and Lithuanians, all of whom demanded large ransoms as the price of sparing its inhabitants. The Jews paid heaviest, and yet to no avail; for the Lublin ghetto was destroyed. Polish troops took all they could carry as loot, and finally set fire to it. The flames spread to the rest of the city, and for two whole days Lublin was a sea of fire. The Jews had taken refuge in the synagogues; but while men blocked the exits others threw lighted torches on to the roofs and thousands of people were burnt to death.

As the smoke of war cleared, the ghetto at Lublin was seen to be in ruins. Every synagogue and prayer-house, every private house, the famous Talmudic academy: they were all destroyed. Hundreds of other Jewish settlements met with the same fate or worse.

The history of the Polish Jews in the decade between 1648 and 1658 is the account of a graveyard. Blackened ruins and charred corpses lay all around, and Jewry seemed to have suffered a mortal blow. Three times in the past it had faced disaster: during the Crusades, at the time of the Black Death, and when it had been expelled from the Iberian peninsula. But this fourth calamity overshadowed all the others.

In the first place, the casualties were greater; though the exact number of people killed is unknown, it must have been nearly half a million. Compared with the six million Jews butchered by the Nazis in occupied Europe in the 1939-45 war this may not seem many; but at the end of that war there were eleven or twelve million Jews, at least, still left, whereas in 1657 the total world population of Jews was only about 900,000. It was the lowest since biblical times, more than a thousand years before Christ. Some 700 settlements had been wiped out altogether: not one Jew had survived in the eastern Ukraine, and only one in ten of the population of Volhynia and Podolia, the two regions which had borne the brunt of Chmielnicki's onslaught.

DESTRUCTION

Those were the casualties. The survivors are another story; for in fact they were, after all, to make history. All at once, every Jewish settlement in western Europe found itself overrun with refugees from the east, fleeing before the terror of the Cossacks, the Muscovites, and the Polish liberators. Rabbis, scholars, and elders turned up in Frankfurt, Hamburg, Amsterdam, London, and Venice, and were followed by an endless succession of exhausted, starving and weeping exiles who had lost all they possessed.

It was as if Polish Jewry had exploded, filling the world with its splinters. The catastrophe had shaken the cornerstone of Judaism, and it is not surprising that it was called the 'Destruction of the Third Temple'. The gloom of despair settled over Israel.

The flow of Jewish refugees was not without consequences for the West. For centuries the stream had gone from west to east; but now it had suddenly changed its course and turned back. Before 1650, the great majority of west European Jews had been of Sephardi origin; now, however, the pattern was altered, and before long ninety per cent of the Jews of Europe were Ashkenazi. Moreover, those who crossed the Atlantic and founded, in America, what is now the largest centre of Jewry in the world, were Polish-Lithuanian Jews.

The Polish refugees changed the whole appearance of western Jewry. Wherever they went they took with them the characteristics that had been typical of the Polish settlements. There are those who say that they brought the Middle Ages over with them into the modern world.

The first news which came out of Poland was as black as night, and every one of the refugees had terrible tales to tell. But it is characteristically Jewish to see a ray of morning light even when the night is blackest; and so it was now.

One of the refugees from Poland was a Talmudic scholar, named Nathan Hannover. He is the author of the best contemporary account of what took place in Poland, in his book *The Deepest Abyss*, which was published in 1653 in Venice. What makes this book so interesting is not so much the eye-witness account of the disaster as the remarkable optimism which animates it. The author sees behind the veil of misery to the deliverance to come.

His expectation is indicated on the title-page, where the year of publication is given as *Bi'shnath biath Ha'meshiah*—The Year of the Coming of the Messiah. Like a good mystic, he also operates with letters and numbers. Chmielnicki's name in Hebrew is *Hmil*; but the letters also stand for the initials of *Heble Meshiah jabo le'olam*, or 'the birthpangs of the Messianic age'. Also, the Hebrew letters in the word *biath* have the numerical value of 413, which stands for the Jewish year 5413, corresponding to 1653 in the Christian reckoning. Hannover had seen the massacres in Volhynia and been deeply shaken by them; yet he was filled with hope, for it was clear, not only from what had taken place, but also from the numbers, that the Messiah must be near.

Hannover was only one among many. In every country, in the smallest of synagogues, the congregations intoned the newly composed *kinnot* and *selihot*, or lamentations and penitential prayers, and their tears would flow as freely as the blood had done in the ghettos of Poland. These mournful elegies play, in almost identical terms, on the same theme, and once again it is concerned with numbers; not, however, with Hannover's 1653, but with 1648. The fate of the whole world was seen to hang on this date. To take a single example:

'In the year 5408 (1648) I was filled with the hope that I should see Aaron's successor, the high priest of the shrine. But faith turned to lamentation. Instead I saw our whole people—laymen, Levites, and priests—brought as a burnt offering.'

It had been widely believed among Jews that 1648 would be the year of the coming of the Messiah. As it said in the Zohar:

'In the sixth millennia, after the passing of four centuries, all the inhabitants of the underworld shall awake to new life; for it is written: "It shall be a jubilee unto you; and ye shall return every man unto his possession".'

The point is that the numerical value of the letters in the word 'it', in the quotation from Leviticus, is 5408, or the year 1648. To a Cabbalist there could be no doubt about it. Instead of jubilation, Judaism had seen the destruction of its greatest centre. As the pious saw it, all this misery and disaster, these onslaughts by Gog and Magog, could have only one interpretation: they were what the mystics called the *Heble Messiah*, or 'woes of the Messiah', which would precede His coming.

In this light they saw Nemirov, Tulczyn, the entire bloodbath of the Ukraine, as the prelude to the great cataclysm from which a purified and redeemed Israel would emerge. The homeless wanderers who poured into every corner of Jewry in western Europe brought this profound conviction with them.

The ground had been prepared. It had been ploughed by the Cabbala; and the mystical dreams of Luria had sown the seeds. The ascetic exercises, the fasting, penitence, ecstatic prayer and meditation had germinated them and made them grow.

A wave of mystical hope ran through the tortured and scattered people, such as had not been seen since the days of Bar Coch-Bar. The great day was seen to be at hand.

A decade after the destruction of the Third Temple the curtain rose on a Messianic movement that was to leave an indelible mark on the minds of the Jewish people. We shall now consider Sabbatai Zevi, the false Messiah.

X

A VISION THAT FADED

THE loud notes of the ram's horn proclaimed in every synagogue in the world the birth of a new year. It was *Rosh hashana*, the first day of the year 5408 after the Creation, or by Christian reckoning 1648. On that morning the eyes of countless worshippers shone with the light of a new hope. Every Jew who had studied the occult wisdom of the Zohar—as hundreds of thousands had—knew that 5408 would be the first year of the Messianic age.

As so often in the past, mysticism bridged the gulfs which separated different religions, in this case Judaism and Christianity. With the same burning faith, Christians in England were looking forward to the year which contained the momentous three sixes, symbolical of the beast in Revelations, which together with the mystic thousand formed the date 1666. The mystics among Cromwell's Puritans, the Fifth-Monarchy Men, saw visions of the millennium, with the coming of the Jewish Messiah and Jesus Christ. We have already seen how such a faith inspired Manasseh ben Israel, and how England had opened her doors to the Jews. We will now trace the strange course of events that unfolded between 1648 and 1666.

It is the story of Sabbatai Zevi, the man who presented himself as the Messiah, and who, everywhere where there were Jews, found enthusiastic followers, until that incredible moment when the Messiah failed and became a Moslem. It was only a vision, and the vision faded.

The town of Smyrna is a place of ancient origin which ceased to exist when Mustapha Kemal created modern

A VISION THAT FADED

Turkey in the early 1920s. It was there that he overthrew the Greek armies which had tried to establish a Greek empire in Asia Minor; and for three days and nights Smyrna was a mass of flames. Where it had stood Kemal Pasha built Izmir. At the head of the Gulf of Smyrna, forty-six miles from the open sea, there is now a modern city with broad and monotonously straight boulevards, modernistic blocks of houses, and, standing by the busy harbour, an immense statue of Kemal Pasha.

Yet the Orient cannot be changed by merely altering its appearances; Izmir is still Smyrna, presenting still the same silhouette of confused roofs, minarets, and cypresses. And whoever finds his way into the narrow, overcrowded streets sees life as it was lived centuries ago. Sitting on the hard, uncomfortable chair of a pavement café, sipping a diminutive cup of scalding-hot Turkish coffee, I have watched the same scenes that were enacted when Sabbatai Zevi grew up in these streets 300 years ago, and it was easy to evoke the past and see the events as they occurred.

Sabbatai Zevi's family were descended from Spanish refugees. His father, Mordekai, had been a poor poultry seller, who had come to Smyrna and set up in business at a lucky moment. War broke out between Turkey and Venice, foreign firms transferred their headquarters from Constantioople to the more remote and peaceful Smyrna, and Mordekai obtained the agency for a British firm. An able business man, full of initiative, he knew how to seize his opportunities and he doubtless had more than one string to his bow, supplying goods to both belligerents. He had soon built up a fortune, which he assumed was the reward of Heaven for his son's piety.

The boy was born in the year 1626, the date being the ninth of Ab, the anniversary of the destruction of the Temple, and it was a fact that was to influence his life. A solitary, introverted boy, he had no friends and never played like other boys. There were plenty of things in the bazaar to interest an alert boy: colourful piles of fruit and other wares on offer by noisy stallholders shouting one another down; the shoemaker seated on his table, sewing shoes and using his bare feet as well as his hands; caravans of dirty camels, striding majestically through the streets heavily laden with figs from the surrounding valleys, their bells ringing to warn pedestrians. The boy saw nothing of all this, but would be lost in reverie about the life which lay beyond it all. If, however, he saw suffering—a blind child, a leper, a starving dog—this strange boy's eyes would fill with tears.

At the Talmudic school he was just as remote. Though quicker than his companions to understand and answer the sophistries of the rabbis, he remained essentially unimpressed and even as a boy rebellious.

He found his mental nourishment in the mystic marriages, the transmigration of the soul, the communion with the dead, and the asceticism of the Cabbala; and he used to flog himself, fast, bathe in the cold water of the gulf on winter days, and spend his nights praying in the burial ground. Only by killing the body could the mind, according to this doctrine, both survive and acquire supernatural powers, such as predicting the future, performing miracles, and cohabiting with the celestial spirits.

He would listen trembling to the mystics when they told excitedly of how the Messiah would arrive. He would appear, they said, before the sultan in person; and without the use of force, only by singing, would get the crown from his head and lead him away in chains. Then for nine months the Messiah would disappear and Israel would suffer a nameless martyrdom; but at the end of those intolerable months the Messiah would return, riding a celestial lion which would have a bridle of ten seven-headed serpents, and leading the ten lost tribes from across the River Sambation. The Temple would thereupon descend from Heaven and the Jewish people would be able to resume their sacrifices and continue them for ever. Jerusalem would be the queen of the earth and the capital of the world.

Sabbatai Zevi grew up into a strikingly handsome man, tall, with fine, dreaming eyes and a magnificently flowing black beard, and his voice captivated all who heard him speak or sing. He wore the required black turban which distinguished Jews in Turkey from the Moslems, who wore white ones. In the streets he attracted the attention of the girls, who would put a red rose in their ear-rings or honeysuckle in their hair as a sign that they were willing to join him under the wedding canopy. But Sabbatai had no eyes for these charming creatures in baggy trousers and open blouses who were not obliged, like their Turkish sisters, to conceal their enthralling faces behind muslin veils.

Like every normal Jew, Mordekai regarded the unmarried state as sinful, and when his son was fifteen procured as his bride one of the prettiest girls in Smyrna, the daughter of a leading merchant. Obeying his father's wish, Sabbatai married her; but ascetic as he was, he never touched her, preferring the Cabbala to her feminine charms. Not surprisingly, she demanded a divorce, which Sabbatai was more than willing to grant her. His father found him another bride, one who was even prettier than the first, but with the same result.

Such mortification of the flesh, so exceptional in the Orient, aroused attention, and the young man who was so proudly superior to the attractions of women began to find disciples.

Leading his followers into the country near Smyrna, Sabbatai initiated them into his mystic experiences. In his mellifluous voice, which quivered with nostalgia and mystical emotion, he sang in strange melodies the songs of Luria. The erotic feeling that in his life he denied was expressed in the songs, which like the passionate declarations of love in the Song of Solomon described man as the mystic bride of the Messiah. This unhealthy atmosphere provided all the conditions of suggestion and auto-suggestion which made his followers see him as the promised Messiah.

The year 1648 brought cruel accounts of the disaster in Poland, as ship-loads of captive Jews arrived at the Black Sea ports where they were dragged ashore by the Tartars and put up for sale in the slave market, the Jews of Smyrna ransoming them as far as they could. To the young zealot they embodied the woes of the Messianic age, and he saw himself as the one who would bring the great national emancipation. The date agreed with the prophesies; for according to these, the Messiah would be born on the anniversary of the destruction of the Temple, which was the 9th of Ab, Sabbatai's birthday, in the year 5408, or 1648.

The day arrived, and he gathered all his friends together. As they sat tense and expectant, waiting to hear what he had to say, he stepped quickly forward, and opening his lips spoke the single pregnant word:

'JAHVEH'.

His followers listened horrified, the blood chilling in their veins, as he uttered the name of God, for it was forbidden except on the great Day of Atonement, and then only the high priest, in the holy of holies of the Temple, might pronounce it. The 'unique' name, the *Shem Ha'meforash*, was generally concealed behind the four letters JHVA, of the Tetragammaton, as it was called by a Greek word.

Once again Sabbatai spoke the word:

'JAHVEH'.

Then, all at once, the tongues of the others were loosened, and they responded:

'Messiah! Messiah!'

There was wild excitement in the Jewish community of Smyrna when they heard the news, and the rabbis united in condemning Sabbatai Zevi's presumption. He merely replied that no one could deny him, who was about to rebuild Jerusalem, the right that the high priest of Jerusalem had possessed.

To the Jews of Smyrna this was the limit; and they solemnly excommunicated him. He shook the dust of Smyrna off his feet and began his years of wandering.

In those days Jews were the only people who could travel where they liked without much difficulty. Wherever they went, they would find people of their own race. The ties of kinship assured them a welcome, and in the Hebrew language they had a common tongue. A special welcome was given to the scholar, who would be lodged in the best room and presented with rich gifts when he left.

Thus wherever he went Sabbatai Zevi found friends, and they paid him enthusiastic homage. Though there were people who would have no dealings with him and who condemned him in the synagogues, they were few in number and got fewer as time went on. Reports of the new Messiah travelled far and wide. Judaism began to awake to a new life.

Among the inhabitants of the Jewish quarter of Constantinople there were adventurers and swindlers, some of whom made a living by making 'old' parchment scrolls and selling them as great discoveries. One of these men, seeing in the new star which had arisen in the Jewish sky an opportunity to boost his business, showed Sabbatai Zevi a document which he told him had been found buried in an earthenware jar. The text in Old Hebrew said:

'I, Abraham, dwelt alone in a cave for forty years. I wondered that the age of miracles never came. Then I heard a voice which said: "Know that in the year 5386 there shall be born to Mordekai a son whose name shall be Sabbatai. He will conquer the great dragon, and is the anointed and chosen one of Israel".'

The words made a deep impression on Sabbatai, and they also became widely known.

One of the biggest Jewish communities at the time was in Salonica, where thousands of Spanish Jews had settled. Their thirty synagogues dominated the city, towering above the minarets of the Turkish rulers and the spires of the Greeks. The sultry air of the Cabbala hung low over Salonica. There Sabbatai Zevi was eagerly received, and it was there he chose to enact the next scene in his strange drama. He announced his marriage in the city's largest synagogue.

The crowds waited outside the synagogue, some holding lighted torches, others singing and dancing, and when the bridegroom arrived they followed him inside, filling the building to overflowing. Sabatai Zevi stood under the marriage canopy, wearing the white shirt of a bridegroom, the one which also forms his shroud. But there was no bride.

A servant of the synagogue then brought in the Torah, placing it on a low table at Sabbatai's side. It was covered with gold and purple embroidery, from it hung a gold chain, and it was shielded by a plate on which were silver bells that tinkled when it was carried. Then, as he placed the gold ring on the end of the roll, Sabbatai Zevi pronounced the solemn words of marriage:

'I bind myself to thee in accordance with the Law of Moses and Israel.'

An astonished murmur ran through the synagogue, and some protested, horrified at this profanation of Israel's greatest treasure. The Cabbalists, however, understood this strange symbolic act. The Torah is in fact the daughter of Heaven, as the Messiah is its son; and now they were being united. In Salonica, however, the orthodox were the stronger party, and once more Sabbatai was excommunicated. Once more he became a wanderer.

In Cairo there lived a man whose name was Joseph Halabi, which means Joseph 'of Aleppo'. He was Government mint-master and tax-farmer, yet for all his wealth was a humble mystic who mourned for Zion and looked forward to the Latter Day. Beneath his purple he wore a hair-shirt, and he fasted, spent his nights in prayer, and flogged himself. Sabbatai Zevi found in him a zealous believer, who more than once assisted him.

Sabbatai's goal was, however, Jerusalem, where he intended to consummate his mission. At first he lived there quietly, at the same time attracting an increasing amount of attention. On moonlit nights he would pray until dawn in the burial ground; he sang Cabbalistic songs, with their mixture of earthly and celestial love; and in the streets he distributed sweets to children, thereby gaining the sympathy of their mothers. Meanwhile, he awaited the great miracle. The year 1666 was fast approaching, and a sensational event, which given a little good will could be interpreted as miraculous, now occurred.

A Turkish pasha suddenly levied a heavy extra tax on the Jews of Jerusalem which they had no means of paying. Sabbatai seized the chance and announced that he would arrange for it to be paid; and, hurrying to Cairo, he placed the matter before Halabi. The words were hardly out of his mouth when Halabi said:

'I will pay for Jerusalem.'

Sabbatai returned to Jerusalem in triumph, and was greeted with the words:

'He went out as a messenger but returned as the Anointed.'

Sabbatai Zevi's friends regarded this event as the vital turning-point in his career. From that day nearly every Jew hailed him as the Messiah. They came from all directions to see him; he was as 'tall as the cedars of Lebanon' where he prayed and sang, and thousands of eyes watched his every movement. He then performed another of those unusual and symbolic actions which impressed the masses, sealing a bond between himself and the Polish Jews in their tragic fate.

A few years earlier two Jewish women had found, one summer morning, a sixteen-year-old girl lying almost naked on her father's grave in the town burial ground. When they asked her who she was she replied to their astonishment:

'I'm the Messiah's bride.'

In broken sentences she told them that her name was Sarah and that ten years before her parents had been murdered by Cossacks, she herself being saved and taken to a nunnery, where she had lived from the age of six. But she had hated the nuns and the Christian faith that had been forced upon her, and during the night her father's spirit had appeared and led her through closed doors to his grave. The women took the girl to the baths, where everyone admired her exceptional beauty.

'Where is the Messiah?' she asked.

'He has not yet come,' they replied.

'Then I will go out and find him,' Sarah said.

Leaving Poland she arrived in Amsterdam, where she had a brother. But she could not settle there; with her eccentric nature and lack of mental balance, with its obvious pathological features, she repelled people. So moving on, she went to Leghorn, where, under the Italian sun, the flower of Poland began to unfold. Every man who saw her at close quarters was infatuated by her. Nor was she one of those girls who always refuse; indeed, malicious rumours were soon circulating. She did not marry any of her many admirers, however, for she was the appointed bride of the Messiah.

News of her reached Sabbatai Zevi, and suddenly the scales fell from his eyes. Here was the woman for whom he had waited all his life. When critical friends reminded him of Sarah's reputation he replied that God had revealed her to him in a dream, and that the prophet Hosea had also by God's command married an immoral woman. He who was to deliver Israel should of course marry a daughter of one of the victims of the Messianic woes in Poland. So sending for Sarah, he courted her, and no sooner did he set eyes on her strange and remarkable beauty than his heart was on fire for her. No woman had ever appealed to his senses in the past; but Sarah did now. She was to be the woman in his life; and her absolute belief that it was the Messiah she had married probably impelled him to go further than he might otherwise have done.

Next he obtained a prophet, an excitable young man called Nathan of Gaza, who had been nurtured on the Cabbala. He hailed Sabbatai as Messiah, sent hysterical letters to communities in the East and the West, and, predicting that the sultan would humbly yield to him, described all the details of the Messianic age to come.

In company with Sarah and Nathan, Sabbatai now set out on his last journey.

Hailed as a ruler, accompanied by a large bodyguard, and followed by a steadily growing crowd of disciples, he passed through Asia Minor, stopping only briefly on the way, and with his native city of Smyrna as his first destination. Arriving there a few months before the momentous year 1666, he found the whole city in a state of rejoicing. The Jews there seemed to have forgotten that they had excommunicated their famous son only a few years earlier; and when he entered the synagogue on New Year's Day the rams' horns were blown to welcome him, and the congregation rose and cried out the words of homage:

'MESSIAH! Long live our King!'

The city's Jews went into a delirium of joy. They fasted and made public penance, tortured themselves by pouring boiling wax over their bodies, flogged themselves, and fell into epileptic fits; even children fainted as they babbled the Messiah's name. Costly apparel was hung from windows in the streets where Sabbatai Zevi went, and carpets were laid before his feet. All this is reported in despatches sent to London by the British consul.

Rarely has there been a mass psychosis like that which now developed, and those small number of Jews who kept their heads fled the city in fear of their lives. Every Jewish shop was closed; for there could be no point in doing business when you were about to leave for Jerusalem and see the Leviathan waiting at the Messiah's table. Parents made haste to marry their children; for it is part of the doctrine of the Cabbala that the Messiah will not come or his epoch dawn

A VISION THAT FADED

until all the souls that God has created have found their earthly bodies. It was thought essential to give birth to as many children as possible in order to hasten the day; and in Smyrna itself 700 boys and girls of ten were married off.

The Messianic movement spread now like wildfire, lighting up every Jewish settlement in the world. Sabbatai Zevi issued a manifesto, addressed to all Jews, and beginning with the words:

'I, Sabbatai Zevi, the first-born of God and the redeemer of Israel, send greetings to all the sons of Israel. Peace be with you!'

In it he proclaimed that their grief should be turned to joy, their fasting to gladness, and that every day was to be celebrated as a day of the new moon; for now with their own eyes they saw the fulfilment of the ancient prophesies.

Jews obeyed him. Old men danced for joy in the streets and synagogues of London and Amsterdam. New prayer books appeared with the Messiah's name printed on the title-page. The initial letters S.Z. were written in gold above the Torah shrine. Dealers on the London stock exchange wagered ten to one that Sabbatai Zevi would be King of Jerusalem in two years. Even the rationally minded Spinoza wrote, in a letter which still exists, that the Jews might reasonably look forward to becoming once more the chosen people of God and founding their own State. There were rumours everywhere. According to one of them, a ship had been seen off the north coast of Scotland, flying a silk flag with the inscription 'The ten tribes of Israel', and its crew had spoken only Hebrew.

The feeling which inspired these demented people was that the God of the Old Testament was no longer a Being abstract and remote, but had suddenly become a handsome and lovable man, whom one could see and converse with. The God who for thousands of years had been hidden behind dead books and symbols was now incarnate, and an ancient desire had become flesh and blood.

At one stroke Sabbatai Zevi had won over all the ghettos of Europe. Emissaries came to Smyrna from distant countries in order to pay homage to the Messiah and lay rich gifts at his feet, and even Christian communities, nourished on the visions and hopes of Revelations, were swept up in the wave.

All Europe was agog with expectation of something great that was about to occur.

The year 1666 arrived. This was to be the year of reckoning, when the sultan's empire would crumble as the Messiah sang, just as the walls of Jericho had fallen at the blowing of the trumpets. Then Sabbatai Zevi performed one more of those symbolic acts which none could resist. Summoning his closest followers, he proclaimed them kings and shared the kingdoms of the world among them.

Then, followed by all his kings, he boarded a ship that was to take him to a meeting with the sultan in Constantinople. It was the period of winter storms, and the Messiah was seasick; and neither the ship nor its passengers made an impressive sight as they sailed into the Golden Horn. Their reception, too, was quite different from what they had expected.

They had barely dropped anchor when two chaloupes of the Turkish navy, heavily manned with troops, hove to alongside. The grand vizier had made his plans to meet what was clearly a case of high treason, and the pasha who led the troops leapt aboard. His first act was to give Sabbatai a resounding slap in the face. Instead of striking back, Sabbatai, following an earlier precedent, turned the other cheek, and thereby earned a certain amount of respect among the Turks. The entry into Constantinople, however, was anything but regal, and the excited Jewish masses were soon disappointed.

Still, the end was not yet; and strange to tell, the Jews regarded Sabbatai's misfortune as a confirmation that he was indeed the Messiah. Seeing him dragged off in chains, they recalled Isaiah's prophesies of the sufferings of the Messiah. Such concepts have little prominence in Jewish thought; but possibly inklings of Christianity were here mixed with hopes of the Apocalypse.

After two months spent in a prison cell, Sabbatai Zevi was transferred to the castle of Abydos on the Dardanelles, and prison at once became a palace, for the governor realized that there was money to be made out of him. Jews called Abydos the Migdal Oz, which means Tower of Strength, and they flocked there from the capital to catch a glimpse of Israel's prince. Soon emissaries began to arrive from London, Amsterdam, Venice, Frankfurt, Prague, and Lublin, seeking

A VISION THAT FADED

an audience of him. So the governor began to make a charge for admission, and in a few months had earned a fortune. It was rumoured that janissaries who came too close to the Messiah fell down dead, but that he recalled them to life by word of mouth. It was also rumoured that his chains turned to gold, and that he gave this to his guards, and, furthermore, that he could pass unhindered through the locked prison gates.

Then came the harsh reality. Sabbatai Zevi was removed, without warning and under armed escort, to Adrionopolis, which was the residence of the great Mohammed the Fourth. There he was met by the sultan's physician, a seceded Jew, and told his fate: Mohammed desired to see one of Sabbatai Zevi's miracles. He was to be bound naked to a stake and archers were to shoot at him. If the arrows turned aside in their flight, the sultan was ready to recognize his authority; for it was written: 'Fear not the arrow which flieth by day'.

Confronted with this threat, Sabbatai Zevi recanted. Stepping up to the sultan, he took off his black turban and flung it on the floor, and then asked for a white one. He had acknowledged Islam.

Why, it may be asked, did he capitulate? Was it simply that he wanted to live; or were there other reasons? Possibly in his confusion he believed he was being guided by God to save his people from the sultan's vengeance. Possibly the sultan had ordered the destruction of his rebellious Jewish subjects.

Sabbatai Zevi's motives at that vital moment are inexplicable, but what is certain is that he provided the sultan with an unprecedented triumph. The Jewish God had gone over to Islam! He was richly rewarded with the honorary post of chief doorkeeper, carrying the title of Mehmed Effendi.

From then on he sank into obscurity, but it is known that he died in poverty and solitude a few years later, in a small town in Albania.

The excitement he had caused, however, did not die with him. His disciples made every imaginable excuse for his doubtful conduct, some saying that the Messiah must know all aspects of human life, including its most degrading ones, before being lifted up in glory, while others declared that it was a double, and not the real Sabbatai, that had betrayed them. There are still some who think that he did not die, and that one day he will return, while some have claimed to be reincarnations of him.

Most Jews, however, were ashamed that the man they had taken for the Messiah had so miserably failed them, instead of bravely going to his death; and disillusion and disappointment spread through the ghettos, resulting in even greater degradation than before. Nevertheless, mysticism did not die with the vision that faded. It turned into new channels and continued to work on the Jewish mind.

Sabbatai Zevi rose like a meteor, leaving a bright trail across the sky, and in his sudden fall leaving a night that seemed twice as dark. He could also be likened to a mirage in an unending desert, to which many men eagerly hurried forward, only to find it an illusion and the desert as hot and parched as before.

It is unlikely that he was an imposter. At least he did not set out to get rich. Men brought gold and women laid their jewels at his feet; yet he never stooped in order to pick them up.

He seemed to them a proof of their deliverance, and there is no doubt that he saw himself as God's anointed. Possibly he also doubted, and certainly his sudden collapse suggests that his great assurance had perhaps been undermined.

It would require a psychiatrist to get to the bottom of this remarkable psychosis, this singular product of suggestion and auto-suggestion, which developed from the tangled web of the Cabbala.

It is easy to be sceptical about such amazing credulity; yet that, too, is part of the pattern of the ghetto 300 years ago, and a manifestation of its deep nostalgia. But though dreams may fade like the mirage, the wisdom of Proverbs is none the less true:

'Where there is no vision the people perish.'

XI

NARROW PATHS

THE war against Cossacks and Swedes had broken Poland's power and wealth. Burnt-out cities and looted provinces told the tale of what had occurred. The process of dissolution, soon to lay the country waste, was in full development. Magnates and nobles were at war with one another, building their own strongholds, keeping private armies, and even conducting their own foreign policies.

In the Sejm every little noble could determine the nation's destiny; by means of that caricature of political liberty, the *liberum veto*, he could consign it to ruin. By uttering the words *Nie pozwalem* (I do not allow), any member of the chamber could nullify even the most necessary decision. The Sejm was paralyzed, and nothing paved the way for Poland's decline more than the *liberum veto*. A whole century before disasters overtook the luckless country, resulting in its division among covetous neighbours, a historian spoke these words of warning:

'God created the world by the single word "Become". We destroy Poland with the single word "Veto".'

And a politician characterized the situation in the bitter words:

'Poland's foundation is disunity.'

It was the bitter fate of Jewish culture in Poland to follow the country in its degeneration. Jewish life might have had a finer flowering in Poland even than in Spain, if Poland itself had been a dynamic and progressive country. Poland, however, was decadent, and its Jews were to experience the medieval conditions their ancestors, centuries earlier, had fled from in Germany during the Crusades and the Black

Death. The first victims of the disastrous social strife, they were driven into the most abject poverty by the nobility and the jealous guilds and companies of the middle classes. The old spirit of tolerance which had marked the days of Poland's greatness gave way to gross fanaticism in the Church and a cruel superstition which led to bloodshed and the stake.

A subsistence had to be found, however, and we now see perhaps the most temperate people in the world occupied as innkeepers. The serving of spirits was a privilege which belonged to the landowners, and they leased it to the Jews. The latter, excluded from virtually every other occupation, could find nothing else. Just as in western Europe they were known as moneylenders, so, after the war, when drinking became a national vice, innkeeping became characteristic of them in Poland.

Further disasters were to befall them when Charles the Twelfth, 'the meteor of the North', launched a lightning campaign against Poland and conquered large parts of it. As before, the Jews tried to remain neutral while Swedes, Saxons, Russians, and Poles occupied the cities in their turn. Once more they bore the brunt of taxation and suffered under a succession of penal attacks.

On top of everything there were the *haidamack*. The word *haidamack* is Russian and means 'highway robber', and it was given to bands of marauding Greek Orthodox peasants who, in the name of their faith, attacked both Roman Catholic landowners and the Jews. At times it was almost like open war.

The disastrous climax came in 1768, when a forged decree by Catherine the Second which circulated among the *haidamack* ordered the extermination of landowners and Jews. The peasants obeyed it with alacrity. It was their common practice to hang a Pole, a Jew, and a dog from the same tree, placing on it an inscription which said: 'All of one faith'.

Those who were able fled to the fortified town of Uman, which was so small that it could barely contain the thousands of refugees. History repeated itself there, when the Poles purchased their own freedom at the expense of the Jews'. Indescribable scenes were enacted in the streets, as the *haidamack* cut down the Jews, threw them on their spears into the street, and rode over them on their horses. When the streets were blocked with corpses, they flung them over the walls, to be devoured by the roaming dogs, which saved the trouble of burying. Three thousand Jews took refuge in the synagogue and made ready to defend it; but the attackers blew in the doors and murdered them to a man.

When no more Jews were left alive in Uman, the peasants turned on the Poles; and when the governor claimed that they had been guaranteed their liberty, the headman replied:

'You sold the Jews to me; and I have sold you to the Devil.'

It has been estimated that 20,000 Poles and Jews were killed in Uman; and what happened there was only the climax to hundreds of similar events in other parts of Poland. People were drowned like dogs in the Dniester; died of starvation on the steppe; or were carried off as slaves.

That some of the Jews managed to survive was due to their organization and mutual solidarity. The Council of the Four Lands, holding regular meetings, did what it could to protect Jewish interests, and it succeeded, with an effort and at great cost, in thwarting plans to turn Jews on the estates into serfs.

During these hundreds of years Jewish history in Poland is one long succession of afflictions and humiliations. In university cities where there were Jesuit colleges Jews had to purchase their freedom from horseplay, and on the estates had to submit to every indignity at the hand of the owners.

The blackest chapter is the succession of accusations for ritual murder made against them by priests. The kings sought to protect them and sent an emissary to the Pope, who issued a Bull which condemned the charges. But it was a virus that could not be eradicated. Any lie, no matter how big, will be believed by some, if it is often enough repeated.

Worse than outside enemies is dissolution from within, and the Polish Jews did not escape that either. A critical period began, with some of the early symptoms of decay. The movement of Sabbatai Zevi had taken its toll. After the disastrous decade between 1648 and 1658, the country was strewn with the ruins of shattered Jewish settlements. The survivors lived in abject poverty that was without comparison in western Europe. Having nothing to hope for on earth, they turned their gaze to Heaven, and Sabbatai Zevi seemed like a messenger from there. Not even his betrayal could extinguish the light that he had lit in their darkness.

The aftermath of Sabbatainism set off one of the most dangerous crises that Judaism had ever experienced. Though it managed to survive without lasting injury, the pathological course is not without significance.

The regions most badly harassed by the Cossacks lay in the extreme south, bordering on the Turkish empire, and there the terrorism had prepared the soil for all kinds of fanaticism. It was there, in 1726, that Jacob Frank was born; a man destined to present an even greater psychological problem than his master Sabbatai Zevi, and one who was to inspire an insane fanaticism. Only an unhappy state of affairs enabled it to develop, and if I refer to it, however reluctantly, it is because it belongs to the history of the ghetto.

Jacob Frank's father was an artist, but the son's only means of livelihood was the peddling of fancy goods and imitation jewellery. This occupation took him abroad, and he spent long periods in Constantinople and Salonica, the twin centres of Sabbatainism. It was there that he received the name of Frank, which was commonly applied to Europeans. There, too, he found his way into the semi-Moslem sects into which Sabbatainism had degenerated.

When after a few years he returned home, the pedlar had become a prophet of a new and singular faith. He rejected the rigid discipline of the Talmud and raised the Zohar to the status of a new Bible—or at least such parts of it as suited his purpose. God, he proclaimed, is one and yet three. Besides the old God of Judaism there was the Messiah, who had already come, and the Shekina, or Radiance of God, which Frank interpreted as the feminine side of the godhead.

With this last he placed eroticism, in its most vulgar form, at the centre of religion; and behind a veil of religious mysteries, he gave free rein to every instinct and the most extravagant sensuality. It was remarkable that these excesses, picked up in the brothels of the Mediterranean, could become popular in Podolia and Galicia. That licentious practices, so alien to Judaism, could have any success there at all was a striking indication of the misery of the Jewish proletariat.

NARROW PATHS

Frank's propaganda was certainly a success, and soon he was being called 'Holy Lord', the reincarnation of Sabbatai Zevi, and the second member of the trinity. The third member, or *Matronita*, to use Frank's Ladino name, was of course a good-looking woman; and she was soon the focus of the orgies into which the drunken meetings of the sect degenerated. According to Frank, those who wished to enter into the halls of sanctity had first to pass through the 'gates of immorality'. The whole movement ended in a gigantic scandal.

Thousands of Jews had come to attend the local market, and at the inn Frank and his followers were celebrating their mysteries. They had carefully drawn the curtains, but unfortunately they had overlooked a crack in the door, and soon a crowd had gathered to watch the strange spectacle of the 'congregation', men and women, dancing naked on tables and chairs, as they sang psalms and worshipped Frank as the Messiah. The news quickly spread, and the outraged people broke down the door. They included a rabbi, and soon a Christian judge, too, appeared on the scene. Those inside were arrested and taken before the court.

Frank was able to prove that he was a Turkish subject, and so he escaped with deportation, but the rest were heavily punished. They were pretty stories which came out at the trial. Women tearfully confessed to having had relations, with the consent of their husbands and under the cloak of religion, with many different men. All who had taken part in the proceedings and refused to do penance were excommunicated by the rabbinical court, and the sentence was published in every settlement in Poland. As a further precaution, the court forbade anyone under thirty to read the Zohar and fixed the age limit for reading the books of Ari Luria at forty.

Those who were excommunicated were, as always, completely isolated. They were forced to give up their houses and shops, merchants refused to deal with them, they were excluded from the synagogues, and no one would speak to them; to walk in the street was unsafe. There was a case of some Frankists who were seized and shaved, so being made to look ridiculous among their long-bearded fellows.

As on many other occasions, the Jews who had been expelled entered the Church, which was only too pleased to accept them. The bishop, though he knew that when Frankists spoke of the Messiah they meant Sabbatai Zevi and not Jesus Christ, took them under his protection, perhaps because he saw a beginning of that general conversion of the Jews which the Christian Church so ardently desired.

At the same time, he extracted all the publicity from it that he could, and, among other things, organized a public debate between orthodox rabbis and anti-Talmudists, as the followers of Frank were termed. Though the rabbis naturally refused to take part, they were forced into doing so; and at the end of the debate the bishop declared the anti-Talmudists the winners, and ordered the Talmud to be publicly burnt. Every copy was confiscated and a fire was lit by the public executioner in the market place; then holding each volume so that the crowd could see the Hebrew letters in which it was printed, he consigned it to the flames.

By this time Frank had had a further revelation, according to which his disciples were to tread in the master's footsteps. Just as Sabbatai Zevi had adopted the religion of his environment and become a Moslem, so the Frankists were to join the Christian Church. The Frankists had cut themselves off from their own people, and were about to sever the last ties which bound them to their past. They desired to demonstrate their servility; and when they achieved wealth and prosperity they had their revenge on their late co-religionists.

The baptism of the Frankists was the event of the year. Distinguished nobles sponsored the leaders, who automatically became Polish noblemen themselves. Frank was baptized in Warsaw Cathedral in the presence of the entire Court and with the king as his godfather. The Church, however, soon came to realize that it had been deceived; for the Frankists formed a separate sect, marrying only among themselves, and continuing to honour Frank as 'Holy Master'. When, finally, it was reported that on a journey to Turkey he had conducted himself like a Moslem the authorities struck, and he was arrested and spent thirteen years in prison.

It is a mistake to make a martyr of a man if you want to forget him and his doctrine. The renown of the imprisoned master was inflated and his influence grew even greater.

Curious crowds went to visit his prison, and, bribing his guards, he managed to smuggle out fresh mystical injunctions.

The first partition of Poland in 1772 led to Frank's release when the town where he was imprisoned became Russian. He then went to Vienna, where, at the court of Maria Theresa, fortune once more smiled on him. The future Joseph the Second fell in love with his pretty and intelligent daughter, Eva; and he was able to live in luxury on the gifts that were collected and sent to him by his poor followers in Poland.

After his death, Eva Frank lived at Offenbach in Germany, where she became the centre, or 'Holy Lady', of the sect. With the years, however, the number of pilgrims and gifts declined and the sect died out; its last, scattered members were absorbed into their Christian environment and no trace was left by it on Judaism. It had been devoid of religious or moral substance, and was no more than an interlude in the history of the ghetto. We shall hear no more about it in this book.

The Jews of Poland went forward to their uncertain future along paths that were narrow, but they trod them with firm footsteps. It was they who, surviving every crisis, maintained Jewish traditions at their strongest and were able to draw upon their reserves to inspire their fellows in other countries right down to recent times.

A splendid example of this power of survival and self-renewal is provided by the celebrated Elijah of Vilna. As in all such cases fact has to be sifted from legend, but at the same time we must avoid straining after an exaggerated objectivity. A man who for centuries has supplied material for folklore must be one of those rare characters in whom legend and reality are personified.

Elijah of Vilna came of a devout family. His great-grandfather was Rabbi Moses, surnamed Krämer, who, like all learned Jews, earned his living by his hands, being, as his name implies, a shopkeeper. The rabbi was popular, and so the community provided him with plenty of custom; but Rabbi Moses, when business was good and there was enough money in the till to keep them for the rest of the week, would tell his wife to shut up shop, saying:

'It would be unfair to other shopkeepers if I exploited my position as rabbi to capture their business.'

It is ironical that such a man should bear the surname 'Shopkeeper'.

Elijah was born at Vilna on the first day of the Passover in the year 5480, or 1720 according to the Christian reckoning. He was his parents' firstborn, and as the latest of a long succession of learned rabbis he was destined to excel all the others. The newborn baby was said to have been 'beautiful like an angel', and to see him was to worship him, it was declared. These good looks he retained throughout life, and were in his old age a source of wonder. He was also an infant prodigy, able to read the Torah and the Talmud without a teacher before he was six, and giving his first sermon in the synagogue before the age of seven.

The facts of his life can be briefly stated. Following the custom of Jewish scholars, he travelled widely as a young man in Poland and Germany, visiting other settlements and meeting famous men. He had planned to visit the Holy Land, but abandoned the project at Königsberg, when he realized that it would be impossible to travel by ship and observe the rules of eating. On returning home, he married, following the rule that 'eighteen is the marriageable age'. Hannah, his bride, was of course a rabbi's daughter. They were never well off, and indeed for long periods they starved. A story is told about this.

When Elijah was old and famous he received a visit from a young Talmudic student. The latter had written a scholarly book and wanted a testimonial.

'My son,' Elijah said, 'you must face reality. If you wish to write scholarly books you must be prepared to hawk them from door to door, as a peddlar peddles his pots and pans. And you must be prepared to starve till you are forty.'

'And what then, after forty?' the young man asked hopefully.

To which Rabbi Elijah replied with an encouraging smile: 'Then you will be used to it, my son.'

It was a subordinate official of the community at Vilna

who for long periods was the cause of Elijah's poverty. This man was a swindler, who pocketed most of the money which the community allotted to their famous rabbi, and though Elijah eventually became aware of the fact, he never reported it; for it says in the Talmud that to shame a man is like shedding blood, and to shed blood, even in order to save life, is forbidden. In sparing the cheat he did not consider that he was doing a great deed; he was simply glad to serve God.

He was, moreover, a great benefactor, who would gladly sell his furniture in order to help a poor family, or give away the family's last meal to a hungry beggar at the door.

Following the ancient rule that the first forty years of a scholar's life should be spent in amassing knowledge, and the next forty in sharing it with others, Elijah isolated himself and devoted himself to his studies, eating only what was essential, sleeping for only two hours a night, and never discussing trivial affairs. It was said at his funeral—and it is hardly an exaggeration—that he had written seventy books. Most of these must have been written in his 'student period', when he would annotate every book which fell into his hands. He was the typical perpetual student who never finished studying, but who read in order to progress ever further towards the goal of wisdom and goodness.

At the age of forty he abandoned to some extent his isolation, and opened a small synagogue, where he conducted the services on his own lines. During the week he ran it as a seminary, where he gathered a number of disciples. A gifted teacher, he had a quickness of comprehension and the ability to inspire his audience intellectually as well as spiritually. About his own inmost life he was always reserved, since otherwise, as he would say, it ceased to be 'inmost'.

He had a good Jewish sense of humour, and he also had the precious gift of self-irony. When a disciple once asked him how he always had an apt illustration ready when a subject was discussed, he replied:

'I will let you into my secret. One day, a young nobleman, who was an extremely good shot, saw on a whitewashed wall a long row of targets, with a bullet right in the middle of each of them. He could not help wondering who the crack shot could be, and he was astonished to find that he was a ragged and barefooted boy of eleven.

'"What made you such a good shot?" he asked.

'To which the boy replied:

'"Well, you see, first I shoot a bullet at the wall, and then I draw the target round it!"

'And that is exactly what I do,' Elijah said. 'I don't look for suitable stories, but when I hear one I save it up. In due course I build a sermon round it.'

His wit could also be caustic. The community at Vilna bestowed upon him the honorific title of *Gaon* (supreme authority), and as such frequently consulted him. It was tacitly agreed that he was not to be inconvenienced by attending meetings on routine affairs; and on one occasion when he had been summoned to a meeting he learnt to his annoyance that the subject was a proposal to prohibit poor country Jews from coming into Vilna to beg.

'How dare you summon me for such a matter?' he asked angrily. 'You told me a new by-law was to be discussed.'

The chairman said in surprise:

'But that is what it is, Rabbi Elijah.'

'You call this a new by-law?' Elijah replied sharply. 'Why, they had it in Sodom and Gomorrah 4,000 years ago.'

Rabbi Elijah had never attended a learned academy and so was happily free both from accepted prejudices and conventions. Rather uniquely, he combined a critical mind with mysticism, the intellectual as well as the emotional side of his character being strongly developed. In him the two sides of the Talmud, the *Halachah*, or legal practice, and the *Haggadah*, or legend, were united.

In his exegisis he employed the notorious method of *pilpul*, but so far adapted it that it ceased to be merely sophistry— 'the school of dialectic fencing', as it has been called. Grappling with the most complex of problems, he destroyed many a house of cards that had been erected by Talmudic exposition.

His sense of mysticism made him a wide reader of Cabbalistic writing, but he imposed narrow limits upon it. When Hasidism (which is the subject of the next chapter) appeared, it went too far for Elijah. The Vilna *Gaon* and the fervent mystics of Hasidism clashed; and it is Elijah's historic achievement that Hasidism was to some extent checked.

Elijah of Vilna is one of the last great figures of the ghetto; and he pointed forward to a world outside it. A healthier atmosphere surrounded him than was usual in Judaism at that time. Realizing that reality is more important than interpretation, he taught his disciples to study mathematics, astronomy, and anatomy, an approach that was exceptional for a teacher of the ghetto.

At the same time he stood firmly on the faith of his ancestors. Let us conclude this sketch of Elijah, the great *Gaon* of Vilna, with a quotation from his works:

'The Torah is to the soul what the rain is to the field. The rain makes the seeds of the earth to grow and bring forth both useful and noxious plants. The Torah helps the man who strives to self-perfection; but it also increases impurity in the heart of the man who neglects to cultivate his mind.'

XII

HASIDISM

It was a sabbath evening in Jerusalem, in the district of Mea Shearim, a name which means 'a hundredfold', in the sense of the seed which returns a hundredfold crop. Mea Shearim is one of the oldest quarters of the Israeli sector of Jerusalem, and it was built with voluntary contributions collected in thousands of synagogues all over the world for the accommodation of pious Jews who settle there to pray, and whose prayers are blessed with a hundredfold return. Mea Shearim is one of those places where the spirit of the ghetto has survived in the atomic age. The narrow, winding streets teem with talkative people, and the men, as already mentioned, still wear the Polish dress of their ancestors. Time there stands still. The inhabitants of Mea Shearim live in order to pray and expound the Torah and the Talmud according to ancient principles, and no sophistries are too esoteric to gain credence.

On many a sabbath evening I have walked through these streets on my way to the synagogue, and, glancing through a window, have seen the sabbath table laid out, the candles burning, the two loaves and the bottle of wine standing ready, as the household awaited the husband's return from welcoming Queen Sabbath at the service.

The synagogues of Mea Shearim resemble the synagogues of every other city; yet at the same time they differ from them just as Jewry differs in the various countries of the world where it has put on the local dress, without anywhere abandoning its real character. Nowhere are Jewish similarities and Jewish differences so clearly displayed as in Mea Shearim, where every Jewish type can be seen, as if in a museum. In my short walk between synagogues I would pass from one continent to another and leap across centuries. Here there are Yemenite Jews and Jews from Bokhara and the Caucasus, squatting on their fine Oriental carpets; and of synagogues there are plain German ones, picturesque Italian ones, and primitive North African ones. The two that I most like to visit, however, are true copies of the Polish village synagogues of 200 years ago.

There men serve God joyfully, their faces beaming with delight and their eyes shining. While praying they rock to and fro and clap their hands together like castanets; and when they have finished they spring to their feet and, holding one another by the hand, dance chain dances, swinging round and round in God's house. When they can dance no more they break up and return to their places; then out come the pipes, and before long the synagogue is filled with tobacco smoke. Next someone will produce a bottle of spirits, and when a glass is filled a piece of celery will be added to give flavour and the contents will be consumed with honey-cake. 'Why not?' they say to the astonished visitor who remarks on this strange form of worship. 'David used to dance in front of the ark of the covenant; and is there any reason why the smoke of tobacco should seem less pleasant to the Lord than the smell of myrrh and aloes?'

It is not only in Jerusalem that Jews worship in this way; they also do so on New York's East Riverside, in the East End of London, and in Istanbul's Jewish quarter. It is a relic of Hasidism, which was inherited from the Jews of Poland.

The word *Hasidism* (or *Chasidism*) comes from *Hasidim*, which means 'the pious', and it is the name of a religious revival, perhaps unequalled in history, which expressed itself in an upsurge of hope, joy, and love, often passing to wild jubilation and fanaticism. Coming, as it did, at the right time, it fell like dew on despairing hearts. As we have seen, the Jews of Poland had sunk into misery; and few people could have been in greater need of fresh hope than they. Crushed and scattered by brutal enemies, they could gain no consolation from their leaders; for though they obediently listened to the learned expositions of the Torah and the Talmud, they found them dead doctrine which failed to supply the spiritual nourishment that they needed. Chasing phantoms, they found themselves lured into bottomless morasses. Then, at long last, Besht came, and they knew that he was one of them. He knew them, too, and he lit a candle for them in the darkness; unlike the rest, he gave them bread instead of stones. The name Besht, however, calls for an explanation.

Baal Shem is Hebrew and means 'Master of the Name', since Shem is the sacred and unmentionable name of God. In Poland there were Jews who had gained control over *Hashem*, the 'Name', and could work miracles with it, healing the sick, casting out devils, averting the evil eye, or investing charms with magic powers which they retained even when sold. Such a man was called a *baal shem*. It was a name of ill-repute, for most *baal shem* were little more than quacks.

Besht, though he had started like the rest, was, however, to be relied upon, and to distinguish him from the others he was called Baal Shem-Tob, which means 'Master of the Good Name', and which by Jewish custom was abbreviated to Besht. The name conceals a lovable character, the man who founded Hasidism, the movement that lives on in Mea Shearim.

Born in 1700 in a remote village of Vallachia, he was originally named Israel ben Eliezer. Little is known about his life, for he is another of those personalities in whom fact and legend are inextricably interwoven. But his character and achievement are so astonishing in themselves that legend is perhaps the only method of indicating them. I will therefore recount his saga as it has circulated for the past 200 years. Though many of the details are exaggerated and much is pure invention, I feel sure that the general gist of it is true.

The legend begins even before he was born. His father, Eliezer, was taken prisoner by the Tartars and sold to a prince; but his subsequent history was similar to that of Joseph in Egypt. In a hazardous war he gave the king good counsel; and after his victory the king rewarded his captive slave by making him his minister and giving him his daughter in marriage. Eliezer, however, remembered that he had a wife at home and did not approach the princess; and when she wonderingly inquired why, he said he was a Jew and already had a wife. At this the king released him and sent him home laden with gifts; and during his journey God appeared to Eliezer in a dream and made him this promise:

'Because you were strong and pious, you shall have a son who will light up the eyes of Israel.'

After many vicissitudes Eliezer at last arrived home; and though by now over a hundred years old, nevertheless had the vigour to beget a son. When, soon after, he died, the only inheritance he had to leave to the boy was these words, spoken on his death-bed:

'Always believe that if God is with you, you need fear nothing.'

The boy was an orphan, his mother having died at his birth, but by Jewish custom he was brought up and educated by the community. Israel, however, disliked school, and used to play truant and spend most of his time day-dreaming in the forests. Such a dislike of knowledge and such a love of nature were alien to the spirit of the ghetto, but they were characteristic of Besht.

In his youth he made a living by conducting boys to and from school, and one day they were attacked by a wolf. The children fled in terror, but, remembering his father's words, Besht plucked up courage and drove the wolf off. Here is the point of the legend, for the wolf was none other than Satan, who had seen how Besht had influenced the children and had taught them to pray, and who therefore was determined to stop him. The story is typical of Besht, who all his life loved children, and who liked nothing better than teaching them to pray. His heart in fact went out in sympathy and affection to all creatures, including those who were despised, among whom he numbered, like Jesus of Nazareth, publicans and sinners.

Strangely enough, this *Am Ha'aretz*, or ignoramus, of low birth, won for his wife the daughter of a respected rabbi. The old man had been impressed by Besht's character and had also been told in his dreams that he was to give him the hand of his daughter, Anna. The papers were all in order, but Besht had yet to visit the home, when suddenly the girl's father died; and arriving unknown and poorly dressed at the house, he was taken by Anna's brother for a beggar. Horrified to find that this was his intended brother-in-law, he tried to persuade his sister to give up the misalliance; but she kept her word, and neither she nor Besht had cause for regret.

On the rugged eastern slopes of the Carpathians where, on one side, the mountains rose to great heights, and on the other there were broad green valleys, the young couple made their home in a poor hut, and there they lived for many years, he digging clay in the mountain-side and she taking it on horse-back for sale in the town. The horse had been a wedding present from Besht's brother-in-law. There, in the shade of the great mountains and the solitude of the forests, he devoted himself to prayer and contemplation and prepared himself for the work he felt called upon to perform.

Besht also observed the rule which prescribed study up to the age of forty, and led no social life until it was reached. Then, settling in the small town of Miedzyboz in Podolia, he made that his headquarters and the centre of Hasidism.

In his mountain retreat he had acquired the art of a *baal shem*: had learnt the curative properties of herbs, the healing of the sick, and the prescribing of charms. It was soon evident that this was no ordinary *baal shem*, however, but a righteous and godly man, one to whom it was more important to heal souls, especially those of the oppressed, the erring, and the sorrowing.

Besht's words struck fire, and in a few short years he had a following of tens of thousands. Spreading from town to town and from district to district, the movement soon numbered hundreds of thousands, most of them humble people who drank in his words, finding in them fresh hope in their miserable predicament. Hasidism seemed to bring with it a new climate of warmth and enjoyment such as the Polish Jews had never known. The movement swelled into a flood which, flowing through the ghettos, created life where there had been only death.

Besht never attacked either the Talmud itself or the scholars who had spent a lifetime in studying it. Yet he read little himself, believing, as he did, that the mysteries of life are to be solved not by learning, but by simplicity.

The closer one studies Hasidism the more it is apparent that it was in every essential foreign to the Judaism whence it sprang, since it is based on a pantheist philosophy. God is everywhere, in good and evil, and nothing is foreign to Him, what we call sin being only that which is imperfect and incomplete, and absolute evil being non-existent.

It was the speculations of the Cabbala, the old mysticism of Ari Luria, that had sprung to new life in Hasidism. Probably Besht did not realize the ultimate consequences of his doctrine. But he was engrossed in mysticism, and he took from the Cabbala what he wanted, popularizing its ideas, and dispensing from them what suited the masses. The following story is extremely characteristic of him:

While on one of his journeys he stayed at the house of a childless couple and was hospitably treated, and in return he promised that they should have a son, invoking as he did so the unutterable name of God, and saying that it would grant them the vigour which they had so far lacked. Scarcely had he committed this dreadful sin when a voice from Heaven declared that he had forfeited his lot in the life to come. Another man would have been crushed, but Besht cried out:

'Blessed be Thou, Lord, for Thy mercy! Now only do I know that I can serve Thee with a pure heart, knowing that by doing so I do not hope for reward in the world to come.'

We have seen the great rejoicing that was manifested in Hasidic services; and rejoicing is indeed one of the principal characteristics of Hasidism. 'Serve the Lord with joy,' it is written; and 'Come before Him with song.' So Hasidists always sing when they are congregated; and they are convinced that this is the surest means of driving away care and temptation.

It is not a restrained joy, but is gradually worked up into ecstasy; for they do not pray in order to obtain favours but to be one with God. It is this exaltation, this underlying idea of merging into the eternal, which supplies the immense joy. Ecstatic enthusiasm which leads to this result is called in Hasidic terminology *Hitlahavut*; and the mystical union with God, *Devekut*. As Besht says:

'The angels rest in God, and the sanctified strife towards Him. Therefore, the sanctified stands higher than the angels.'

There is another aspect of Hasidism which must be referred to. Most mystics before Besht, and certainly Luria and his followers, considered tears an essential element of true prayer, and asceticism the way to union with God. Not so Besht.

'Weeping,' he says, 'is evil; for one should serve God joyfully. Only the tears which spring from joy are good.'

He also rejects all forms of asceticism as evil, and indeed takes a far healthier view of life than the mystics who preceded him, since he demands thought for the body as well as the soul.

A strangely magnetic personality, Besht started a revolution which transformed the lives of hundreds of thousands. He did not do so by great oratory, for in that he was of small account; but he was a man of the people, and it was to the people he addressed himself, using simple words and metaphors which ordinary people could understand. His personality remained influential long after his death, especially by reason of the stories, and indeed the mythology, which clung to his memory, as well as the clear and concise maxims which he was remembered to have uttered, and which were passed on from generation to generation. The following is a typical example:

A father complained to Besht:

'My son has become a stranger to God. What am I to do for him?'

To which Besht replied:

'Love him the more.'

Hasidism ended like all religious revivals. It achieved great results, but in time it grew rigid, becoming only an organization without inspiration.

There was also a debased form which came to be known as Zaddikism, from *zaddik*, or 'righteous'. Hasidism had its outstanding leaders, men whose prayers were more than usually fervent, and who were sure of achieving a special approach to God. They were credited with miraculous powers, among them that of enabling childless women to bear children. Such a man was called a *zaddik*, and was held in great honour.

There was a *zaddik* who received a visit from a stranger, who said:

'I have come, not to hear you speak, but to see you undo your shoe-lace.'

HASIDISM

He meant that what mattered was the way a teacher lived, and not what he said. To the man of faith the teacher was the embodiment of the Torah itself.

But the *zaddik* became an institution, and that is always fatal. When he died his son inherited his skills, activities, and reputation. Dynasties of *zaddik* arose. Soon there was no room for newcomers; and only the descendants of the great were acceptable. They, however, were honoured, and pilgrims flocked to them with gifts. The *zaddik* lived on the fat of the land.

He also became a favourite butt of Jewish humour, which made great ironical play with the miracle man and big prayer. Here is one of the jokes:

While on his way to the synagogue one sabbath, a 'miracle rabbi' saw young Simon near his father's house, eating a ham sandwich, and so committing a double sin, first in eating meat and butter together, and secondly, and far worse, in eating pork. The good rabbi was very angry, and he prayed that his father's house should fall down on Simon.

On arriving at the synagogue, however, and on thinking the matter over, he realized that, strictly speaking, the fault was not Simon's but his parents, who must have neglected his education. To allow Simon to die when the house collapsed would thus be unfair; and so he hastened to say a new prayer:

'Do not let Simon's house fall down.'

The house did not collapse; from which fact it is clear that the rabbi had the power to pray so that God would listen.

Another story relates to a timber merchant, who had bought a forest, and to whom, therefore, it was important that there should be plenty of snow that winter, to enable him to remove the felled timber on his sledges. He therefore requested a miracle rabbi to pray for the snow, giving him as a gift a *pidjon*, or 333 guilders. Snow in Hebrew is called *sheleg*, and the numerical value of the word is 333. Happy at the prospect of making good money out of his new forest, he gave the rabbi's servant ten guilders.

There was no snow that winter; but, on the contrary, it was rainy, and all the timber rotted. The timber merchant therefore accused the rabbi of being an impostor. The rabbi replied:

'I cannot understand what happened. I prayed for snow; and as your *pidjon* had the same numerical value as snow, we should have had snow. Did you, by the way, give a *pidjon* to anyone else besides me?'

'Well,' stammered the merchant, 'I must confess that I gave ten guilders to your servant.'

'Ah, there you see!' the rabbi said satisfied. 'It is all your own fault; 333 plus 10 makes 343. That is the numerical value of rain!'

Hasidism, and later Zaddikism, had the greatest success in southern Poland, where Jewish misfortunes had been greatest. The movement did not go uncontested, and in fact there were powerful disputes between the Hasidists and their opponents. The great leader of these was Elijah of Vilna, and the encounter no doubt was mutually stimulating. In it the conflict, latent in Judaism, between doctrine and life, mind and heart, had been stirred into activity.

In spite of its debasement, Hasidism proved a source of inspiration to numberless Jews. Underlying its rather absurd pretensions there were deep layers of positive values which deserve respect. They can perhaps best be characterized by means of two opposing statements by great Hasidic teachers:

One of them is:

'The real slavery of Israel in Egypt was that it had grown used to it.'

And the other:

'An old rabbi said to his sons: "My life has been blessed because I have never needed anything until I have had it."'

Though these two statements seem to conflict, since one of them alludes to the dissatisfaction which drives men to pray, and the other to the peace and security which do not call for prayer, they are in fact mutually connected; like the two arches of a Gothic cathedral, which, opposing each other, yet support the vault above them.

Hasidism was to prove the last but not least of the fruit borne by the ghetto. It was at any rate the brightest and most colourful.

XIII

LIVING RUINS

THE coach for the airport drove through the ancient gate of Istanbul at approximately the point where the Turks stormed into the city 500 years ago and an hour later we were airborne and the minarets of its 496 mosques had vanished into the distance. Far below lay the Aegean Sea, a deep-blue chart dotted with flat, yellow-brown islands, and soon we were over Athens, the Parthenon and the Acropolis looking like tiny dolls' houses. Continuing our flight over Corinth and the Pelopennese, in a couple of hours we were over Rome, where the geometrical profiles of the Vatican and the Arch of Titus glittered in the bright spring sunshine. It is astonishing that it is possible in one day to visit Istanbul, Athens, and Rome.

I came from the Wailing Wall of Jerusalem and was studying Jewish history, and so my first walk in Rome took me to the Arch of Titus. This beautifully designed triumphal arch symbolizes the clash between two of man's most important centres, Jerusalem and Rome. Rome proved the stronger, and Jupiter overthrew Jehovah on the day that Titus and his armoured legionaries stormed the white Temple in Jerusalem and laid waste the Holy City.

It is nearly 1,900 years ago, but on that May evening as I stood by the commemorative arch it was as if it had all happened only the day before yesterday. The last golden rays of the sun brushed the top of the brown masonry of the Colosseum and fell obliquely on the ruins of the Forum Romanum. The breeze waved the spring flowers that were peeping up among mouldering stones and a solitary nightingale sang mellifluously in the tall plane-trees between overturned pillars.

Inside the triumphal arch the scene of the victorious Roman entry is carved so lifelike in marble that I seemed to hear the tramp of iron-studded legionary boots on the stone bridge. The river Jordan is shown personified as a venerable old man being carried on a barrow, while Jewish prisoners are being driven towards the sacred vessel, the golden table of shew-bread, the ark containing the Law, the silver trumpets that initiated the festivals, and the seven-armed candelabrum that was named after the arch. Floating above all these are the Roman eagle-banners, and the goddess of victory is seen crowning the emperor's son who burnt down the Temple.

But the pictures are motionless, and the events depicted happened long, long ago. It is nearly 1,900 years since the emperor's slaves built the arch to commemorate his triumph, and the mighty Flavian dynasty has for centuries been material for school history books. The triumphal route and the Forum Romanum lie in ruins, and nothing is left of what once ruled the world: only ruins and crumbling symbols of a remote worship which holds no message for men living today. A past great and magnificent, yet nevertheless a past.

Leaving the arch of Titus I walk down to the river and follow it as far as the island with the Quattro Capi bridge. There I turn into the old, narrow streets that were once the Roman ghetto, and where Jews still live. And what do I see? Pictures of the same seven-armed candelabrum are scratched on the house walls as on the triumphal arch. Here, however, they are alive: symbols of something that *is*, that exists and survives. And to this day descendants of those Jews whom Titus led in triumph that far-off day still live in these houses. Inside the synagogue the same pictures as on the arch decorate the walls, including the table, the ark, and the trumpets. Beneath the images of these objects from the Temple, which Titus looted and carried off to Rome, the Jewish people, who were not destroyed, pray to the Jehovah who proved stronger after all than the Capotiline Jupiter. Power and inspiration can never be judged close at hand; and only the millennia and the long view tell who is right.

Curiously enough, it was from these same streets that the

LIVING RUINS

triumphal procession started out on that day when Rome celebrated the victory over Jerusalem. Near the fish market close to the edge of the ghetto stand the ruins of Octavia's peristyle, the magnificent portico with the double colonnade erected by Augustus in honour of his sister. Some of the Propylaea are built into the church of St Angelo in Pescaria, which the Jews were obliged to attend on their sabbath in order to hear the conversion sermons.

On this spot stood the aged Emperor Vespasian and his two sons, Titus the victor, and Domitian who was to succeed Titus as emperor, watching the triumphal procession as it moved off, the legionaries parading past the lord of the world, the stooping Jewish captives following, and the looted treasures raised aloft so that the emperor and his sons could see the spoils of victory. Then, when the procession had passed, the imperial party entered their chariots and brought up the rear, the cries of the jubilant populace ringing in their ears. We know exactly what happened on that day, for we have a minute-by-minute account written by a Jew in the emperor's suite who witnessed it all. His name was Flavius Josephus, a renegade and an imperial sycophant, yet at the same time one of the greatest historians in the world. It is a brilliant record he has left of that day.

It is this ancient link between the people of Israel and the Rome that drove them into exile which makes the Roman ghetto perhaps the most remarkable of all the ghettos in Europe. Many another grew famous for the learning and the scholarship which it nurtured, but none has Rome's age or can share its importance at one of the great moments of Jewish history.

That, however, is its one and only distinction; for there scholarship never flourished. Neither the Torah, the Talmud, philosophy, nor the Cabbala was studied there to any notable extent. Yet one thing it did have. Its history is a record of almost incredible tenacity, which has endured for many centuries. That this spurned people, the descendants of captive slaves, should have gone on being Jews in these narrow, humid, and disease-ridden alleys, is a mystery.

They occupied the most exposed position of any. They were the first people the Romans met when they returned home after the victory at Jerusalem; and they lived in the shadow of the Catholic Church, close to the Popes who were the vicars of that Christ the Jews had crucified, and they were reminded of the everlasting guilt of that deed.

At the edge of the ghetto there stands, to this day, a large church, facing the synagogue and displaying in gilded letters a quotation from the Bible. The quotation is in Hebrew, so that Jews may read it in their own sacred language, and, what is more, it is from their own Old Testament:

'I have spread out my hands all the day unto a rebellious people, which walketh in a way that was not good, after their own thoughts; a people that provoketh me to anger continually to my face.'

In their ghetto they lived like pariahs, herded together in their congested corner, surviving every fresh turn of fate, and not least the monotony of their impoverished existence. They lived hopelessly and yet in hope, as a Jew must who is familiar with the promises by the prophets of One who is to come. They were powerless to meet their enemy and return him an eye for an eye and a tooth for a tooth. So they entrenched themselves behind the barriers of their misery and the tenacity and the traditions of their domestic life. There is no rational explanation of how they managed to survive. All they owned was their graves, and indeed barely those. Of none were Byron's words more true than of them:

> The wild dove hath her nest, the fox his cave,
> Mankind their country, Israel but a grave.

Living ruins, they have been called. That is what they have always been, and still are today. Stout women sit chatting there on the pavement, a rag-and-bone merchant walks off carrying a sack over his shoulder, black-eyed children play together or call for their mother, who has forgotten them in conversation with a neighbour. In the street pigeons pick grains of corn, and bed-linen hangs out of the windows. Here are the homes of mattress fillers and fishmongers. The ancient and tumbledown walls and the worn and greasy pavements bear the marks of untold generations. No Spinoza was bred here.

LIVING RUINS

Ruins; and yet living ruins.

Where there is life there is hope; and the Jews of Rome have always, even in the midst of their wretchedness, waited in hope of a great event that would one day occur, and that would come as a gift from Heaven.

When the State of Israel was being founded the Roman ghetto began to stir into life. The sparks had smouldered faintly under deep layers of ashes, and soon they began to flicker. In 1946 the Roman Jews held angry meetings of protest against the British Government's anti-Zionist policy. In November, 1947, they danced in the streets when they heard the news of the United Nations resolution on the Jewish State in Israel.

On May 14, 1948 the flickers broke into flame. When it was announced that David Ben-Gurion had proclaimed the State of Israel their joy knew no bounds; for they saw the rebirth of the country from which their forefathers had been exiled, the event for which they had prayed and longed for through sixty generations.

In dense crowds they flocked to the fish market; and they marched in triumph along the same route by which the emperor and his sons had seen their ancestors led as captives to the Arch of Titus 1,900 years before.

No Jew had ever passed under that arch; and none could be driven through it. It symbolized Jewry's hour of greatest degradation.

But on May 14, 1948, the people of the ghetto marched singing to the arch, and then, carrying lighted torches, they did march through it. Finally, they danced for joy round it. The stigma of their disgrace had been washed away.

Living ruins: such were the people of the ghetto. But today it is clear that among the ruins there was life; and from it has grown a future.

For Product Safety Concerns and Information please contact our EU representative GPSR@taylorandfrancis.com
Taylor & Francis Verlag GmbH, Kaufingerstraße 24, 80331 München, Germany

www.ingramcontent.com/pod-product-compliance
Lightning Source LLC
Chambersburg PA
CBHW061445300426
44114CB00014B/1838